# MY ANIMALS AND OTHER FAMILY

## Clare Balding

**WINDSOR**
**PARAGON**

First published 2012
by Viking
This Large Print edition published 2013
by AudioGO Ltd
by arrangement with
Penguin Books Ltd

Hardcover     ISBN: 978 1 4713 3033 9
Softcover     ISBN: 978 1 4713 3034 6

British Library Cataloguing in Publication Data available

Printed and bound in Great Britain by
TJ International Limited

For Alice

Until one has loved an animal, a part of one's soul remains unawakened

—Anatole France

# CONTENTS

# Candy

The first face I can remember seeing was Candy's. She was my protector and my companion, my nanny and my friend. A strong, snuffling, steady presence.

I looked into her big brown eyes, pushed my pudgy fingers into her cavernous wrinkles and smelt her stale breath. It was an all-in sensory experience. I was home.

I pulled her ears, lifted back her lip to examine her tiny teeth and gripped her rolls of fat, but she never snapped, never growled, never even gave me a warning glare. Candy was a saint and she knew her role in life. She was put on earth to guard me and she would, to the end of her days.

Candy was my mother's boxer, and the pecking order was clear—in terms of affection and attention, Candy came first and anyone else, new baby included, came second. Candy loved my mother without question and my mother needed that from someone, even if it was 'only' a dog.

Candy was what they call a red-and-white boxer: a deep-chestnut colour in her body, with a white chest, white around her neck and across her face. Her eyes sagged, her titties swung low and loose and her girth was wider than was strictly desirable. But as far as my mother and I were concerned, Ursula Andress could move aside—she had nothing on Candy.

When she was excited, Candy's whole body showed it. The move started in her stub of a tail and proceeded to her hips, which would rotate from side to side, making it virtually impossible for her to walk. Her body shook with delight and her lips drew back in an unmistakable grin. Most of the time she was rather matronly and sensible, but when she was happy, she was delirious.

I adored her and she responded with an immediate, unquestioning sense of duty. She would lie by my side, move if I moved and allow herself to be a living, breathing baby-walker as I used her to climb to my feet, wobbling on my plump, short legs as she pulled me gently forward. When the strain got too much and I collapsed on to a nappy-cushioned backside, she would sit and wait for me to get going again. She didn't much like other people coming near me, particularly men, warning them off with a withering glare.

Candy seemed to be the only one who was pleased to get to know me. The day that I first came back from hospital, Mum put the basket down on the floor and left me there. Bertie, the aloof lurcher with pretensions to grandeur, had a quick sniff, cocked his leg on the side of the basket and demonstrated exactly what he thought of it all. He stuck his head in the air and walked off, never to give me a second glance.

Candy, on the other hand, planted herself next to me, and there she stayed. It was a comfort, now I think about it, that she was so protective. You see, I was a disappointment from the minute I popped out, and there wasn't a thing I could do about it.

'Oh,' said Grandma, a woman routinely described as 'formidable', 'it's a girl. Never mind, you'll just have to keep trying.'

Robust and six feet tall, my grandmother was a daunting presence. Her hair, neither long nor short, was 'done' once a week by a woman called Wendy, who came to the house. Grandma wore no make-up, believing it to be 'for tarts and prostitutes'. Her favoured formal uniform for race days was a raw-silk dress and matching coat, tailor-made to accommodate her unfeasibly large bosom, and non-patterned, because patterns accentuated the mountains. Sensible court shoes, a spacious handbag to hold wallet, glasses, diary and binoculars, the outfit topped off with a matching beret or—in the summer—a silk turban-style hat.

During the week Grandma would wear a calf-length skirt with a plain-coloured polo neck or cardigan. She never wore trousers. Once upon a time she had been a competent horsewoman,

3

but she gave up riding when the side-saddle was discarded. She refused to countenance the idea of riding 'astride' and did not approve of women wearing jodhpurs.

She didn't much approve of women, full stop, especially women with 'ideas above their station'.

Grandma came from a family of statesmen, prime ministers and patriarchs. Her grandfather was the 17th Earl of Derby, but, as the daughter of his daughter, she would inherit little more than a nice collection of jewellery and a strong sense of entitlement. Her childhood had been split between a town house in London, an estate at Knowsley on the outskirts of Liverpool (now Knowsley Safari Park) and a villa in the south of France. Her mother, Lady Victoria Stanley, had died in a hunting accident when Grandma was just seven years old. Perhaps that accounted for her lack of maternal instinct.

None of the children got much attention, but the boys at least had the advantage of registering a presence. For the one girl in the line-up, early life was a losing battle.

My mother had had one staunch ally during her childhood years: her father. Captain Peter Hastings could trace his lineage back to the House of Plantagenet, which included Henry V and Richard the Lionheart. Deep in that family tree was also a mysterious link to Robin Hood. As far as my family are concerned, Robin Hood is not a fictional figure. He was Robert, Earl of Huntingdon.

He existed, and he still does. And not just in Hollywood films but in the middle names of my uncles. Every one of them is Robin Hood, and Uncle Willie—William Edward Robin Hood—is the 17th and current Earl of Huntingdon. It is a title that is worth very little in material value—there is no stately home and no land to go with it—but it has a certain historical magic, I suppose.

Uncle Willie, my mother and their two brothers did not see much of their parents. Nanny took care of the children's everyday needs and a nursery maid was ever present. They got under the feet of Mrs Paddy, the cook, and mimicked Stampy, their butler. The household bristled with staff.

The children ate, played and slept in the east wing of the house. They were presented to their parents in the drawing room of the main house at exactly six o'clock every evening: William, Emma, Simon and John, in that order. All present and correct. All sent to bed.

My grandfather is the reason that we lived at Park House Stables in Kingsclere, a village on the Hampshire/Berkshire border. His uncle was a brewery magnate called Sir William Bass. Sir William had no children and was concerned that the Bass name was threatened with extinction. So he asked my grandfather if he would consider adopting Bass into his own name.

Grandma was appalled.

'I will not have any part of that common beer name,' she said. 'You can if you wish, but let it be your business.'

My grandfather duly changed his name by deed poll to Captain Peter Hastings-Bass, and all of his children's surnames became Hastings-Bass. My grandmother steadfastly remained Mrs Priscilla Hastings. Most people called her Mrs Hastings. A few close friends called her Pris. Two naughty nephews dropped the 'r' and got away with it, but woe betide anyone who called her 'Prissy'.

'I am not Prissy. Not to anyone!'

In return for the adoption of the name, my grandfather inherited the Bass family fortune on Sir William's death. In 1953 he used it to buy Park House Stables and the surrounding fifteen hundred acres on the southern outskirts of Kingsclere. It had the benefit of downland turf on Cannon Heath Down that had never in its history seen the blade of a plough. It was deep, lush, springy grass—perfect for gallops. There were just over fifty stables, onsite accommodation for the employees and a house big enough for an expanding family and domestic staff.

It was a magnificent house. The short drive, between two Lebanon cedar trees planted in the middle of perfectly maintained lawns, led up to a front door that stood twelve feet high and seven feet across. A stone vestibule protected it, with ivy-enlaced columns on either side. The north-facing wall of the house was covered with a mature Virginia creeper, while the south side boasted sweet-smelling hydrangea.

The house had huge sash windows that filled the rooms with light. The only room that was dark was the kitchen, where the cook and her army of helpers baked, steamed, boiled and roasted slightly below ground level. The kitchen separated the adult side of the house from the children's quarters.

When guests were welcomed through that front door by Stampy, the butler, his heels would click together on the black and white marble floor. My grandparents shared the main bedroom, with windows to the south and west, their views across the adjacent farmland—also part of the estate—to Watership Down and beyond it to Beacon Hill. Sir

6

William Bass would have been satisfied with the acquisition afforded by the addition of his surname.

My grandfather would only enjoy his new surroundings for a few years. A persistent cough that had been with him for ages worsened, and his skin turned a shade of yellowy grey. As illness ravaged his body, he had to make plans that would last beyond his lifetime.

He employed a twenty-four-year-old American-born assistant trainer in whom he saw something special. He was a good amateur rider, had a rugby-union blue from Cambridge, played cricket and polo. He was handsome, with jet-black hair parted to the side, full lips, dark-brown eyes and clear, fresh skin, marred only by a livid red scar across his left cheek.

He had an extraordinary way with horses and, importantly, he was not intimidated by my grandmother. He had no family money, which might be construed as an advantage, as it made him less likely to leave. The only negative was that he had a reputation for being a bit of a ladies' man. Grandpa was confident he would grow out of that.

His name was Ian Balding. Six months after he arrived at Park House Stables, my grandfather died of cancer at the age of forty-three. It was 1964, the year of the Tokyo Olympics. My mother was just fifteen. Nanny passed on the news of their father's death and the instruction from their mother that none of the children were to cry in public.

The grief belonged to Grandma and to her alone.

In terms of the business, it was two years before the Jockey Club would allow women to hold a trainer's licence. They were banned on the grounds that female trainers might see semi-naked jockeys in the weighing room—and who knows what might have happened if that came to pass! Might they be overcome with desire? Faint from the shock?

Grandma had to allow a man to take over as the trainer at Park House, so she allowed Ian Balding to take on the licence. She remained on hand to help with the owners, many of whom were personal friends, and she had her views on which races the horses should run in, but the management of the business, of the staff, and the day-to-day training of the horses was the responsibility of my father.

Grandma and my father ate dinner together every night. They had breakfast together every morning. He rode out with the racehorses, a flat cap on his head, a tweed sports jacket worn over his dark-beige breeches. Grandma walked or drove with her whippet and her Labrador to stand by his side, binoculars in her hands. They commented to each other on how each horse was moving, how each rider was coping and whether a certain race at Ascot, Newbury or Goodwood might suit. Ian Balding charmed the sensible pants off the widow Hastings. He made her laugh.

Ian introduced her to a colourful array of girlfriends in mini-skirts, tight tops and big sunglasses, their hair piled up high. None of them met with the approval of Mrs Hastings. He worked hard, he trained winners, played cricket with the boys, tennis with the sporty American owners and often drove my mother back to school, much to the delight of her teenage friends. Ian was the only one she could talk to about her father and how much she missed him. She was only fifteen and needed someone with whom to share her fears, her

8

problems and news of school, to test her on her French and talk to about her domineering mother. Ian became that confidant and, best of all, when he dropped her off, her friends would gather round and giggle excitedly as the Cary Grant lookalike took her suitcase out of the boot.

My mother was bright. She excelled in English and history and was an A-grade student. She was advised by her careers teacher at school to apply to Cambridge University. Her eldest brother, William, was already there, at Trinity College. Her younger brothers, Simon and John, would eventually follow. When it came to Emma, however, there was no encouragement.

'Don't be ridiculous,' said Grandma. 'I will not have a bluestocking for a daughter.'

There was no point in arguing. The sixties may have been in full swing, but my mother was locked in a Jane Austen novel where women learned to play the piano, to sew and, if it was strictly necessary, to cook. They could be witty, pretty and well read but God forbid they should be 'clever' or have opinions of their own.

Ian suggested that Emma go to America to visit his family. By coincidence, his little sister Gail had been at prep school with Emma and they had been firm friends. It was the first time my mother had been abroad. Family holidays had always been taken at Bognor Regis, in a rented house within walking distance of the pebbly beach. Crucially, it was not far for Grandma to leave the children and join her friends at Goodwood racecourse. The children came to dread Boring Bognor.

So my mother flew to America, the land of the free—free at least from her mother. When she

9

came back, armed with her own declaration of independence, she went to London to find a job. She grew in confidence, had her own income from work as a secretary and was enjoying being able to make her own decisions, but when she went home it was back to square one. A contemptuous 'What on earth do you think you look like?' from her mother would send her scurrying back to her room to change her clothes to something more conservative. Progress was constantly and consistently blocked.

Ian Balding, meanwhile, was fitting in just fine. He looked good in a dinner jacket and even better in sports gear. He hadn't been in the army so had none of the constraints of officer syndrome and didn't live in tweed or yellow cords. He was different to any man any of them knew—there was a hint of danger about him, yet he looked like a boy scout.

He was far removed from and much more fun than any of the men my mother met in London. She watched the way he dealt with her mother and envied him. He had such an easy manner. She rode with him one morning and, after the racehorses had finished their work, Ian called out, 'Come on, Ems, we're going back this way.'

He headed towards the fence line and popped his horse over a jump about three feet high on to the side of the Downs. Emma followed. They galloped along together, jumping everything in their path—hedges, ditches, post and rail fences. She felt exhilarated—galloping on a tightrope of fear and fun.

Many women had stayed in the guest room of Park House and were certainly worth creeping down the corridor for, but none had quite made Ian feel the way he did that morning on the Downs. As if overnight, Emma had grown up. He had never really looked at her before, not like that.

Three months later, he asked Grandma for permission to marry her only daughter.

'Really? Well, that's very kind of you,' she said.

My father went to telephone his mother in America while Grandma called Emma in to see her.

'I understand you're going to marry Ian. You're a lucky girl.'

'Oh,' said my mother, 'am I? He hasn't asked me.'

He never did actually ask her but, clearly, it had been decided. When he rang America to pass on the good news to his own mother, Eleanor Hoagland Balding said, 'So which one did you choose, the mother or the daughter?'

The wedding was organized by my grandmother. My mother was allowed to invite ten friends. She was twenty, my father thirty. A number of his ex-girlfriends (the ones whose names he could remember and whose addresses he had logged) came to St Mary's Church in Kingsclere to see the great charmer finally tie the knot.

With no father of the bride to call upon, Grandma decided that it would be appropriate for Emma's eldest brother, William, to give her away. My mother was horribly nervous. She had not really had time to think this through. Ian made her heart skip a beat but she wasn't at all sure that she was ready for this. She dreaded the sight of all those women from her fiancé's past, in their miniskirts and trendy hats, their sunglasses and platform shoes. It felt a bit like the ride on the Downs—

dangerous, with the threat of a fall right around the corner.

Her brother William stood with her outside the church door. She looked to him for comfort as he took her hand to lead her down the aisle. The best he could offer was, 'Your hands are sweaty.'

So Ian and Emma, my parents, were married in the summer of 1969. They honeymooned in Cornwall, at a house belonging to a friend of Dad's. They couldn't be away for long because the flat season was in full swing and my father was busy. They stayed for four nights and then they were back to the hectic life of Kingsclere and the glare of my grandmother.

My father gave my mother a horse called Milo as a wedding present. It was a re-gift, really, as Dad had been given him and continued to ride him. By 1970, he'd clearly forgotten that he had gifted him to my mother at all, as he rode him in his own colours and listed himself as 'owner' for the whole point-to-point season.

My mother's life ran to the clock of her new husband. His work was important and all-consuming. The horses were divided into two 'lots' of around thirty horses each. One was exercised before breakfast, the other after. My father got up before six, rode Milo out with First Lot and then went to Park House for breakfast with my grandmother, his assistant trainer and Geoff Lewis, the stable jockey. Then he rode out a different horse with Second Lot and went to the office to plan the entries, speak to the owners, pay the bills and sign the cheques for the staff wages.

There was racing from Monday to Saturday. On Sundays, he played cricket in the summer and rugby in the winter. Or my mother drove the horsebox to Tweseldown or Larkhill or Hackwood Park so that my father could ride Milo in a point-to-point.

His life was frantic, but my mother was lonely. She needed company. So she trawled the adverts in the *Horse & Hound*, the *Telegraph* and the *Sporting Life*. Eventually, the *Newbury Weekly News* came up trumps:

---

### Boxer Puppies for Sale

**3 BITCHES, 2 DOGS**
**Already weaned. Ready for new home.**

*Phone Paul on 0703 556218*

---

'Come in, come in,' he said as he ushered them through the door. 'Now, sit down, the both of you. My, what a handsome couple you make. Cup of tea?'

Uncle Simon blustered and flustered, 'We're not, we're not . . . It's not like that. She's my sister,' not sure where to look.

Paul shimmied into the kitchen to flick on the kettle.

'So, my lovelies, what do you know about boxers? Do you realize how much work they take, how much exercise they need, how they will take over your life?'

He made tea, and for half an hour he told them every detail about the behaviour of boxers. He grilled my mother about the house, where the dog would sleep, how often it would be exercised and what sort of lifestyle it was entering into. My mother was tested further on her suitability to be a dog owner than she had been to be a wife. Forced to think about it more deeply, she knew that this was what she wanted.

When finally allowed to see the litter of puppies, she was captivated. One of the red and white bitches was playing with her brothers when my mother knelt down beside the pen. Paul and Uncle Simon stood back to let the bonding process begin. The puppy looked up at my mother and wiggled her hips. Mum leant down to pick her up, and the puppy seemed to smile. She licked my mother's face and then pressed her velvet head into the soft part of my mother's neck, just below her jawline.

My mother smiled and a tear formed at the corner of her eye.

'Hello, you,' she whispered. 'Where have you been?'

Uncle Simon uttered his first words in an hour. 'We'd like to take that one, please. If it's not an imposition. If we can, that is.'

Paul had watched my mother and understood. She had been a bit stranded, floating on a raft not of her own making.

'Of course. She's weaned, she's had her injections and she's good to go.'

Candy sat by Uncle Simon's feet in the passenger seat of the car. He was wearing open-toed sandals, which was how he realized, as they passed Winchester, that she had peed on his foot. It was the only thing she ever did wrong.

Boxers are such fun to be around. Forever playful, fiercely loyal and always affectionate, they will demand a full part in family life. Mum said that

14

if we grew up thinking that boxers were beautiful, then the whole world would be a beautiful place. She was right.

*       *       *

I arrived about six months after Candy, in January 1971. My father was not present at the birth. It was not the done thing.

I spotted early on that the dogs got lots of attention so worked out that it would be best to be a dog. I crawled to drink from the water bowl—I mean, who doesn't do that? I stopped short of sharing their food, because I was a fussy eater.

During my early years, Candy was queen of our castle and she took her responsibilities seriously. When a photographer came to take an official black and white photo of 'the new baby', he asked my mother to find something for me to play with. I was lying on my front on a rug on the lawn. Candy watched my mother disappear and silently moved in next to me, just to make sure the man with the camera didn't whisk me away. The best photos are of Candy and me together.

Later that day, Mum shut Candy and Bertie, the lurcher, in the house and headed off down the steep drive with me in the pram. She was wearing a new coat, which changed her outline from behind. She heard a noise and, when she turned round, she saw a slightly wonky-looking boxer trotting down the drive, barking a low, gruff warning alarm.

'Candy, what are you doing here?' she said.

Candy looked a bit dazed, as well she might. She had clearly thought that I was being abducted, so she'd thrown herself out of a top-floor window.

She had tried the back door, the front door and all the windows on the ground floor but found them locked. So she'd run up the stairs and discovered one window that was slightly ajar. Pushing hard, she had squeezed through the gap and jumped the twenty feet down to the ground. Her job was to protect me, and protect me she damn well would.

She suffered only mild concussion and recovered quickly.

When Candy was nine years old, my parents took a rare holiday. My mother was persuaded, against her better judgement, to send her and Bertie to kennels. What happened is still a mystery but it seems that Candy had a heart attack. She died before my mother returned.

Mum has never since sent a dog to kennels. It wasn't the kennels' fault, she knows that, but she still frets that Candy must have felt abandoned and confused, that she wouldn't have known she was being left there only for a fortnight, that she must have panicked and weakened her heart with anxiety.

## 2

# Mill Reef

The year was 1971. Specify beat Black Secret by a neck to win the Grand National under a jockey called John Cook, wearing the colours of Fred Pontin, the owner of Pontin's holiday camps.

I do this, I'm afraid. Mark my years by Grand National or Derby winners. Sometimes I do it by Olympics—give me a year and I'll tell you where the Olympics were held, but that only works every four years, so Grand Nationals and Derbies are more precise.

In 1971, the Derby winner was a little horse called Mill Reef. He was one of the true greats. He's still talked about as one of the best Derby winners ever. He's also the only Derby winner I've ridden—well, sat on. But there's a photo to prove it and everything. I'm wearing red cords, blue wellington boots, a blue jumper and a red balaclava. I am a vision in red and blue.

I'm leaning forward like a jockey but there's no saddle. I'm turning to the camera and smiling. I have a light grip on the reins and no one is holding me.

Hang on a minute . . . No one is holding me and no one is holding him. What the hell is going on here? I'm barely eighteen months old, I'm on a four-year-old colt who the year before had won the Derby, the Eclipse, the King George and the Arc, and earlier that year had won the Coronation Cup. Alone. There isn't an adult in sight.

He could have bolted, I could have lost my balance and smashed my skull on the floor. Just one step sideways and I'd have been a mess. Clearly that mattered little to the people around the great horse—that is, my parents.

My dad cries when he talks about Mill Reef, because he knows he owes that brave little bay horse everything. I once met a man who bought his first house with the money he won on Mill Reef in the Derby. My father never put a penny on him and yet could claim to have won his career and lifestyle because of him.

Ask my father what happened in 1971 and he'll tell you how disappointed he was when Mill Reef was beaten by Brigadier Gerard in the 2000

Guineas, how easy he was to train, how he had a serenity and inner confidence, how when he first saw him gallop it was like watching a ballerina float across the stage: his hooves barely touched the ground before they sprang up into the next stride. He was neat, compact—some might say small—but he was nimble, agile and fast.

Strong fitness training for racehorses, when they gallop fast in pairs or threes, is called 'work'. It happens twice a week—at Kingsclere, where my father trained, the horses walk for twenty minutes up to the Downs on a Wednesday and a Saturday, and that's where they do their serious work.

Some horses work moderately and improve on a racecourse; others show it all at home and are disappointing on race day. Mill Reef was so good at home that he needed one horse to lead him for the first half of the gallop and another one to jump in halfway to stay with him to the end. No horse was good enough to stay with him for the whole length of the gallop. When he got on a racecourse, he was even better.

Dad will tell you how he got stuck in traffic on the way to Epsom and had to run the last two miles to make sure he was in time to put the saddle on Mill Reef for the Derby. He might admit that he had a funny feeling that Mill Reef was going to win the greatest flat race of all, but even he didn't know that this wonderful horse would do it so easily.

What he will forget to tell you, if you ask him what else happened in 1971, is that I was born.

*      *      *

No one was prepared to rush my grandmother out of her home, so she took her time. When she was ready, Grandma built a new house across the road and painted it pink. We called it 'The Pink Palace'. There she would reign for a further fifty years.

The rooms at Park House were used as living quarters for the stable staff, and it acquired an air of faded glory. Now in a new house not far away, my mother was removed from the workings of the yard, and a safe distance away from Grandma, but she was also disconnected from her husband, who worked every day of the week.

My mother might see him if he popped in to change, but often he jumped in the shower, pulled on a suit and dashed off to the races. He would come back in time for evening stables and then, finally, some time after seven, he would arrive at the house with a large board that looked like a ladder of narrow slats. 'The Slate' was sacrosanct.

Into each horizontal runner on the board, he would slide the name of a stable lad, and either side of it the name of a horse. The horse to the left of the name would be his ride for First Lot and the name to the right of it the one he would ride out Second Lot. The names of horses and lads were printed with a Dymo Maxi printing gun. It had a wheel with letters on it that would imprint in white on to coloured plastic tape. The horses were colour-coded according to their age, and the human names were all in blue.

It took a fair amount of planning, and on Wednesdays and Saturdays there was 'work' to be sorted out. My father did not like to be interrupted while he made his lists on paper with his all-colour Biro: black for the date and for the horses' names;

blue for the riders and their weight; green for the gallop to be used, the distance to be covered and the instructions; red for the comments (written afterwards) on how they had worked.

## Wednesday, 30 August 1972

| Seven | 7f |
| --- | --- |
| Merry Slipper | Joe Bonner  8st 3lbs |
| | Lead, good bowling canter |
| Mill Reef | John Hallum  9st 7lbs |
| | Strong even canter, track in behind |

In the summer of 1972, Dad had planned a strong, bowling canter for Mill Reef on the Seven Gallop (so named because it was seven furlongs in length). Not a full piece of work—he wasn't ready for that—but a gallop fast enough to ascertain how well he was and how much fitness work he would need before he could run again. John Hallum, who always rode him at home, was on board and set off behind Merry Slipper, who was going as fast as he could. Mill Reef—or Jimmy, as John called him—was swinging along in his usual fluid way.

It was and still is quite rare for a Derby winner to be kept in training as a four-year-old, but Paul Mellon, the American philanthropist who owned him, believed that racing was about being a good sport. The latest Derby winner is the headline horse—he can earn millions in his first season at stud. The risk of keeping him in training is that he may not improve or, even worse, he might deteriorate and therefore devalue his earning potential as a stallion.

In this case, the gamble of keeping Mill Reef in training had turned out well—he had won a Group 1

21

race in France that spring by ten lengths and the Coronation Cup in a tight finish at Epsom in June. Dad was worried about the way he'd struggled in that race and got the vets to check him over. He was found to be suffering from 'the virus'. He was sick.

'The virus', as all trainers call it, is an unspecified illness that can sweep through a yard, affecting all the horses to a greater or lesser degree. How it is caused is a mystery, and even stranger is how it suddenly disappears. The symptoms are hard to spot because the horses are generally fine at home. They work well, they eat up, they look healthy in their skin but, when it comes to racing, they run out of puff at the crucial stage and abruptly look as if they are treading water. Most ordinary horses finish nearer last than first when they have the virus. Mill Reef still managed to win, but he wasn't right.

So he was given time over the summer to recover, and this gallop in late August was part of his preparation for another tilt at the Arc de Triomphe in Paris on the first Sunday of October. It's the most stylish, glamorous occasion in the racing calendar. I have presented the Arc on television many times and I love it—as a sporting event, as a fashion parade and as a reminder that the French do things with such, as they would say, *élan*.

When Mill Reef careered away with the Arc in 1971, he was the first British-trained winner since 1948 and, if he could retain it, he would be the only British-trained horse *ever* to win back-to-back Arcs. It was with this elusive challenge in mind that Mill Reef was winging his way up the Seven Gallop early that morning.

My father was sitting on a horse further up the gradual incline so that he could watch the final, fastest two furlongs and assess the fitness of his star. The heat was not yet in the sun. It was a bright day, the grass slightly browned by the summer months. My father loved the view from up there. He could look north from the height of the Downs, right across Berkshire and Hampshire, as far as Reading, sixteen miles away. He loved it there. He was a lucky, lucky man.

That bubble was about to burst and, for the first time in his life, neither his luck nor his charm would save him.

He heard the distant pounding of hooves. Mill Reef and his lead horse, Merry Slipper, came thundering by, their nostrils flaring, their coats gleaming like polished mahogany in the early-morning sun. John Hallum was crouched over Jimmy's neck, his soft peaked cap turned backwards so that it didn't blow off in the wind, his reins tight, holding the horse together as he lengthened his stride and quickened his pace. He was moving well, looking good and, with a satisfied smile, my father turned to watch the next pair coming up the gallop.

As he followed that second pair with his eyes, sweeping his gaze from right to left, he noticed something strange. The first pair of horses were not at the top of the gallop as they should be, gently pulling up to a trot and turning to walk back along the track. Instead, one of them was standing to the side of the gallop, with only three legs on the ground. It was—oh God, he thought, it couldn't be—it was Mill Reef.

John Hallum was holding him, trying to keep him calm as the other racehorses galloped past.

Dad's heart stopped. He started shouting at the work riders coming up the gallop, *'Pull up! Pull up!'*

He then turned and cantered with dread towards John and Mill Reef.

'I heard a crack, Guv'nor. It's not good,' said John, his quiet voice faltering.

The horse, whose galloping motion was so smooth and so easy, had suddenly juddered. John had realized in an instant that something was badly wrong and pulled on the reins immediately to stop Mill Reef doing further damage to himself.

John, the man who loved and cherished this horse even more than my father did, was cradling Mill Reef's head into his chest to stop him moving, stroking his face and whispering into his ear, 'It'll be all right, Jimmy. It'll be all right.'

Mill Reef had fractured the cannon bone between the knee and the ankle of his front left leg. He was holding it above the ground, a look of confusion in his eyes, pain searing through his body.

Most racehorses will not stand still when they are hurting—they thrash, they bite and they try to gallop away from the thing that is causing them pain, injuring themselves further in the process. Mill Reef stood still. John kept whispering in his ear, telling him that the pain would stop soon, that he was a champion, that it would be all right.

Both John and my father knew that it would not be all right. They knew Mill Reef would never race again.

When a human breaks a leg, they can recover on crutches, taking the weight off the bad leg and allowing the bone to heal. A horse can't do that and, for most, the suffering is too great to make an operation viable. In 1972, it was rare, if not unheard

24

of, for a horse with a fractured cannon bone to survive.

My father and John both understood the gravity of the situation. Mill Reef had to be saved, whatever the cost. This wasn't just a commercial decision. Their world had revolved around that horse since the day he had arrived in the yard. If my father knew anything about love, he knew he loved this horse.

Time must have dragged for the next hour. Grandma had been watching work and drove back in her car to the yard as fast as she could. She organized for the horsebox to get to the top of the Downs and sent for the vet. Riders often fell off on the gallops but, thankfully, accidents are not an everyday occurrence. Perhaps once or twice in a season there would be a serious injury, but the chances of this happening to the best horse in the yard were 100:1. It was utterly shocking that it should happen to not only our best horse but the best horse in the country.

All that time, John kept talking to Mill Reef— not as a Derby winner, a champion, a superstar, but as Jimmy: his friend, the horse that he adored.

More remarkable than the way in which this beautifully balanced racehorse had, on the course, sailed past those stronger, bigger and more muscular than him was the way in which he allowed himself to be saved. He trusted John and he trusted my father, so he hobbled up the ramp into the horsebox and was gently taken on the short journey back to the yard.

John talked to him all the while and stayed by his head as the vet examined him. 'He knows what he's doing, boy,' he murmured into Mill Reef's ear.

'He'll sort you out.'

The vet did sort him out, but the horse would have known nothing about the plate and the three screws that were inserted into his front leg until he came round from the anaesthetic. The whole operation was done on site, in a large square room that had once been a chapel. Paul Mellon had instructed my father to do whatever it took, at whatever cost, to save the horse. When my father had called him in America, Mr Mellon's first question was, 'Poor John—is he all right?' He knew how much his horse meant to the man who every day groomed him, fed him, mucked him out and rode him.

The recovery room was covered in the thickest, freshest straw, banked up at the sides. Mill Reef was never alone. Either John, my father or Bill Palmer would sleep in there with him while he lay with his left foreleg in plaster.

Eventually, Mill Reef could stand and, as his recovery progressed, so the attention increased. He had hundreds and hundreds of cards on lines of string in the recovery room, and the BBC had a live TV link-up with my father during Sports Personality of the Year in December 1972 to see how the patient was progressing.

The plaster was eventually removed, and Mill Reef could walk. He hobbled at first, unsure of how to put one leg in front of the other, but as he realized that it no longer hurt to place his weight evenly on all four legs, so he gained in confidence. Shortly after that, I was lifted on to his back and the photograph was taken. A last snapshot of Jimmy at home.

With every day that Mill Reef gained in strength,

26

so John Hallum knew that his time with him was running out. Mill Reef's life had been saved, but his racing career was over, and that meant his stay at Kingsclere was coming to an end.

John went in the horsebox with him to the National Stud and wept as he kissed Mill Reef goodbye.

'It's all change for you now, my boy. What a life you'll have,' he explained to his friend. 'Mares will come and visit you, so you be polite and always say thank you.

'This is your lovely new home in Newmarket, with all you can eat and huge fields to gallop in. You'll want for nothing, I promise you, nothing. I'll come and visit you to see how you're getting on, you see if I don't. Be a good boy now, Jimmy. Be a good boy.'

John was true to his word, and every time Mill Reef heard his footsteps approaching and his gentle voice he would whicker in recognition and fondness.

A film, *Something to Brighten the Morning*, was produced, with Albert Finney doing the voiceover, to tell the story of Mill Reef. He was the champion cut down in his prime, the perfect little package who had taken on and beaten bigger beasts. He had faced his toughest battle of all away from the racecourse, and he had won that too.

After Mill Reef had retired to stud, Mr Mellon wrote to my father.

'Dear Ian, I'd like to do something special for you as a friend,' he proposed in his elegant handwriting, 'and I would prefer to do it now rather than waiting until the day my will is read. Mill Reef brought me so much pleasure and you were masterful with him. I'd like to set up a trust fund for you and your children. You can do anything you like with it and, if you're careful, it will last long beyond your lifetime.

'I do hope this will be useful to you, and in any case it comes to you with my warmest affection and regards, and my continued thanks for all you have done to make racing in England a tremendous pleasure. Yours ever, Paul.'

My father read the letter again and again. He could hardly believe it. He carried so much guilt for the way in which Mill Reef had broken his leg. He questioned himself endlessly—what if I hadn't used that gallop? What if I'd sent him up second rather than first, would it still have happened? Not that he would have wished such a painful and life-threatening injury on any horse, but the question remained, why did it have to be him? Why the best horse he would ever train? Why?

Yet here was Mr Mellon—he was always 'Mr Mellon'—thanking him and offering him a life-changing reward. My father knew that he would never have a chance like this again. Owners were not all as philosophical and as altruistic as Paul Mellon. He wrote straight back, 'Thank you. That is an extraordinary offer and I would like to use your generosity to fund my children's education. Emma and I have no savings to speak of and can't afford to send them to the best school, but we will make sure they make the most of this opportunity. Thank you so much.'

Eighteen years later, when I was at Cambridge University, I sent Mr Mellon a letter to express my gratitude for the education he had funded.

He sent me a postcard back with a picture of

28

Clare College on it. He had studied there and used their black and gold college colours as the inspiration for his racing colours. It read:

*A picture of Clare for Clare,*

*You need not thank me. I have watched from afar and you have more than fulfilled your side of the bargain. Be lucky, be happy and stay true to yourself.*

*With much love,*

*PM*

As for Mill Reef, he passed on his brilliance to his progeny and, in doing so, became a champion sire: his son, Shirley Heights, would win the Derby in 1978. He eventually died in 1986, of heart failure, the year before another son, Reference Point, would also win the Derby.

There is a statue of Mill Reef at the National Stud, where he spent the majority of his life. Under it is an inscription from a speech that Paul Mellon gave about him. The last line reads: 'Though small, I gave my all. I gave my heart.'

There is also an exact replica of that statue in the new yard that my father built the following year. He called it the Mill Reef yard. New visitors to Park House are shown that statue and told the story of the greatest horse he ever trained—the horse who encapsulated the mighty swing for Dad from a charmed life to the brutal reality of a world where everything would not always go his way.

Sometimes, early in the morning or when

evening stables have finished, you will find my
father standing alone looking at that statue.

# 3

# Valkyrie

Our house was high up on a hill, about four furlongs from the stables as the crow flies. Sorry, I do that too—measure things in furlongs. In London's Oxford Street, when asked for directions, I told a tourist that Selfridges was two furlongs further on. It made sense to me.

A furlong is 220 yards, four furlongs equals half a mile and eight furlongs a mile. So the stables were about half a mile away, down in a hollow, protected by the Cannon Heath Down on one side, Cottington Hill behind and by our hill on the north side. Our house was called The Lynches. I have no idea what that means and, as far as I'm aware, it was never owned by anyone called Lynch.

It was not an attractive house. It had been built in the 1930s according to the fashion and had been bought for £25,000 by my parents from Granny Hastings, my mother's paternal grandmother.

The windows had latticed lead crossing them, which prevented the light ever flooding through them the way it did at Park House. The back of the house had the rise of the hill just behind it, meaning that light from that side came only into the top-floor windows. The bathrooms were new and colourful. My parents' bathroom was avocado, the bathroom I used was apricot and the guest shower was dark green. They all had carpet on the floor, something that continental Europeans think so unhygienic.

The kitchen was modern, with Formica tops and a cork floor. I liked to scrape away at the cork, like a dog scratching. It came up in satisfying chunks. It didn't take long before the floor looked like it had acne, with miniature potholes all over it.

The saving grace of The Lynches was the most incredible south-facing view, right across the 'Starting Gate' field, the four-furlong woodchip gallop called 'the Chippings', the peat-moss gallop called 'the Peat Moss' and the grass gallops called 'the Near Hedge' and 'the Far Hedge'. The names were not an attempt at subtlety or post-modern irony. They said what they were and they did what they said.

So far so good, but this is where it gets confusing.

The gallops we could see from the windows of The Lynches were the gallops 'down below', as opposed to the gallops up on the Downs. Learning that 'up' is 'down' and 'down' is 'up' is confusing at any age, but when you're only just mastering the language, it's hopeless. This was where the horses were exercised on regular, non-work days. It was also where the younger horses were educated before they were allowed to make the hike to the Downs for their first exams.

The Starting Gate field was where the practice starting gates, or stalls, were kept. The young racehorses would be driven through them on long reins, then ridden through them and finally galloped out of them from a standing start, as if at the beginning of a race, so that by the time they got to the racecourse, they knew what they were doing.

Looking across the sweep of green, divided by hedges or tall lines of trees, the stud paddocks were to the right. This is where the foals were born and first learned to gallop on their spindly, tottering legs. They didn't have Candy to help them get going, so I think it was harder for them than for me. Beyond those paddocks were the ancient red-brick buildings of the stables. Built to house the growing list of horses tended for by the great Victorian trainer John Porter, Park House had been designed with the express intention of keeping thoroughbred racehorses fit, healthy and relaxed.

With thick brick and stone double walls to keep them warm in winter and cool in summer, the spacious boxes were largely hidden from view so that no horse could get upset or distracted by the goings on outside. Whereas, nowadays, stables are built to give horses fresh air and a view, back in the 1880s, it was all about keeping them safe, quiet and away from prying eyes. It worked for John Porter, who was the most successful trainer of his day, with seven Derby winners, chief among them Ormonde, who, in 1886, won the Triple Crown of 2000 Guineas, Derby and St Leger.

\*     \*     \*

This entire fairyland for thoroughbreds was far, far away from me. I lived up on the hill in a room that the subsequent owners would use as a broom cupboard.

It had a bunk bed and bars on the window. There was a chair in the corner, and I'm pretty sure I had a chest of drawers, but there wasn't space for anything else.

I lay on my top bunk and stared out of the window at the big mast on top of Cottington Hill. It had red lights that burnt throughout the night. We called it the 'television mast' and you could see it from miles away. Even now, as I drive towards Kingsclere from Ashford Hill, I feel the pull of home when I see that big, ugly mast.

The huge garden spilled down the south-facing hill towards a clump of trees. There was hardly a flat patch on it, but it was great for pretending to be a sausage roll. I liked to wrap my brother Andrew in a blanket and roll him down the slope. When he reached the bottom, he emerged from the blanket blinking and swaying. Nearly always, he fell over. I enjoyed the sport of 'sausage rolling' far more than he did.

My father had proved that he could train racehorses and, thanks to the exploits of Mill Reef,

34

he had become champion trainer in 1971. He was the hot new kid on the block, and most of the owners were satisfied. They loved to feel part of a sport, enjoying success in what was essentially a high-stakes form of poker.

There was no knowing how good a horse might be, however fine its breeding, however knowledgeable its trainer and however talented its jockey. A champion racehorse is a unique being, and it's due partly to nature, partly to nurture. Equally, its development is part science, part art, because reading a horse is an instinctive thing. You can look at charts, consult stopwatches and plot programmes, but knowing whether a racehorse is ready to give of his best is based on intuition.

Some of the owners understood horses. Others understood business, or fashion, or music. There were American philanthropists, Canadian businessmen, British entrepreneurs, members of the aristocracy and the odd dodgy dealer who liked to pay his bills in readies and always tipped the stable staff double the standard amount. There was also Her Majesty the Queen.

Twice a year, in the spring and autumn, the most high profile of my father's owners came to the yard to see her horses. She always arrived early to see First Lot on the gallops and then have breakfast. This caused a kerfuffle. We relocated to the dining room, and my mother asked Mrs Jessop, our daily, to come in early to help with the breakfast. I practised curtseying for days—is it left leg behind right or the other way round? I'm still not sure.

It was OK when we were young because we could get away with not knowing how to behave. We also had Valkyrie to fall back on. The Queen would be thrilled to see her and, if we were with her, all was plain sailing.

You see, not long after I was born, the Queen had given my parents a gift. Knowing that the children of a would-be jockey turned trainer would most certainly want to ride, she gave us Valkyrie.

Valkyrie was a sweet-natured old girl, round and dark and fluffy, with a long tail that trailed the ground and a long, dark-brown mane. She was patient and wise, a proper Shetland pony schoolmistress whose first job was to teach me manners. She had no time for tantrums, shouting or foot-stamping. If she thought I was not behaving well, she would simply back me into the wall of the stable and pin me there until I calmed down. This could take minutes, it could take an hour, but she wouldn't budge until I had settled down and said sorry.

Valkyrie would do what she wanted to do, so the trick was to make her want to do what *I* wanted to do. She taught me the first and most important lesson of my life: if you want a pony, a horse—or a person—to do something for you, it's better if you ask nicely. If you are patient, kind and consistent, you will reap the rewards.

Valkyrie had taught both Prince Andrew and Prince Edward how to ride and had no doubt trodden on their toes as well. She may also have backed them into the corner of the stable when they were being naughty. Valkyrie was her own woman and would not be subject to anyone, Royal Family or commoner. I suspect that is one of the reasons the Queen was so fond of her.

When Her Majesty came to assess her blue-blooded racehorses at evening stables, I was

36

dispatched to get Valkyrie. At the end of the line of gleaming, fit, polished blue-bloods with their lads in spotless matching jackets and caps would be this little hairy Shetland pony with her equally scruffy-looking rider, neither of whom ever quite got the hang of the curtsey. The Queen smiled, crouched down and always had a long chat with Valkyrie, who generally remained well behaved. As soon as the inspection was over, Valkyrie dragged me towards the racehorses' feed room, knowing from one illegal visit that she would find sugar beet, oats, chopped carrots, freshly pulled grass, racing nuts, molasses and all sorts of goodies that she was never allowed. She was a strong old girl and I had no chance on the end of a rope, so one of the lads had to take over and haul her away from the treasure trove of fine foods.

Valkyrie was permanently on a diet. Not because she was fat—she was, but it didn't really matter, all Shetlands are pot-bellied—the diet was for her various ailments, which needed to be controlled, including laminitis and sweet-itch. Laminitis is a disease of the foot that, if managed well, need not cause serious problems, but it meant that Valkyrie could not be turned out in a field of lush spring grass, as it would cause a nitrogen-compound overload that would trigger an attack. I understood none of this, of course, so thought it most unfair that she wasn't allowed to enjoy the lovely green grass.

The sweet-itch was more obvious and rather more unattractive. It was caused by an allergic reaction to insect bites, which clearly caused her great discomfort, as she always rubbed her neck and backside on the nearest fence post as hard

37

as she could, losing lumps of mane and tail in the process and leaving bald, red, sore patches of skin. My mother did her best to keep her in the stable as much as possible, to douse her with anti-fly spray so that she didn't get bitten when she was out being ridden and with ointments to soothe the broken skin if she did, but Valkyrie's summer look was never her best.

I started to ride her at roughly the same time I started walking. I had a soft red leather saddle with a bar on the top to hold on to, and I had no fear because I didn't know there was anything to be afraid of. I knew this was where I should be, where I felt comfortable and where I was at home. I was born to ride.

My brother arrived in December 1972, the year that Lester Piggott won the Derby for the sixth time on Roberto. My father was at a party at the Argentine Embassy the night my mother gave birth, but the next day he picked up his wife and their son to bring them home. Grandma was at The Lynches with a bottle of champagne. She kissed my father and patted my mother on the shoulder.

'Good girl. Well done. That'll be that then,' she said, looking at my father with a silent signal that two children were quite enough now they had one of each. The fact that she herself had gone on to have two more boys after the allotted 'one of each' was quietly ignored.

Andrew was a calm baby. He didn't go in for tantrums, crying fits or sleepless nights. He was good in all the ways in which I had been bad. He had a sweet nature and he loved his food, gobbling up everything that was within reach.

I wasn't much interested in him as he couldn't

really *do* anything, and yet he seemed to get so much attention. It was strange.

*　　　*　　　*

During the winter, Valkyrie had been to visit a Shetland pony stallion called Cornelius. They seemed to like each other and, eight months later, she was even fatter than usual.

'There's a baby growing inside her,' my mother explained.

I thought it odd that a baby like Andrew could be growing inside Valkyrie, but figured that, if my mother said it was true, it must be.

Eleven months after her date with Cornelius, Valkyrie gave birth to Parsifal, known as Percy (the Wagner connection passed me by). Percy slipped out smoothly in the middle of the night and, by the morning, he was standing on the tiniest legs I had ever seen, feeding from Valkyrie's swollen teats. He was lighter than her in colour, with a reddish hue to his main body and a darker mane. Mum said he would be 'bay'.

Percy's nose, in the concave space between his mouth and his cheekbone, was the softest thing I had ever felt. I scratched the front of his face and looked him square in the eye.

'Percy, you are going to be my brother's pony. I think you will be a good boy and he will love you.'

The last part of that was true. Andrew did love him, but Percy was as far from being 'a good boy' as it was possible for a pony to be. Where his mother was warmth and sunshine, Percy was darkly evil. He bit, he kicked and, just as you'd got him into a nice bumpy canter, he loved to jam on the brakes and try to roll. If you hadn't already fallen off, the only suitable exit was to jump off before you found yourself squashed underneath him.

Percy looked as if butter wouldn't melt, but he was a little bastard. Andrew spent most of his early years being bullied by a pony no taller than a large dog. It must have been humiliating. On the plus side, he fell off a lot. My father had told us that to be proper jockeys, we had to fall off a hundred times. We took our father at his word and, as we were both keen to impress him and desperately wanted to be 'proper jockeys', we set our minds on the challenge ahead. Andrew and I worked out that to get up to a hundred falls, we would have to commit ourselves fully to the project. Ten falls a day seemed too many, but five was manageable and off we went. Or, to be more accurate, off we came.

'That's one more. I'm going to be a *proper jockey*!'

Our mother was always in charge of our riding, but she did not understand why we were gleefully falling off so often. Dad had not been allowed out alone with either one of us since the one and only time he had been told to 'mind Clare gets home safely'. He had handed Valkyrie over to Billy, one of the young boys working in the yard, smacked my pony on the backside and watched as we trotted off. I was barely two and a half. We headed out across the Starting Gate field, back in the direction of The Lynches. Billy was in a hurry. He didn't much like being given the task of childminding, and did not realize that I was bumping along, hanging on for dear life.

I held on for as long as I could but, as we gathered speed, I couldn't keep it up. I fell off.

40

It took Billy a full furlong before he realized I wasn't there. When he turned to look, I was in a crumpled heap in the middle of the field. I didn't cry immediately, mainly because I was in shock, but when the tears came they came thick and fast.

'Come on now, don't you be making a fuss,' Billy said. 'Up you get, straight back on. That's what happens when you have a fall. Got to get back in the saddle. Straight away.'

I cried all the way home as he held me in place. My mother took one look at my face, which had turned quite pale, and knew it must be serious. She sent Billy on his way, seething with anger that my father had been so irresponsible. She whipped the tack off Valkyrie, turned her out in the paddock with the shortest, least succulent grass and carried me into the house.

I was still in pain and couldn't move my shoulder, so she left a note for my father:

Make your own lunch. Gone to hospital with Clare.

P. S. You are a bloody idiot.

My parents had a friend who was a doctor at Basingstoke Hospital Accident & Emergency. We would come to know him well. He X-rayed my shoulder.

'I'm afraid it's broken,' Dr Elvin explained to my mother. 'Collar-bone. Should take a couple of weeks to mend. Can't do much more than try to control the pain, and I'd advise you, Emma, not to let the children anywhere near Ian.'

The good news was twofold. My bones were so soft that the break mended quickly, and Dad's other rule was that 'to be a proper jockey, you have to break your collarbone'. I had already done it and I hadn't even turned three. This was a serious head start. Dad took until he was over fifty-five to break *his* collarbone and, by that age, it really hurt and took ages to mend.

*  *  *

It was 1976, the year of the long, hot summer. An Italian jockey called Gianfranco Dettori, father of Frankie, won the 2000 Guineas on Wollow. Andrew and I decided we wanted to be cowboys or, more specifically, rodeo riders. I had a full cowboy outfit but decided that, for the purposes of authenticity, Andrew should borrow it and try out the rodeo riding. I had noticed that there were no female rodeo riders and, therefore, it had to be him.

Even at the age of five, I would certainly not have turned down the opportunity of doing something just because girls weren't meant to do it. No, I wanted Andrew to go first for a good reason.

We had worked out that what made the rodeo horses buck was a 'flank strap', a piece of leather tied under and round their flanks and touching the sensitive skin at the top of their hind legs. We duly found something that would do the trick and tied it round Valkyrie so that Andrew could reach back and pull on the strap and it would tickle her under her tummy and cause her to buck.

Well, Valkyrie had always been the mildest-mannered old lady in the world. Trying this on Percy would have been suicidal. But Valkyrie would look out for us. Putting her head down for grass was about her only vice. Or so we thought.

Good Lord, we had no idea what a mean and moody mare lay underneath that calm exterior. Andrew walked over in his chaps, plastic gun in holster and red neckerchief in place. He pulled down the tip of his cowboy hat and said, in quite a good American accent, 'I'm a rockin' rodeo rider!'

I helped him get on and led Valkyrie out into the field behind the house. I stood back and shouted, 'Hold on to your hats, folks, because here in the stadium for you tonight we have Cowboy Andrew and his bucking bronco Vixen. It's *rodeo time . . .*'

Andrew reached behind him and pulled the flank strap. Valkyrie, aka Vixen, went berserk. Totally and utterly bonkers. She galloped from one end of the field to the other, bucking with every stride. Andrew started screaming. His face was bright red. He was terrified. For all the falls we had practised taking, nothing quite prepared him for this, and I don't know whether it was a bail-out or a fall-off, but it was a relief to see him hit the deck.

We caught Valkyrie and took off the flank strap as quickly as we could. We led her quietly back to the stables and, when Mum asked why Andrew looked as if he had been crying, he said, 'Clare hit me.'

I didn't argue. It was better than the truth, and Mum was so used to it being the reason for his tears, she didn't question us further.

We decided not to tell the Queen about the rodeo incident.

Andrew's most spectacular fall came when we were galloping full pelt up the straight four-furlong woodchip strip that was used for the racehorses. It was a rare treat to be allowed on it, and we were doing our best impressions of Willie Carson

(Andrew's favourite jockey). Suddenly Percy stopped and Andrew, in the midst of head-down Carson-like pumping, carried on. He ended up face first in the woodchip. Percy had dived off sideways on to the grass and was merrily munching his way to a broader girth.

I was laughing, as I thought Andrew had done it on purpose. He hadn't. I was keeping count of his score and told him that he was up to number fifty-six. He didn't respond. His round face looked up, covered in brown bits of wood. He was crying. He was bruised and battered, but he hadn't broken anything. Not this time.

My mother got fed up with us falling off before we even got into the sixties and told Dad that he had to do something.

'It doesn't count if you're falling off on purpose,' he said, in his important voice.

'What?' we responded together.

'Sorry, but it's not the same. Falling off is something that happens by mistake, not by design. You can't just go round falling off all the time. It's dangerous, and your mother doesn't like it.'

'Oh,' we said.

It was rather disappointing—all that effort and none of it counted.

However, it did teach both of us not to be afraid of falling. It's funny how not being scared of something means that you no longer try to fight it and, in not fighting it, you find it doesn't control you.

Dad inadvertently taught us not to avoid doing something because we might fall or fail. Do it, enjoy it and, if you fall, so what? You'll get straight back on again.

# 4

# Bertie

They say a person's choice of dog reflects their personality. Some dogs, all too clearly, look like their owners—or owners can grow to look like their dogs. My favourite image from Crufts was a tall, sleek woman with long hair running alongside her Afghan hound, his ears falling up and down against his face as her hair did the same. They fell into the same rhythm, with blond locks flowing, lolloping across the arena in perfect symmetry.

My mother had her boxer. She was warm, protective and slightly smelly. Candy, that is, not my mother.

My father? Well, he had a lurcher. A proud, dismissive and vicious killing-machine called Bertie.

Dad, with his jet-black hair and olive skin, always used to tell us that he was a pot pourri of different bloodlines. He said he had Gypsy blood through his great-grandfather, a horse dealer in Leicestershire, and we had no reason to disbelieve him. Dad could never have lived in London or worked in an office. For one thing, he is always slightly too loud and too obvious with his observations on other people.

'Honestly, why on earth would you let yourself get like that?' he will say in a stage whisper about anyone who carries an ounce of excess flesh. This is not helpful in a crowd.

He hates to be inside and, if he could, he would spend all day out in the elements—he's not much interested in talking to people. Animals, however, fascinate him. There is something intuitive about the way he is around horses that makes me believe he has Gypsy blood. I certainly think that his ancestors lived and worked with horses and dogs.

Dad's father, Gerald Balding, had spent his childhood on the backs of various ponies and horses, improving them so that they could be sold by his father for a profit. His Uncle Billy had taught him and his brothers to play polo. They rode long, with one hand on the reins, turning their ponies by placing the reins on the side of the neck. The ponies and the boys learned fast as they galloped around the big field in Leicestershire, hitting a ball with a mallet.

Billy Balding taught them to be decisive and

strong, to 'ride off' each other, to take their line and commit to it, to be forceful with players but sensitive with their ponies, never yanking them in the mouth or exhausting them. They would hop from one pony to another, the skill of fast interchanges being as valuable as hitting the ball accurately.

In polo, there is a handicap system so that really good players can form a team with overweight, rich businessmen and make them feel as if they are contributing something. The best player is rated 10 and effectively makes his team start at −10 goals, while the worst player is rated +2 so his team starts with a 2-goal advantage. The handicaps of the four team members are added up to create a team handicap, and teams of similar ability will be pitted against each other.

Gerald Balding became a ten-goal player. The Gerald Balding Cup is still played at Cirencester Park in his memory and, to date, no British player has matched his ability.

In the 1920s and '30s, he made the most of a golden age for polo—a thundering, fast sport that married danger and excitement with wealth and privilege. With a stroke of good fortune that would later be mirrored by his son, Gerald met and befriended an American multimillionaire who became his patron. Jock Whitney was a friend of Fred Astaire, was at times romantically linked with Tallulah Bankhead and Joan Crawford, had inherited $20 million from his father and was mad for horses.

Whitney owned Easter Hero, the Cheltenham Gold Cup winner of 1929 and '30 who was also runner-up in the Grand National. Somewhere along the line—family history does not relate when or where—Whitney discovered Gerald Balding's talent for polo so asked him out to New Jersey to help instruct the socially ambitious, wealthy young men who were taking up the game in droves.

Gerald encouraged his brothers Barney and Ivor to follow him to a land where they would not be limited by lack of money or social connections. They were single, handsome Englishmen with good manners and a way with horses. As far as the New Jersey set was concerned, the Balding Brothers were the most eligible new bachelors in town.

There is a photo of the three of them leaning on their polo sticks, all with slicked-back coal-coloured hair, wearing pantaloon-type breeches with black leather boots and short-sleeved shirts. They looked like movie stars. They played at the Meadow Brook Club in Long Island, cheered on by pretty, well-connected young women. Special trains from New York would arrive with thousands of spectators. They were living the Great Gatsby lifestyle, and yet they had inherited nothing, apart from exceptional ability on a horse.

Gerald spent the spring and summer months managing and playing for Jock Whitney's Greentree team. In the late autumn, he headed out to India, where he played polo for the Maharajah of Jaipur, who himself was a ten-goal player.

Gerald represented England in the Westchester Cup, the big polo match against the USA, in 1930, '36 and '39. Along the way, he married an American called Eleanor Hoagland and, by the time he headed off for the Second World War, he had seen the birth of his eldest son, Toby, in 1936 and my father, Ian, in 1938. When he returned from the war, he and his family moved to England, where he started to train racehorses, with Jock Whitney as his major owner.

\*      \*      \*

Many of our dogs and horses were given family names. Dad's first lurcher was called Billy, after his Great-uncle Billy who had taught his father how to play polo. Bertie was named after his grandfather, Albert. Bertie was the colour of August wheat, with a smooth, velvety head and a broken, rough body of hair. His eyes were pale brown, his nose aquiline and his knobbly tail had wisps of hair hanging down from it. I thought he was a domesticated lion, and I was wary of him. He was not warm and cuddly like Candy. He would raise his lip if I came too close when he was in bed. He didn't actually bite me, but he would snap at the air to make sure I knew it was his space.

He liked my father, and when Dad walked into the room he would be delirious with joy. He wagged that thin, bony tail so ferociously that it smashed against the furniture and split. Even if you like Jackson Pollock, you probably don't want a bloody imitation of his art on your kitchen walls. Consequently, Bertie spent many weeks with his tail tip taped up.

The word 'lurcher' comes from a word in Romany, 'lur', meaning 'thief' and, my God, Bertie had that bit nailed. If you so much as glanced out of the window while eating, he would whip a potato off your plate, slinking away before you had even noticed.

Once, during Royal Ascot, when my parents had

49

important owners staying, my mother had laid out the starter for a dinner party. It was Parma ham and melon. Mum thought she would get ahead of the game so that she could enjoy pre-dinner drinks with the guests but, by the time they came into the dining room, there was just melon. Each and every piece of Parma ham had been delicately and thoroughly removed. There was not a shred of evidence left, to the point that my mother genuinely thought she had forgotten to put the ham out.

Bertie was in his bed, pretending to be asleep, one eye half open to survey any potential fall-out. I wouldn't have put it past him to have planted half a piece of ham in Candy's bed while she snored, so that she got the blame.

A lurcher is a mixture of a sight hound, usually a greyhound, with a type of terrier or pastoral dog. They were invented in Norman times to get round some daft law that said that only the gentry could own smart, majestic breeds like the wolfhound or deerhound. Commoners were effectively forbidden from owning a sight hound, in case they used them to poach game.

Well, the commoners came up with something even better: the speed and eagle-eyed vision of the greyhound or whippet with the brains of a Bedlington terrier or a collie is a lethal combination. They are hunters by nature, with the ability to run, turn, jump fences, catch and kill their prey silently. They will also retrieve, bringing a hare or a rabbit back from miles away. They are stealthy, cunning and ruthless.

By the twentieth century, they had become the favourite breed of the Romany Gypsy and had learned to be good around horses. Perhaps that is why they became so popular among the racing set. There was also a rumour that they had been trained to run back home shortly after they had been sold, so that they could be sold again and again. For the first year we had Bertie, my parents kept expecting him to disappear back to his breeders, and I wouldn't have minded much if he had.

Bertie was the perfect companion for my father. They could roam the countryside together, Bertie shadowing my father's horse, galloping alongside him, jumping fences with him and stopping to admire the view. He liked to take off suddenly with a spurt, his teeth bared into a manic grin as he enjoyed his own grace and speed. Sometimes he did this alongside the racehorses and, if a two-year-old could keep up with Bertie for half of the straight chippings, then everyone knew it would win a race.

In full flow, the lurcher has a wild and raw beauty. The power is all in the quarters, the hind legs coming either side of the forelegs and then exploding the body forward in a series of leaps that blur into a galloping motion. Bertie's back thighs were thick and strong, his head held straight and low, his commitment total. The trouble was that he was easily distracted. He might see a rabbit or a hare as he was belting up the gallop and, within a millisecond, he would turn and throw himself into headlong pursuit.

He took wire fences, hedges and ditches in his stride, oblivious to where the hare might lead him. All he could see was the target, and all he felt was the need to destroy it. He would spin this way and that, changing direction to cut off the hare and, as he got close, he would fling himself forward, sinking his teeth into the back of its neck, rolling and diving

51

as he did so and breaking the hare's neck with one flick of his own.

It was brutal to behold.

The strange thing was that he wasn't hunting to eat—he rarely if ever tried to eat his prey—he was hunting because he had a taste for the kill. Something inside him went 'ding' when he saw a rabbit, a hare or a deer, and he was off. No amount of roaring from my father would bring him back, until he returned, however long afterwards, with a hint of pride in his eyes and a dead animal in his mouth. He dropped it at my father's feet and waited to be congratulated.

Bertie was an alpha-male dog: a hunter, a killer, a thief and a rascal. Added to the mix, he was also impossibly handsome.

The lurcher, as a breed, became so popular in racing circles that, in Lambourn, the Valley of the Racehorse, a group of enthusiasts set up the Lambourn Lurcher Show. My father would not ordinarily have gone to a dog show if you paid him, but the Lambourn Lurcher Show was different, and Bertie was a canine reflection of him. He had to show off his boy.

Bertie won 'Best in Show' for five years running and became the most sought-after lurcher stud dog in the south of England. Oh, that his human children had ever made my father as proud!

\*       \*       \*

Dad spent most of his life in a distinctive uniform: dark-brown breeches, tight around the calves, baggy around the thighs, jodhpur boots, a short leather or cotton jacket and a flat tweed cap. Neither he

52

nor any of the stable staff—'the lads', as they were always called—wore crash hats or back protectors. Some rode out bareheaded, others with caps like John Hallum's that were turned backwards on the gallops.

Dad always liked to ride with the racehorses. In the winter he would be on one of the jumpers, and in the summer on a 'hack'—a retired racehorse who was settled enough to stand and watch the others but fast enough to gallop after a loose one if a lad had fallen off. Every morning around eighty horses would be fed, groomed, ridden, washed off and given a pick of grass. Dad knew each one by name, could recite its breeding, where it had run so far and where it was likely to run next time. With time, he learned how certain horses might react, what distances would be most suitable or what ground was preferable, because he had trained their sire or their dam.

We had about forty employees, all of whom lived on site. They were in charge of two horses each, and they fed them, groomed them, mucked them out and rode them. On work mornings, a jockey or one of the senior work riders might take over the duties on the gallops but, day to day, each lad 'owned' his two horses and was responsible for them.

If they were single lads, they had a room in the Hostel, in the centre of the three yards, where they had their meals cooked by Harvey and Joyce, who would also, if not actually do their washing, gently show them where the washing machine was. Some lads arrived as thirteen-year-olds, having left or been thrown out of school. They needed surrogate parents, and Harvey and Joyce became just that.

The senior or married staff lived in cottages

around the place. Some had been built by John Porter, some by my grandfather and some by my father. They had to live nearby because of the hours. They were up at 6 a.m. in the winter, earlier in the summer to avoid the heat of the day, riding until midday and then either going racing or coming back for evening stables at 4.30 p.m. They worked every Saturday morning and alternate Saturday evenings and Sundays. Christmas or New Year could be taken off, but not both together.

During the seventies, the number of female employees increased and Park House was divided in two. The back wing of it, where my mother and her brothers had slept under the care of Nanny, was sealed off from the rest of the house. That provided six rooms for girls so that they could be safe from randy little corridor creepers in the middle of the night.

My father always said his job was like that of a headmaster. He was always putting out one fire or another. Two lads would have got into a fight because one said the other looked like a sack of potatoes in the saddle; a young girl would come to him worried she was pregnant; or a married lad claiming his wife was having an affair with the farrier; a would-be jockey felt frustrated because he wasn't being given a chance to ride in races; another was homesick.

I am not sure that Dad would have made a fully fledged counsellor, but he was honest in what he said and thought. He was also practical— encouraging all the young lads to play football in the summer and enter the Stable Lads' Boxing Competition during the winter months so that they channelled their energy into sport rather than petty arguments or sexual conquests.

Back at home, however, my father had little clue how to deal with a temperamental toddler and a baby who wanted milk all day long. He never changed a nappy in his life, never got up in the middle of the night to see why one of us was crying and he certainly never made us a meal.

Oh, that last bit's not true. He once made me beans on toast.

'This will be the best beans on toast you have ever had,' he said as he covered the toast in a layer of butter.

'Mmmm,' I said, wanting him to know how much I appreciated it.

'Isn't that good? Doesn't it taste yummy? Is it the best meal you've ever had?'

'Yeth'—my mouth was full—'ith the beth'd ever.'

For weeks, my father talked about having given me the most delicious meal I had ever had. He did the same with the dogs. One of his jobs around the house—no, his only job—was to feed the dogs. He did this with the concentration, the effort and the chaos of a Michelin chef. A raw egg, left-over vegetables, thinly sliced meat and stock were added to the combined dog mix that said all over the bag that it was a 'complete meal' and didn't need any extras.

'Oh diggy, dig dogs,' he liked to sing as he concocted the dogs' food. 'Oh diggy, dig dogs, yummy, yummy, yum yum.'

As he put down their bowls, he told each dog how lucky he or she was to have such a special meal, made by him. They didn't much give a hoot and my mother got annoyed with the mess he made and the effects of the raw eggs. Dad didn't realize that his 'job' was meant to include washing up the dog bowls, but he was whistling a happy tune on his way to the office by the time they'd finished eating their banquet.

I wanted a hot chocolate before I went to bed. Mum was busy doing something so I asked my father.

'A hot chocolate, you say? A hot choccy chocolate? Well, I shall make you the *best* hot chocolate you have ever had. Oh yes I will.'

He was humming to himself as he poured the milk into the kettle to boil it. As he flicked the switch, even I knew this was a mistake.

'What the hell have you done?' My mother's voice was incredulous as she surveyed the spewing foam of milk coming out of the mouth of the kettle.

I stood staring at the kettle, clasping my blanket close to my face and sucking my thumb.

'She wanted hot chocolate.' My father motioned at me, as if it was my fault.

'So you put the milk in the kettle?' My mother could not believe he had been quite so stupid.

'Yes. It needs to boil, doesn't it?'

There was no apology, no contrition. As far as my father was concerned, it was a fault with the kettle or the milk if they didn't get along. It certainly wasn't his problem.

'Where were you anyway?' He turned on his heels and headed outside. 'I'm taking the dogs out.'

That was his way of ending any conversation in which he did not wish to play a part. The dogs were his shield, the end to a dinner party, the excuse to avoid washing up or the reason for not hanging around at someone else's party.

Mum sighed and cleaned up the mess. I

continued to suck my thumb and determined that, in future, I would either wait for my mother or learn how to do things for myself.

*      *      *

When Andrew first arrived, he came with his own nurse. I was impressed, not so much because she was a proper nurse with a uniform and everything but because I knew she was a really good rider. In fact, she had ridden at the Olympics and had won Badminton Horse Trials. Her name was Jane Bullen, and she had ruled the world on a little horse called Our Nobby. As Jane Holderness-Roddam, she would win Badminton again on Warrior.

Jane kept her eye on Andrew, and I played innocent, even pretending to be interested in his ability to crawl or to grip anything that came towards him. I studied him carefully, watching as he developed his set habits. He was always hungry and was becoming impressively strong. When I tried to poke his eyes (purely to see what they felt like), he grasped my finger and squeezed until I screamed.

After Jane came a nanny called Liz. She had wild grey hair and a florid face. She came from Ireland and would phone home once a week to have long conversations in a language I couldn't understand, but I liked it when she read me stories and put on different voices. I liked it even better if she made the stories up—that meant that I was in them, and so were Andrew, Valkyrie, Bertie and Candy.

I also liked Liz because she talked to me as if I was a grown-up and, in my head, I was. Even at the age of four I was mature enough to know that you should never put milk in the kettle.

# 5

# Flossy

Although Candy was my protector, she was not *my* dog. She belonged to my mother, and my mother belonged to her. So when Candy had her first litter of puppies, I attached myself to the one who attached herself most strongly to me. This puppy liked to suck on my chin and my earlobes as I held her up to my face. Sometimes we would just fall asleep together in the corner of their pen.

The puppies had their own shed in the garden.

It was called, naturally, the Puppy Shed. Inside, the floor was covered with newspaper, there was an infrared light for warmth and a large square wooden tray with cushions in it—a handmade dog bed for a mother and her puppies.

My puppy looked like her mother, with a reddish, chestnut-coloured body, white chest and a little streak of white down the centre of her eyes leading to her black button nose.

We called her Flossy. Andrew said that Flossy was lazy and that she was always making smells. It is true, she did more than her fair share of 'bottom burps', but to me she was perfect.

I am looking at a photo of me as a three-year-old. I am wearing a royal-blue tank top with green edging, a white polo neck, a slightly grumpy look on my face and a studded leather dog collar around the crown of my head. It was my homage to Flossy. I was one of the pack and would curl up with Flossy in her bed and drink out of her water bowl. I tried sucking on the odd Bonio biscuit too, but they weren't quite sweet enough for my taste.

I loved the Puppy Shed. It was peaceful in there. No shouting, no strange people turning up unannounced. No pens or papers we weren't allowed to pick up or things we weren't allowed to touch. I could listen to the gurgle of the puppies as they drank Candy's milk or watch them sleep all piled up on one another, their fat little tummies pointing to the sky. A whole day in the Puppy Shed could slide by unnoticed.

If I got bored, there was always a challenge I could set my little brother.

'Quick, quick, I'll time you,' I would urge Andrew to fetch my hanky, which I needed to hold in my hand as I sucked my thumb. 'Let's see if you can do it quicker than yesterday.'

Usually I wouldn't bother to start the stopwatch but would make a big show of stopping it and telling him he was just outside his record time, so would have to try again tomorrow. The competitive streak was strong in us both, so any challenge would have either a time to beat, a mark to surpass or an intrinsic sense of danger.

We were also creative. We decided that the Puppy Shed, our new favourite playroom, needed sprucing up. The paint was flaking off and it was a boring cream colour. I had spotted a pot of turquoise paint in a cupboard under the stairs with some brushes. It was a sign. Not to use it would have been a crime.

Andrew was going through a phase of calling himself 'Alan'. A child psychologist might deduce that he was trying to carve out his own identity, but I think he was just being weird for the sake of it.

I climbed the stairs to share my artistic plans for the Puppy Shed. He was in his room, sitting in the corner, licking the radiator.

'Andrew, what are you doing?' I asked.

'It's Alan,' he replied, deadpan.

'OK—Alan—what are you doing?'

'I'm licking the radiator.' He looked at me as if I was stupid. In this situation, I hardly thought it was *me* who was the stupid one.

'I can see that. Why?'

'It tastes of tea,' he said.

'Does it?' Now I was intrigued. Curiosity was my strong suit and my downfall. Andrew/Alan was still licking, smiling away to himself.

So I knelt down beside him and leant towards

the radiator. I stuck out my tongue and let it touch the white paint. What had tempted him to taste the radiator in the first place? Strange child. Yet here I was, about to copy him.

The radiator did not look that appetizing. I tried to fake it, making an elaborate licking motion with my tongue, keeping it an eighth of an inch away from contact. Andrew put his head on one side and looked at me.

'You're right,' I said. 'It tastes of tea.'

'You wouldn't know,' he said calmly. 'You didn't lick it.'

That was a red rag to a bull. I couldn't bear him to be enjoying an experience that I was not having. So I leant right into the radiator and licked as if it was the sweetest lollipop in the world. I licked and licked and licked. I did it with such intensity and force that I lost any sense of feeling. It may well have tasted of tea, but I wouldn't have known.

After a minute or two of ferocious licking, I sat back. Andrew was staring at me.

'Wow,' he said. 'That was a lot.'

My tongue did not feel right at all. I opened my mouth and stuck it out. Andrew gasped. My tongue was covered in blood. I had licked so hard that I had hundreds of little cuts all over it. The taste of blood in my mouth, combined with whatever was on the radiator, made me feel quite sick. I ran to the bathroom, where my mother found me vomiting.

'What have you been doing?' she asked.

'She was licking my radiator,' said Andrew. This was, after all, the truth.

'Now why would you do that? Ridiculous girl.'

I couldn't speak because my tongue had swollen up. I pointed at my brother and started to say

61

'Andrew—'

He said, 'It's Alan,' and walked out of the bathroom.

My mother made me gargle TCP, which stung like mad, and then she sent me to my room.

You might have thought that I would have learned an important lesson from this—that it is always worth following your own instinct instead of following another person. If the crowd are throwing themselves over the cliff and you know they will fall, do not copy them. Yes, that would have been a very good thing to have locked away in my head and brought out in times of need. Sadly, I learned nothing of the sort.

When I was eventually allowed out of my room, speech was still difficult. I found my brother and motioned to him that we needed to do some painting. I thought it would be the perfect way of getting back into my mother's good books: do something really positive and helpful. The puppies would like it, Candy would like it and Mum would be so impressed.

That was the plan.

Andrew and I carried the large pot of turquoise paint between us. We grabbed as many brushes as we could find, including a large broom, which I thought might be good for the bits we couldn't reach. I had seen the painters doing the high bits with a brush on a pole that looked a bit like a broom.

The puppies were pleased to see us, and Candy heaved herself up, careful not to tread on any of her offspring, to say hello. Her lips eased back into a wide-mouthed grin, her head was on one side, and her backside was swaying as she wagged her stump of a tail.

'Hello, girl, we've come to do thum decorating,' I said, with difficulty.

Andrew helped me rip off the lid of the paint pot, and we went for it. I have to confess that, even now, I am wary of paint and I'm sure it goes back to that day. Within seconds, there was paint *everywhere*—on our clothes, in our hair, on the puppies, on Candy. I had no idea that paint could be so intrusive.

The colour was much brighter than it had looked on the side of the pot, and it was hard to get a really smooth finish, especially with the broom. We soldiered on for an hour or so before we heard our mother calling us in for tea. I stood back to admire our handiwork and, as I did so, a shadow fell across the floor.

There was a figure standing in the doorway. It was taller than my mother, wearing a skirt and a turtleneck sweater. The shadow had its hands on its hips. Andrew was facing the door.

'Hello, Grandma,' he said, cheerfully. 'Look what we've done.'

I turned around, slowly, hoping that our enterprise would find favour. My grandmother made a sort of whistling noise with her nose. It was a strange sound, but I knew it wasn't good. She did not look happy. She did not look proud. She looked quite the opposite. She turned on her heel and marched back towards the house, meeting my mother midway across the lawn.

'Your children are out of control,' I heard her say. 'They are feral little urchins. I will come back when you have sorted them out.'

My mother approached the Puppy Shed.

'Oh God. Oh my dear God. I'm so sorry, Candy,' she said to her boxer. 'I'm so, so sorry.'

Her voice was still and quiet.

'Leave it. Leave it all. I will tell your father about this.'

That's when I knew it was really bad. I wanted to argue our case, to reason with my mother, but my tongue was so sore that I could only communicate through sign language—and that didn't seem to get my point across. It's not as if we were trying to be deliberately naughty. We had been trying to help. We really had.

Mum marched us back into the house, and the next hour smelt strongly of white spirit. She had to cut paint out of our hair, throw away our clothes, wipe us down with cotton wool doused in white spirit and then put us in the bath. She left us with Liz, the Irish nanny, as she disappeared to clear up as best she could and wipe paint from the short coats of the puppies.

When my father got back from evening stables, I could hear him laughing downstairs.

'Ian, it's not funny,' I heard my mother say. 'You should have seen the state of them. You're going to have to do something. My mother said they were feral—feral, for God's sake. She wouldn't even stay for tea.'

I heard my father climb the stairs, and I was breathing quickly as he opened my door. I was frightened he was going to spank me so I pretended to be asleep. I wanted to tell him that we weren't really furry. Or at least we hadn't meant to be. I didn't know why it was a bad thing to be furry, but clearly Grandma didn't like furry children. My tongue was still throbbing. I opened my eyes a little

64

bit and saw him standing there with his hunting crop by his side. I held my breath. He tapped it against his leg.

'I know you can hear me,' he said. 'Make sure you say sorry to your mother in the morning, and don't do it again.'

With that, he shut the door. I couldn't sleep for ages and, when I did, I dreamt I was swimming in a pool of paint.

We were banned from the Puppy Shed for the next week, which was torture. We both said sorry to Mum, who just shook her head sadly. Grandma didn't come to see us for ages and, when she did, she took one look at my head and said, 'What have you done to her hair? She looks like a bloody lesbian.'

\*     \*     \*

Andrew and I were keen to hone our skills as jockeys. My mother said we were only allowed to ride Valkyrie for an hour every morning. We both thought our Shetland pony would have preferred to spend all day with us, but Mum said something about 'abusing her good nature', which I never really understood.

'What is going on?' It was my mother.

Andrew and I were in the middle of the kitchen, with Valkyrie.

'She's come in for some lunch,' I said matter-of-factly.

I was brushing her mane as she tucked into a bowl of cereal. Andrew was picking his nose and looking slightly confused.

'It was Clare's idea,' he said, under his breath.

'Look, Mummy, she loves Shreddies,' I said, by way of distraction. 'And she's really comfortable. She wanted to see where we live and we couldn't stop her.'

It was bad timing, as I'm convinced my mother was coming round to the idea of Valkyrie having lunch with us every day, but the pot-bellied pony lifted her tail and dumped a steaming pile of poo on the kitchen floor.

'*Take her back to the stable. Right now.*' My mother did not raise her voice often and, when she did, it was scary. What she usually did was count to ten. I would often wait until she got to eight, just to be sure she wasn't joshing, but there was no count this time. It was to happen right away.

'Can't she finish her Shred—'

'She most certainly cannot.'

I pulled Valkyrie's head, with difficulty, out of the bowl and trudged out of the kitchen with my pony reluctantly in tow. Andrew stayed where he was, disowning any part in the project, while I stayed with Valkyrie in her stable, telling her about all the other rooms in the house and how I would have taken her upstairs to see my bedroom except that she wouldn't have been able to fit through the door.

Some hours later, Liz came to get me and, when I returned to the kitchen, the floor was sparkling clean.

\*     \*     \*

Dad was keen on a golfer called Tom Watson but cross with the England cricket team because they had lost some big series to Australia. Red Rum had won his third Grand National. A big, flashy chestnut with white socks and a white blaze down his face called The Minstrel won the Derby under a driving finish from Lester Piggott. Andrew was upset because Willie Carson, his favourite jockey, had finished second.

My father was trying to consolidate the position he had earned courtesy of Mill Reef, but even that early in his career he knew he would never enjoy another season so perfect. If you have trained the best horse anyone has ever seen, it would be sheer arrogance to expect another one like him to come along.

So he did the best with what he was given, and with people like Paul Mellon, the Queen and the Canadian millionaire Bud McDougald, who bred their own stock and liked to see them race in their own colours, life was good. He was a top-ten trainer and he was based at a place that was horse heaven on earth.

There is a book called *Kingsclere* that was published in 1896. It is by John Porter, the most successful trainer of the Victorian era and the man who put Park House on the racing map. Between 1863 and his retirement in 1905, he trained twenty-three Classic winners, including seven Derby winners. All of them were prepared and cared for on the gallops of Cannon Heath Downs and the stables of Park House.

When he first arrived at Kingsclere, Porter asked a shepherd what sort of country it was.

'Well, zur,' came the reply, 'I can tell you that in a very few words. It is too poor a country to live in and it's far too healthy to die in. We just hangs on as long as we likes, and then we comes up here and

67

gets blowed away.'

We had a gallop man a bit like that shepherd. He was called Jonna Holley and was a big, round man with a weather-beaten face who spent all day patrolling the Downs, either on his tractor or on foot, repairing the divots made by the hooves of horses thundering up the gallops. I liked Jonna. He didn't say much, but he kept an eye on all of us and he knew the Downs, the sheep in the fields and the buzzards that swept overhead. He was a man of the land. He didn't come to the stables except to fill up the tractor with diesel, and yet he knew every horse and every rider.

What were the Downs made of? Chalk, grass, a few trees and Jonna.

The only things Jonna wouldn't have known were the stables. They were indoors, and he didn't do indoors. The design of the yard was precise. The boxes were twelve feet wide, deep and high; the floor had to be made of a material that does not allow a horse to slip; and there should be no sharp edges.

'In fact,' wrote John Porter, 'there should be no projections or sharp rises in any part of the stable where a horse can possibly injure himself. He is sure to do this if there is half a chance.'

Every decision, whether it was the design and placement of hayracks and ventilation shafts, drainage, the paving or the material that is best for roofing, was made with the health and welfare of the horse in mind.

*Kingsclere* outlines best practice for feeding racehorses, with high-quality oats, a few beans or peas for flavour and some chaff (cut hay) to help them chew. They should have a bran mash twice a week, carrots now and then, and fresh grass. Porter was a stickler for tidiness and expected the horses and their stables to look perfect morning and evening.

The horses came first at Park House, but the staff who worked there in the late 1800s were also well treated, by comparison with other yards. Mr Dollar tells John Porter that in many racing establishments the lads 'have to perform their ablutions in the stables bucket with the aid of the sponge and cloths that have been used for grooming the horses'. At Kingsclere, they had bathrooms, lavatories and a dormitory, as well as a recreation room and a dining room where their meals were cooked by 'The Captain'. It amazes me how little has really changed.

There is no longer a curfew with lights out at ten o'clock every night, nor a requirement for the lads to go to church on Sundays, but the daily routine is much the same: feeding, morning exercise, grooming, grazing, rest for the horses in the afternoon, evening stables when all the horses are inspected, and an evening feed.

The dedication of the trainer was, and still is, complete. There are no short cuts with racehorses, no decisions that can be made by others, no substitute for knowing your own horses. Good staff are essential: a wise Head Lad, a supportive assistant trainer and a lively Travelling Head Lad, who is in charge of the horses when they leave the stables for racecourses around the world. These are all essential, but the trainer needs to be on top of it all.

John Porter felt the same about the responsibility of being a trainer in 1894 as my father did eighty years later:

He can see nothing through other eyes. He must make a separate study of each horse; find out his constitutional peculiarities; watch daily, even hourly, the progress he is making, so as to have his charge in perfect condition on the day of his race. He must not be a week too soon, or a week too late, for that means defeat.

To be a trainer is not a job; it is not even a career: it is a way of life. My father did not really enjoy going on holiday because he felt he should be at home with the horses. He would allow himself a week off, maybe two, in the winter—but from February to the end of November he was working full-time.

I say 'working', but I'm not sure he thought of it that way—it was what he was put on earth to do. Dad only ever paid himself a small salary. Every penny of profit made in prize money would be ploughed back into the business—for new gallops or a new yard, to build a swimming pool for the horses (one of the first in Britain) or to improve the footing in the avenues and walkways so that there was no danger of a horse picking up a stone bruise.

There is an old saying 'No hoof, no horse,' and my father employed a full-time farrier. He had a forge where he shaped the steel shoes the horses wore for their everyday work and the light, aluminium ones they wore on race days. Weight is crucial in racing—the more weight a horse carries, the more he will be slowed down. So it is important to have the lightest shoes possible, but aluminium shoes are fragile, so they can't be worn for longer than about twenty-four hours.

Our farrier was called Speedy. I think this may have been ironic, as he was not the fastest worker in the world. As well as tending the racehorses, he would make regular checks on the horses up at The Lynches, including Valkyrie and Percy. Andrew and I weren't sure about Speedy. He didn't seem to like us much.

'What are you doing here?' I asked as he was getting out of his Ford Cortina. It was bright red, with a black roof. It was a warm day, so the windows were half open.

Speedy slammed the door and looked down at me, his shoulder-length hair falling over a wide-collared shirt.

'What's it to you?' he asked.

I stood my ground and put my hand down to Flossy, who was by my side. I could feel his aggression. Speedy was strapping on the leather chaps that protected his legs while he placed a horse or pony's hoof on his thigh. Hanging from the hook above the back seat of his car was a blue velvet suit.

He went to the boot of the car to get his kit bag of files, hammers, nails and shoes.

'I need to know,' I said importantly. 'You can't just turn up here. What are you doing?'

Speedy was hot, he was irritated and he was in a hurry.

'I've come to chop your pony's head off,' he stated as he walked off towards the stables.

I was aghast. I stood rooted to the spot for a moment and then ran to get Andrew. I even played by his rules to make sure I got his attention straight away.

'Alan! Quick!' I shouted. 'We've got to do something. Speedy is going to chop Valkyrie's head off. He said so. He told me he's going to do it.'

Andrew could see that I was not joking. This was a clear and present danger to our pony's life. We must take action. We crept through to the block of four stables that looked across to Cottington Hill. Speedy was in the first of the stables, shoeing Milo—Dad's point-to-pointer, which was meant to have been his wedding present to my mother.

It would take him a while to get to Valkyrie, so we had time to exact our revenge and still prevent him from doing her any harm.

The gravel parking area by the back door of The Lynches was in the process of being re-surfaced. There was a huge pile of sticky red sand and clay mixture near Speedy's car.

My brother and I looked at each other. We looked at the pile of what I believe is called 'hoggin', and we looked at Speedy's car. I nodded at Andrew and we got to work.

We shovelled as much hoggin as we could through the open windows of the car. I remember enjoying the repetitive motion of going from the pile to the car and back again, watching the red-mulch mound shrink on the outside and grow on the inside. We worked until we were exhausted, and we did a good job.

'Now we need to stop him,' I told Andrew, and we marched off towards the stables. Speedy was about to start work on Valkyrie.

'*Stop!*' I shouted. '*Leave her alone!*'

Andrew joined in: '*Don't do it!*'

'Shh, now,' Speedy said, 'you'll scare the horses.

What is the matter with you two?'

My mother appeared. 'What's all this commotion?' she asked. 'What's wrong?'

'He's going to chop Valkyrie's head off. He told me he was going to. Don't let him, Mummy, don't let him. He's a murderer!'

She looked at Speedy and raised her right eyebrow. He shrugged his shoulders.

'I was only joking,' he said, with nails in his mouth. He bent over and started filing Valkyrie's front hoof.

Andrew and I glanced at each other, and at our palms, which were scarlet from the hoggin. We were red-handed, but we had not yet been caught.

Andrew and I were hiding in the wigwam at the far end of the garden when we heard Speedy roar. It turns out he was due to wear the velvet suit to a party that night. It was his best. It also turns out that red clay and sand doesn't come out, even after dry-cleaning. It's also almost impossible to remove from the stitching of car seats or from the floor surface.

My mother had to buy Speedy a replacement suit. She also had to pay for the car to be valet cleaned. We both got smacked with the back of the hairbrush, but it didn't really hurt, and I always felt the moral victory was ours. Years later, Mum admitted that she thought it was a bloody stupid thing for Speedy to have said.

I stayed in my room with Flossy for comfort. She was big and solid and, when she didn't have wind, she smelt safe. She looked at me with her big, sad face while I told her what had happened, and she licked the tears off my cheeks. She was my best friend.

73

# 6

# Volcano

Growing up is tough if you ride ponies. Getting taller is the hardest thing to deal with because it means you have to move on. Just as you have learned to understand a pony, trust it and love it, you grow out of it and have to build a relationship with a new, bigger pony. One marriage ends and another has to begin straight away. These marriages are not all an equal, happy meeting of minds.

It was with dread that I realized I would not be small enough or light enough to ride Valkyrie for ever. I was six and a half years old; Andrew was not yet five and was riding her son, Percy. They were getting on like a house on fire. By which I mean, destructively.

Percy would do pretty much what he wanted to do, and Andrew would go along with it. Mostly, they were kept on the lead rein, but on the odd occasion they were set free they would merrily head off together in whichever direction Percy fancied, my brother deaf to the shouts of my mother as he bounced along in the saddle. Percy would stop to munch grass whenever he felt like it or suddenly take off at as fast a gallop as his hairy little legs would allow, my brother clinging on for dear life.

This may explain why Andrew is the most conciliatory person I know. He will always take the path of least resistance, hates to have a row and can't bear anyone making a fuss. Even if he knows the option being offered to him is daft or dangerous, he will do it to avoid saying no. He just wants affection, attention and food—a bit like a dog, really.

Whenever I went to talk to Percy in his stable or in the field, his little ears would go flat back, his eyes would narrow and he would grab my jacket, or my jumper, or my bare flesh with his teeth. He picked on small people, or on adults when they weren't watching. I think he did it for a bit of fun, just to watch someone in pain. He was a bully and, like all bullies, he was also a coward. When he had taken a particularly painful lump out of my arm, I told my father that he was a rascal and Dad went out to have stern words. Percy cowered in the

75

corner of the box and, from that point on, if ever he heard my father's voice, he would bolt to the furthest corner of the field.

When the time inevitably came for Valkyrie, who, let's not forget, was a stately older lady when she first came to us, to be eased into gentle retirement, I would like to say I was distraught. I would like to think that I wept into her mane and thanked her for the years of delight she had given me. I would love to suggest that I visited her every day to check her sweet-itch and her laminitis and that I cared for her until the end of her days.

But I didn't. I was like a magpie moving from one shiny thing to another, brighter, shinier one. A horsebox arrived one morning from Dorset and the prettiest, whitest pony I had ever seen came down the ramp into our yard.

'Is he mine?' I asked my mother.

'He is for now,' she said. 'He's called Volcano, and he's a Welsh Mountain.'

He looked different from Valkyrie and Percy. Shetland ponies are small, woolly and hardy. They tend to be between 28 and 40 inches tall or, in horse language, between 7 and 10 hands high. Volcano was much finer, he was taller, his coat seemed thinner and he was so white he practically dazzled. If Shetland ponies were the equivalent of a fluffy, woolly jumper, Volcano was cashmere.

Horses and ponies are always measured in hands, and the reason is simple: it's the easiest way for dealers to be certain a person is not lying about the height of the horse they are selling. A flighty young animal won't stand still long enough to allow itself to be measured with a ruler or a tape, but you can measure it with your hands even if it is moving.

Hold your hand out in front of you, flat. From the outside of your thumb to the outside of your little finger will be approximately four inches. Henry VIII standardized it as a measurement in 1541. It's quite fun to measure by walking your hands, one after the other, up and down or across a surface. The desk I am sitting at is ten hands wide.

My new pony, Volcano, was 12.2 hands high. That's quite tall. He was certainly taller than me at his withers, the bone that sits between the shoulder blades, at the base of the neck. It's the highest non-variable point of the skeleton, so I am told, which is why it's the measuring point for ponies, horses and dogs. The head can move up and down, so there's no point measuring there; the withers cannot.

The Welsh Mountain pony is a survivor. Henry VIII, shortly before he made sure that all hands were four inches in span, ordered the destruction of all stallions below fifteen hands and all mares below thirteen hands. He was worried that England's war horses were becoming puny little things because of cross-breeding with Arabs, which are designed for endurance but are rather dainty and fine boned.

The 1535 Breed of Horses Act was a brutal decree, and many small horses were destroyed. Tough little ponies and horses fled to the higher ground to escape the cull, where they survived in the most extreme weather conditions. The Welsh Mountain pony was one such breed which survived and, in the centuries that followed, it was ridden, took its owners to church in a trap and even pulled ploughs. These ponies can lug great weights, which is why so many were used in Wales as pit ponies, dragging huge cartloads of coal below ground and in the open air.

My Welsh Mountain did not look like a pit pony or a farmer's plough horse. He looked more like an Arab pony, with a slightly dish face and long, dark eyelashes, which he fluttered for effect. Volcano had been ridden by a girl eight years older than me, who had won rosettes galore on him in the show ring. He was adept at hiding his faults and showing off his assets to imaginary judges. He was a 'show pony', with all the beauty but also all the faults that entails. He would teach me that looks weren't everything.

\*       \*       \*

Andrew and I were kept away from the racing yard as much as possible. We lived up on the hill, and our ponies were kept separately from the racehorses so that they could not bring disease into the yard. Racehorses are flighty creatures who will spook at the strangest things—a shadow, a piece of paper or a little pony—so mixing with them wasn't worth the risk. Besides, my father was busy and we were not to disturb his concentration by riding with the string or wandering through the yard.

'Would you listen? This is important,' my father would say to his secretary, or my mother, or Bertie.

He was always in a rush, so other people had to work to his timetable and, if he had graced you with his attention, you had to listen. I remember a discussion with a girl on the way back from school: 'My father's very important,' I said, with confidence.

'Why on earth do you think that your father is any more important than anyone else's?' came the offended tone of the girl's mother, who was driving us, and clearly thought I was in danger of rising above my station.

'Because he is always saying things that are *important*.' I made sure the volume was turned up as well as the emphasis on 'important'.

He was certainly too important and too busy to take much of an interest in my new pony, but I was enthralled. Volcano was so white and so pretty that I felt under pressure to keep him looking perfect. The trouble with grey ponies is that your work is never done. No wonder my mother has always believed white to be impractical. Grey ponies are the hardest work in the world. Every day is Fairy Liquid day.

Soon after he arrived, Volcano managed to cover his hind legs in muck. There was a large brown stain on his backside where he had been lying down in his own droppings, and I decided that I would deal with it. A large bucket of soapy water, a sponge and a wet brush were my instruments of choice, and I got to work. For ease of access and because I was too lazy to do otherwise, I tied his rope around the top of the outside tap.

Volcano stood quite happily as I scrubbed away at his bottom, at his tummy and then at his neck. I thought I'd make a complete job of it and, when I'd finished washing, I realized that his mane and tail looked a bit long and untidy.

The first rule that you learn about grooming ponies and horses is that a mane must never be cut, it must be pulled. This is quite a complicated procedure involving a mane comb and lots of tugging. I didn't really understand why I couldn't just trim the mane like the hairdresser did my hair.

So that's what I did.

I chopped merrily away, singing to myself and feeling proud that I was cutting Volcano's mane in such a straight line. Then I moved to his tail, which I thought would look much better if I trimmed it at the top so that it was thinner and then flowed out to a full tail at the bottom. I had seen this look in *Horse & Hound*, and I knew exactly what I wanted to create.

I stood back to admire my handiwork and noticed that the line I thought was straight was crooked, so I went back to work on his mane. Then I looked at his tail again and it looked all jagged and ugly, so I kept trimming.

I had been hard at work for nearly an hour when my mother appeared. Volcano had been getting a bit bored during this final tidying-up process and was increasingly restless. He pulled back on his rope and, as he felt the resistance, pulled even harder. I tried to grab at the rope, but it was too late. He heaved backwards so hard that he pulled the tap clean off the wall.

Water was gushing everywhere, my mother was shouting at me and Volcano was trotting off down the hill, a dismembered tap dangling off the end of his rope, his mane and tail looking as if they had been attacked by a David Bowie fan paying homage to Ziggy Stardust.

I threw myself at the tap, trying to stop the whoosh of water by laying my body over the open pipe, but it seemed to make it worse. My mother had disappeared. I was shouting for Andrew to come and help me, but he was sensibly staying as far away from this mess as he could.

The water suddenly stopped, and Mum walked

out of the tack room.

'I've turned it off at the mains,' she said. 'Now would you like to explain to me exactly what you've been doing?'

She was using her quiet voice. The one that meant she was *very* angry. This was wrong. All kinds of wrong.

'I was making Volcano look pretty.' I decided just to stick to the facts, keep cool and hold my ground. I could see that he was eating grass on the side of the hill and played for an exit strategy.

'I really must catch him,' I said, knowing that distraction might be my only chance of defence. 'I would be upset if he got any grass stains. I've washed him, you see. All over.'

'So I observe,' said my mother slowly. 'And what exactly have you done to his mane? And his tail?'

I was walking steadily away from her at this point, towards Volcano and relative safety.

'I've tidied his hair up. It was a mess.'

As I approached Volcano and picked up the rope, still attached to the tap, I could see my handiwork as a whole for the first time. Up close, it is so hard to judge what you're doing. Artists must find this all the time—they are painting sections, and it's only when they stand back and take in the whole work of art that they can judge whether they have created a masterpiece.

I made an 'O' shape with my mouth, but I'm not sure the word came out.

My eyes felt as if they were being pricked from behind as it dawned on me that I had not made him look good at all. In fact, I had ruined him. If my mother had been going to get cross, she stopped herself as soon as she saw my face.

My crest was utterly fallen. Even Volcano seemed to know, without looking in a mirror, that his sheen had disappeared. His self-confidence was shattered and he trudged back alongside me to his box, where he took himself to the far corner and stood with his head facing the wall.

Andrew was standing by the box door.

'He looks funny,' he said.

We were going to our first show the next day; the timing of this compounded the humiliation. My mother told me there was no point in entering any of the classes that were judged on tack and turn-out, so I would have to just do the gymkhana classes.

It was the annual Kingsclere show, organized by a Mrs Snook. It took place in a field at the back of the roundabout where the bypass would soon be built to divert traffic from our village high street. A week earlier, my mother had taken me to Calcutt & Sons, where tack and horsey clothes were bought and sold. I was always a little nervous of Calcutt's, because you had to ring a bell before the door was opened, as if you were going into someone's house, and the man who ran the shop looked at me suspiciously all the time, as if I was going to steal something.

My mother took me straight to the room that housed second-hand clothes. She pulled out four or five jackets that looked roughly the right size and made me try them on. How they looked was not as important as how much they cost, so it took a while to find one that was not 'a complete rip-off'. She bought rugs and boots and grooming kit for the horses that were brand new, but for us, used was best.

Of course, the jacket would look better in a year or so, when I grew into it, but as I admired myself in the mirror, turning up the sleeves so they didn't hang below my hands, and pretending to sit so that I could see what I would look like on Volcano, I thought I had never looked finer. It's amazing how much happiness can spring forth from the purchase of one second-hand tweed hacking jacket.

To make up for the hairdressing debacle, I made an extra-special effort to look smart for the show. My father is a manic cleaner of boots. He cleans them so that he can see his reflection in the leather and because, he told me, in his 'important voice', 'There's no point doing something unless you're going to do it well.'

My arms got tired with the effort of it all, I struggled with the instruction to spit and polish, and I got brown boot cream all over my jumper, but Dad said, 'Not bad for a first effort, not bad at all,' and smiled at me.

I felt better.

Before I went to bed I laid out my jodhpur boots, my jodhpurs, a smart white shirt and my new hacking jacket. I left my curtains open so that I would wake up when the sunlight came through the window and, sure enough, I slid off the top bunk before anyone else was awake.

I pulled on my smart cream jodhpurs, my gleaming boots, my white shirt and my jacket. I didn't know how to put on a tie, so I stuffed that in my pocket and ran downstairs. The dogs woke up and immediately wanted to be let out, so I headed out to our stables on top of the hill, with two boxers and two lurchers, even before the lads in the yards at Park House down in the valley were feeding the racehorses.

Volcano was still asleep in his box, lying down with his head stuffed between his front leg and his tummy. He looked like a swan with its head tucked under one wing. Unfortunately, I could see that, once again, he had chosen to lie with his backside in his own droppings.

I tried to ignore the state of his mane and tail as I got him up and started the cleaning process all over again. As far as Volcano was concerned, this was quite a successful attempt at removing dirt. As for me, it was a disaster. My clean, perfectly pressed outfit was now covered in white hair, dirt and manure.

First lesson of going to a competition: don't put on your smart kit until the last minute. It's a bit like presenting on TV. When it comes to Royal Ascot, I don't even sit down in the clothes I am going to wear on air—I wait until half an hour before the programme starts, slip them on in the loo and take them straight off again as soon as I've been counted off air. I learned that trick in 1978, on the day of the Kingsclere Show.

After breakfast, Mum showed me how to load Volcano on to the horsebox. We put the ramp down on the side of a hill so that it wasn't too steep for him to walk in. Mum told me to be firm with him but not to tug. Walk alongside him, rather than ahead of him, she advised, and keep talking to him all the time. He didn't need a lot of encouragement. I'd put a tail bandage on to protect what was left of his tail, in case he rubbed it, and I'd put boots on his legs. Even though we were only going about three miles down the road, I thought it was important to do it properly.

84

Then we piled into the front of the horsebox—me, Andrew, Mum, Candy and Flossy. The lurchers stayed at home, because they don't really like social occasions and they hated being on the lead. Candy and Flossy sat on the long passenger seat between Andrew and me. They looked more human than we did. They even looked left as we inched out of our drive, as if they were checking for traffic.

There were thousands of people in horseboxes and trailers at the show, all of whom seemed to know exactly what they were doing. There were three different rings—one with a showing class for children on the leading rein, one with jumps so high I couldn't imagine how anyone could clear them, and one with a row of poles, a pile of sacks and buckets full of water.

That would be my ring for the day, the gymkhana ring. Like the word 'jodhpur', 'gymkhana' has its etymological roots in India. It means a venue where sporting events take place. It has been adapted in the UK to mean games on horses. Believe me, any game you can think of can be played on a horse.

I watched older kids galloping headlong up and down the field, picking up handkerchiefs from the floor by flinging themselves sideways and down from the saddle. They looked as if their bodies were made of rubber, as if they had extendable hands.

I felt a little rush go through my body as I contemplated doing what they were doing. I was a bit scared, but mostly I was thrilled. The gymkhana would be my métier, my calling in life.

My mother paid £1 to enter me in five classes—the bending race, sack race, egg and spoon race, apple bobbing, and round the world.

The embarrassment of riding a pony with a mane

and tail that looked like Ziggy Stardust's hair soon evaporated as Volcano and I lined up for the first of our five events. He knew exactly what to do, even if I didn't. He took off, weaving himself in and out of the bending poles with the expertise of a snake on steroids. I looked across at my closest competitor with two bends to go and gave Volcano an extra squeeze in the belly. He accelerated just enough to ensure that we won.

There was no time to celebrate, as next up was the sack race. Volcano and I had to gallop to the end of the ring, where I would jump off and into a sack, hopping all the way back while I led him. There was a lot of shouting and a fair degree of chaos as children fell over in their sacks, letting their ponies trot off loose, but I kept my focus and Volcano stayed right by my side. I threw myself over the line like a rugby player scoring a try and managed to finish just in front of a boy who had barged me in the collecting ring.

So the morning went on and, with each race, Volcano and I grew in confidence and trust in each other. We had four red rosettes with 'FIRST' written across them. A 100 per cent record: four wins out of four.

'Right, that'll do,' said my mother.

'What?' I said.

'It's not "What?", it's "I beg your pardon?"' she replied, on automatic response.

'No, I mean—*what?*' I was outraged that we should not be going for the clean sweep of gold medals at the Olympics of the Kingsclere pony world.

'You've done very well,' my mother explained. 'And yes, I know it would be nice to win all five races, but I don't think it would be fair. So you are not going to go in the round-the-world race. You have to give someone else a chance.'

I adopted a look of part confusion, part indignation. 'Are you serious?'

'I have never been more serious,' said my mother. 'You can watch from here and cheer on everyone else.'

Andrew was fingering my rosettes in wonder and saying, 'Wow,' forgetting that he was meant to be holding Candy and Flossy. He was in a world of his own as I fought the urge to scream at the unfairness. I picked up the reins and moved away from my mother, cursing her as I did so. At the edge of the ring, I did furious round-the-worlds, spinning round and round my saddle as the final race of the five unfolded in front of me. A little boy called Harry won and was so happy he cried. I should have been flooded by the spirit of generosity, but I wasn't.

My competitive dreams of a clean sweep dashed, I sulked.

We tied Volcano up to the side of the horsebox, took the boxers and went to watch the other rings. As we passed a stand that caught my eye, I deigned to speak to my mother for the first time in an hour. There was a woman with a board in front of her which said 'Craven Pony Club' and had lots of photos of children on ponies jumping cross-country fences, doing dressage and grooming their ponies. There wasn't a pair of scissors in sight. I begged my mother to sign me up. As soon as I was on the list, I got a book on pony management and a badge to go with it. Mum picked out a tie from the rack at the back of the tent and tied it around my neck. It had a few stains on it from a previous owner.

I was now a member of the Pony Club, and I felt as if I belonged. This would mean I could go to Pony Club rallies, ride in Pony Club hunter trials and, best of all, go to Pony Club camp. This was the most exciting thing that had ever happened in my life.

*      *      *

I wore my Pony Club tie to breakfast the next morning. My father was opening his pile of post at the head of the table. Andrew and I were squashed up together on the bench that went under the bay window. He was sticking his elbows in my face as he ate his Frosties.

'Bloody invitations,' said my father. 'Why do people keep inviting us to things? All the time, people having parties to celebrate this or that. I don't want to go.'

He flung the thick bit of card towards my mother, via me. I picked it up and looked at the swirly writing.

'Ooh, it's a wedding in America. Can we go?'

'I prefer funerals,' my father grumbled. 'At least you can only have one of them.'

'Can I wear my Pony Club tie?' I asked my mother, who was now looking more carefully at the invitation.

'It's your god-daughter's wedding,' Mum said. 'Are you sure you can't come? It's all your family, and you love Sheila. Come on, don't be so miserable.'

'It's York that week,' my father excused himself. 'We'll have runners. Ridiculous time for a wedding.

88

And it's too far to go. Say no from all of us.'

A month later, three of us were on a plane to Denver, Colorado, for the wedding of my second cousin and god-daughter of my father, Sabrina Jewell. I settled into my seat on the plane with *Nancy Drew and the Mystery of Crocodile Island*. Andrew scratched his head and asked the stewardess for more snacks. My mother sat between us so that we didn't fight.

The Jewells lived in a place called Golden on the outskirts of Denver. The Golden Jewells—I liked that. Aunt Sheila, my godmother, had characteristic black Balding hair, scraped back from her face into a big tortoiseshell clip, ebony-black eyes and a cigarette never far from her mouth. She spoke with a deep, gravelly voice.

'Well done, Ems. So pleased you all could make it.' She stubbed out her cigarette and gave us all a hug.

Andrew went back to scratching his head, while I marvelled at Aunt Sheila's style. She led us out of the airport, her heels clicking on the concrete floor, and put on her big black shades as we hit the sunshine.

'I've put you in a neat hotel downtown,' she said. 'I think you'll like it. There's a party tonight out at our house, a barbecue lunch tomorrow at Sam's sister's place and then the wedding the day after. I know you're not here for long, so we're packing it all in.'

That wedding was the first time I had encountered the American side of the Balding clan en masse. They loved a party. Andrew and I were surrounded by cousins, who were so funny and friendly and just seemed to want to like everyone.

89

There were a lot of names to remember, but I loved the feeling of belonging.

We checked into the Sheraton Hotel in Denver. I had never seen such a big hotel or such a massive room, with three queen-sized beds and a bathroom the size of our kitchen. I jumped from bed to bed, wishing that I could share it all with the dogs. Mum decided that Andrew and I needed our hair cut if we were to look the part at the wedding.

The scream from the hotel hairdresser could have cracked glass.

*'Oh my God!* It's alive! His head is alive!'

I looked up from my basin to see the girl who was combing my brother's hair paralysed with fear.

'Get him out of here. Out of here right now.'

She was shouting at my mother, who looked thoroughly confused.

'He has lice.' The hairdresser's voice had gone all wobbly. 'We haven't had lice in Denver, Colorado, since 1967. How dare you bring your infestation into this hotel? How dare you?'

The woman seemed delirious. My mother explained to her, in a calm voice, that there had been an outbreak of nits at his school and that it was very common in England.

'Well, it is not common here. And I will not have it in this hairdresser's. Get out. *Get out!'*

The woman was pushing Andrew out of the door. Mum followed him and called at me to follow, so I got up from my basin, hair covered in shampoo, and walked, with as much dignity as I could muster, through the door. After I had rinsed my hair in the lobby loos, our promised exploration of downtown Denver became a hunt for lice shampoo. Surprisingly, it was not hard to

90

find because, despite the hairdresser having told us they had not had a case of head lice in Denver for over a decade, the pharmacy had three shelvesful of anti-nit products.

When we got back to the hotel, there was a man in the foyer who seemed to have been waiting for my mother.

'Ma'am,' he said, with gravitas. 'Ma'am, I am so sorry to trouble you, but I'm afraid we have a problem. You cannot stay at this hotel.'

My mother looked appalled.

'Why?' she said. 'What's happened?'

'I am not at liberty to explain but we have removed your cases from your room and you will have to leave immediately.'

'Well, that's not your prerogative,' my mother replied. 'We have things in the safe in that room and I insist on retrieving them.'

A sort of scuffle dance broke out between the hotel manager and my mother as she made for the lift and he tried to stop her. My brother and I followed behind.

'Stop scratching!' I hissed at Andrew. 'It just makes it worse.'

My mother stepped into the lift, and the hotel manager went with her but, as my brother got in, he made a little squeak and got out again.

'I shall wait for you here,' he said.

As we got out of the lift on the sixteenth floor, we saw yellow and black tape across the door of our room. There was also a sign: 'DO NOT ENTER!' it read.

'What a load of nonsense.' My mother tore down the tape as she slotted the card into the door. 'You'd think it was a crime scene.'

91

Inside, there was a notice on the bed: 'ALL STAFF MUST WEAR GLOVES. INCINERATE ALL LINEN.'

You could see why they hadn't had a case of head lice in over ten years—they were thorough. We hadn't even slept on the beds yet.

Mum retrieved our passports from the safe, checked that all our belongings had been picked up, and we headed back to the foyer. The humiliation for my mother was complete, but Andrew and I felt as if we had been in the middle of a soap opera. It was so exciting that Andrew had forgotten how much his head itched. My mother made a point of shaking the hotel manager's hand as we left, even though he didn't seem that keen.

The Sheraton had rung round all of the hotels in Denver warning them about a family called Balding with head lice. We finally found a room at the Ramada and checked in under the name Jewell.

I remember the wedding being held in the garden and Sabrina arriving in a horse-drawn carriage; the cake being made of profiteroles; Andrew trying to undo cousin Flora's dress, which was laced all down the back. But, most of all, I remember Aunt Sheila's laugh when my mother told her that we'd been thrown out of our hotel because Andrew had nits. She doubled over and put her hands on her knees she was laughing so much.

She introduced us as 'the nit clan' and started laughing every time she repeated the story, which she did all week. I loved that trip, despite the nits—or because of the nits, I'm not sure. Andrew, however, is still nervous about checking into hotels in Denver, in case they have him 'on record'.

By the age of eight, I was pretty proficient as a rider, but the next step was to learn to jump properly— not just being on the leading rein and hanging on tight as we trotted over a small pole attached to two big crosses (a cavaletti pole). I wanted to fly through the air, to leap over ditches, rubber tyres, hedges and timber poles. I wanted to take off and soar, suspended in time, before landing the other side. Jumping on my own would be fun.

Dad was always out jumping things. My mother jumped things. It was a grown-up thing to do, part of what would make me a 'proper jockey'. All forms of riding are based on the harmony between horse and rider. Whether it is racing, dressage, show-jumping, cross-country or endurance riding, both the horse and the rider have to understand what is going on and, in an ideal situation, both want to do the same thing. Learning to jump on my own was a natural progression. Everyone did it.

What could possibly go wrong?

Volcano was a pretty pony, especially once his mane and tail grew back, and he was superb at gymkhana games, but jumping was something he could take or leave. Usually, he jumped well— neatly and conservatively for four or five obstacles in a row. Then, with no warning, he would jam on the brakes and skid into the bottom of a tiger trap, say. He would stop so suddenly that I had no time to adjust my position or resist the motion that sent me somersaulting over his neck and into the middle of the fence.

This way of parting company was damned

painful, and I started to lose my enthusiasm for jumping. I tried to look for signs from Volcano—a flick of the ears or a change in stride—but it was impossible. It was as if he waited until I was feeling safe and then *wham!* He'd refuse.

I lost my temper and smacked him with my stick. He kicked out. When I turned him round and into the fence again, he started to slide from five strides away and refused to leave the ground. I hit him harder. My mind exploded. I was flying into a tantrum born of frustration. This damned pony would not do the one thing I wanted him to do.

'Clare? Clare! Stop it. Stop it right now.'

It was my mother.

'Give me that stick this instant, you horrid little brat. How dare you beat your pony?'

I opened my mouth to explain, but my mother was not having a minute of it.

'Do you want me to try this on you? Do you?'

Mum was holding the stick above her head, and I didn't trust her not to bring it cracking down on me. My bottom lip started to quiver as my rage turned to shame.

'No, please, no. I'm sorry. I didn't mean to hurt him, but he wouldn't jump.'

'Well, that's because he's had enough,' said my mother. 'You've been out here for over an hour, and he's tired. Take him home right now, and that is the last time—do you understand me? the *last* time—you will ever use your stick in anger. It is there for correction and for safety. It is not to be used in a tantrum. Do you copy?'

I nodded and turned Volcano for home. It was the beginning of the end for us. He couldn't trust me, and I couldn't trust him. Our relationship was broken. We soldiered on for the rest of that year, but Volcano and I had reached the natural end of our journey. He went on to another little girl who wanted to win rosettes in the show ring. They were happy together.

# 7

## Barney

We now had four dogs: two lurchers and two boxers. Bertie was golden, Cindy was brindle, both Candy and Flossy were red and white. Bertie was still aloof and wary of children. Cindy was a dustbin for left-over food and constantly on the search for something revolting to eat, preferably excrement. Candy and Flossy were sedate and sensible, apart from when they were excited.

Then Barney arrived. He was a gleaming ebony lurcher puppy who had found his way into my mother's car when she was visiting a litter of Bertie's puppies.

He was kind, and he was tolerant, so we took full advantage. I lay all over him, playing with him, kissing him, stroking him, until Dad declared, 'For God's sake, leave that poor puppy alone. He needs a rest. Hurrumph,' and then, under his breath: 'We all do. Go and read a book, why don't you?'

Andrew was sitting on the floor, eating something he'd found under the table. I was wearing my favourite multicoloured checked jacket, which must have been bought in America. I tugged it down with both hands at the front, something I'd seen people do when they made a deal, and headed out of the back door. I signalled for Andrew to follow me.

Moments later, I could feel his hot breath on the side of my face.

'I'm scared,' he said. 'How are we going to get down?'

I had laid my jacket carefully on a straw bale at ground level because this was a climb that was unsuitable for business attire. We were now some twenty feet above the ground, on the second-from-top row of bales in the barn. Earlier that week, I had noticed a rope attached to the metal rafters and a plan had hatched. The rope was an invitation.

'Don't be wet.' I adopted my cool, older-sister voice. 'You've seen *Tarzan*. How do you think we're going to get down?'

I flicked my head towards the rope. Andrew said nothing, but I knew he'd do whatever I did. The fact that we both might die didn't occur to him. He didn't do logic.

I adjusted my lucky red neckerchief, sized up the

leap and the angle I would have to hit the rope, spat on my hands and launched myself at it. Andrew screamed.

I hit the rope just right, gripped tight and swung to the other side of the barn. I kicked off the bales, swung back again and was sitting beside my brother, laughing, before he had got to the 'm' of 'scream'.

'Easy-peasy,' I said. 'It's all about timing.'

I took Andrew's podgy little hand in mine. It felt clammy. He looked at me with baleful eyes.

'Do I have to do it?' he asked, voice quivering.

'If you want me ever to recognize you as my brother, yes, you do,' I replied.

It seemed a fair enough request.

I showed him once more how to jump off the bales, grab the rope and swing. This time, I slid down a bit and then, hand over fist, lowered myself to the ground. I stood, feet wide apart like a cowboy, looking up at him. Now he would have to jump, because there was no other way of getting down.

Half an hour later, having exhausted my persuasive vocabulary, I walked away and left him there. If he wouldn't jump, he'd have to stay put. Tough luck.

By lunchtime, my mother had noticed he was missing. He was usually the first at the kitchen table.

'Where's your brother?'

'Who?' I said. I had already cut him out of my life. He was no brother to me.

'Andrew—where is he?'

'Dunno.'

Mum headed out of the back door, across the

98

gravel car park, past the row of four stables and down the slope that led to Hollowshot Lane. I followed at a distance, interested to observe the maternal instinct of a bloodhound. She found him, sobbing, where I had abandoned him.

'There you are,' she said, with a hint of surprise. 'Now what sort of a pickle have you got yourself into?'

Andrew couldn't really speak, he was crying so much. He was terrified, and hungry.

Mum stood on the barn floor with her arms outstretched, begging him to jump.

'I'll catch you,' she promised.

Andrew eyed her from above. He was paralysed. Mum continued to bargain with him until, eventually, he inched himself to the edge of the straw bale.

'You won't catch me, Mummy. You can't. I'll use the rope like Clare did.'

'Clare?' My mother sounded surprised. 'Did Clare know you were here?'

'She made me come up here,' he answered.

Well, that sealed my fate. I thought it hardly my fault that I had foreseen Andrew's keenness to follow me up the mountain but had failed to anticipate his lily-livered attitude to coming down. I hid behind a wheelbarrow as my mother called my name. She was not doing so in a friendly manner.

Soon, Mum turned her attention back to getting Andrew down. She spoke to him softly, coaxing him to jump. Her arms were once again outstretched, but Andrew remained suspicious.

'Come on, darling. On three,' Mum called up. 'One. Two. Three!'

This time, Andrew launched himself like a big

lump of rock towards the rope. His fat little fingers grasped it and he started to slide down. I was now running towards the barn, crying.

'Put one hand over the other, don't slide! It'll burn!'

I was right, but it was too late. Andrew let go. He fell faster than my mother could move back into position to catch him and, as he hit the ground, we all heard the crack.

Andrew spent the next month in plaster, his leg broken in two places. Mum pushed him round in a pram, his leg sticking straight out in front of him. I have a sneaky suspicion that he quite enjoyed all the attention, until his leg got itchy inside the cast. I offered to scratch it for him with a knife, but my mother intervened and effectively put a restraining order on me. I was not allowed within ten feet of my brother.

\*　　　\*　　　\*

It was the summer of 1979. Mum had taken us down to Glorious Goodwood for the first time. We spent the first two afternoons on the beach at West Wittering, and then we were allowed to go to the races. Even though our father was a trainer, Andrew and I did not go racing often: my mother did not believe in children being in the office, and the racecourse was my father's office—as well as the yard, the gallops and the office itself.

Anyway, on this occasion, we were allowed to go racing, and I remember it clearly for a horse called Kris. We stood on the rails about two furlongs from home and, as the horses cantered down to the start, I said I liked the one in the orange colours.

100

'Apricot,' my mother corrected me. 'Those are Lord Howard de Walden's colours.'

They looked orange to me, and they were easy to spot. When the field came back past us, they were flying. I had never seen horses travel so fast, and I was thrilled by the sound they made—I could hear the jockeys shouting at each other, the hooves thundering and the whips cracking. For the first time in my life, racing had made my heart pound. As the field came by again, I could see the orange/apricot colours of Kris surging clear. He won easily and was crowned champion miler of 1979.

The trip to Goodwood was a fun diversion from 'the move'.

The main house that went with the stables—Park House—had lain empty for a couple of years, and my parents decided that it made sense to sell The Lynches and put the money into converting the fourteen-bedroom house that adjoined the yard into a more manageable family home. So they divided it into two, making the back end of it—where my mother and her brothers had lived with Nanny—into permanent staff accommodation. The front end had five bedrooms, four bathrooms, a sitting room, a drawing room, a dining room and a playroom. Even at half the size of the whole house, our end was still enormous.

My parents explained to the dogs what was going to happen. Andrew and I listened carefully, so we knew our parents were taking us all to Park House to have a look around.

The dimensions were amazing, with huge bay windows and high ceilings. You could play tennis in the drawing room. I know because we tried.

I ran up the stairs, with Barney bounding ahead

of me and Flossy puffing behind, to check out the bedrooms.

'Don't take the dogs up there,' my mother shouted from the hall with a sigh that said she knew it was too late. 'Yours is the room on the left.'

I walked into the biggest bedroom I had ever seen, with a sash window in three sections looking southwards towards Cottington Hill. It was the same view I had had from my cupboard at The Lynches, but it seemed so much larger; instead of looking at the television mast from the same height, I was now looking up at it. The hill seemed the size of a mountain from down here.

My new bedroom had a basin in the corner. This gave me real pleasure, as it meant that my toothpaste was now safe from my brother's habit of squeezing it in the middle and not putting the top back on.

Having paced out my bedroom and discovered that it was exactly five times as big as the cupboard I'd had as my room at The Lynches, I explored the rest of upstairs. There was a wide flight of five stairs leading up to another landing, with an enormous mirror on the wall ahead. To the left was the room that had belonged to my grandparents and would now be my parents'. There was a third door on this level, and it was closed. It was stiff and creaky and, as I pushed it back, a layer of dust was blown up in the breeze. On the shelves were rows of shoes, covered in a thick film of dust.

There were brown-leather brogues, black dress shoes, heavy shoes with steel-capped heels, jodhpur boots, long, black hunting boots and velvet slippers. It was a museum of carefully stitched, long-unworn, handmade shoes—the shoes of a man who had long since left us.

Grandma had moved her things out to the Pink Palace, but she had left this strange memorial to her late husband. I closed the door and wondered whether to tell my mother. For some reason, I thought the sight of her father's shoes might upset her.

The next time I opened that door, the space had been transformed into an airing cupboard. I don't know where the shoes went.

We went from a cut-off, quiet existence to being at the heart of everything that was happening.

The 'Old Kitchen', where my grandmother's cook had toiled away in the dark, was turned into a utility room, and a new kitchen was built on the north side of the house, looking out over the drive and next to the office. This became the hub, with an endless stream of people coming through the back door.

Breakfast at Park House was like going to the theatre. It was a mini-drama every morning, with the regulars—my father, his assistant trainer, my mother, a nanny or au pair and us—joined by an ever-changing cast of extras. Owners who had come to see their horses, a jockey riding work, pupil assistants, visiting foreign students, family members—all played their part. When we were more than eight for breakfast, which was often, we moved into the dining room, where there was a little hole in the wall connecting it to the kitchen so food could be passed through.

Andrew and I revelled in our new surroundings. We had a flat lawn for the first time, and it was as big as a football pitch. We built a Grand National assault course from old doors, tyres and branches for Barney to learn to jump. He followed us like a lamb, jumping up at my arm as I ran between 'Becher's Brook' and 'the Chair'.

He was so fast and agile that he made it look easy. I struggled to keep up, leaping across the width of a door that was perilously balanced on two croquet hoops. Barney had sailed over, but I banked it, stepping on the middle of the door. It came crashing down on my foot.

'Ow!' I bit my lip as I winced in pain, trying to be brave in front of my little brother. Barney shoved his long nose into my armpit as I sat on the lawn nursing my left foot.

Later that day, when I still couldn't put any weight on it, my mother took me to Basingstoke Hospital. I had broken my big toe. Andrew had little sympathy.

'Nothing serious then,' my father said when we got home. 'You'll be riding in the morning, won't you?'

I wasn't sure whether it was a question or a command but, as it happened, riding didn't really hurt. Walking did. Running was out of the question. Andrew tried the assault course alone.

'S'not as much fun,' he muttered, and gave up.

We settled into life at Park House quickly, but as it was so close to the racehorses there were strict rules. Andrew and I were not allowed into the yard on our own; we had to have an adult with us at all times. We were not allowed to ride our ponies through the yard, except during breakfast, when all the racehorses were in their stables. We were not allowed to run down the tarmac stretch known as the 'Straight Mile'. This was the main thoroughfare between the yards and led to the indoor school and the swimming pool.

We were definitely not allowed in 'the Colour Room', where all the silks belonging to Dad's owners hung in an open cupboard, as if on display. That was the room where Mill Reef had recovered from his broken leg, and was now the domain of Spider, the Travelling Head Lad. There was a sign on the door telling everyone who entered: 'God help anyone who helps themselves to anything in this room.'

In the Colour Room, Spider prepared the satchel needed for each runner—passport (for the horse, not the jockey), girths, colours, chamois leather, a paper-thin, super-light square of grey polystyrene-type material that acted as a saddlecloth, bridle, grooming kit and bucket. The saddle would belong to the jockey and was as big as the weight being carried by the horse would allow. Some saddles weigh only a pound and are so tiny they are no more than a means of hanging stirrups either side of a horse's back.

As for the swimming pool at the far end of the Straight Mile, we didn't need to be told not to swim in it. It was freezing cold, ten feet deep and circular. Despite a filter system and a boy using a stick with a net to fish out droppings as fast as he could, the water wasn't exactly crystal clear. There was no chlorine, as that was bad for the horses, and there were often 'fragments' floating on the surface.

\*　　　\*　　　\*

That winter, it snowed. The Downs were covered with a crisp, white duvet and my father decided to take advantage. He did not spend that much time with us as children. We did not go on summer holidays together because he was busy, he was always doing something 'important', and in the winter my parents took a break in Barbados with other adults. Having a holiday with children was not my father's idea of fun—at least, not until we were old enough to ski.

The snow on the Downs gave him an idea. He told my mother he was taking us sledging. We all climbed into the white Subaru truck, which had its yellow winter shell covering the back of it. Andrew and I shared the front passenger seat and flung our two sledges into the back of the truck. Dad stopped at the garage and picked up two sections of long rope.

'Right, you two—this will be the best fun ever,' he said when we got to the top of the Downs.

The whole place was still: no birdsong, no horses galloping, no people. All was quiet. Dad tied both ropes to the tow bar at the back of the truck and looped them through the front of our sledges.

'Hang on tight,' he said as he climbed back behind the wheel.

The silence of the snow-clad Downs was split by the roar of a Subaru engine and the screams of two children clinging on for dear life. I don't think my father realized quite how fast it felt behind the truck as he tore up the side of the gallop. Andrew and I kept swinging into one another. The uphill bits were just about manageable but, when we started going downhill, we had no way of stopping ourselves catching up with the truck. I was terrified we were both going to end up as mashed potato underneath the exhaust pipe.

'How's that! Fun, eh?' Dad shouted out the

window. I waved at him, my face fixed in a grimace. Andrew had such a thick Puffa jacket on that he could hardly move. There were tears streaming down his face from the icy-cold wind and exhaust fumes.

'Brilliant. Let's go again!' Dad was enjoying himself, at least. He put his foot down and took off. Andrew was caught unawares and fell backwards as his sledge lurched ahead. His legs spun right over the top of his head as he performed a backwards roly-poly and was left sitting in the middle of the gallop. I was on the same side of the truck as Dad, so tried waving at him to stop, hoping he would see me in the mirror. He did, but, unfortunately, he thought I was telling him to go faster—so he did. I was screaming with terrified urgency:

'*Stop! Stop!* We've lost Andrew. Daddy, stop.'

All he could hear was the roar of the engine, and all he could see was one child behind him, seemingly having the time of her life. Dad was enjoying the challenge of controlling the four-wheel-drive truck as it slid over the snow and was lost in his own dream sequence, pretending he was a rally driver. Eventually, more than a mile away from where Andrew sat crying in the snow, Dad stopped.

My voice was hoarse from shouting, so all I could do was beckon to him and point at the empty sledge beside me. Dad got out of the truck.

'Oh, how did that happen?'

I pointed back down the gallop to a little dot in the snow.

'That's a shame. He missed the best bit,' Dad said. 'Do you want to stay there for the ride back?'

I shook my head as vehemently as I could, and

my father looked rather disappointed when I made a run for the passenger seat. Poor Andrew was all cried out by the time we rescued him. Dad pulled him to his feet and told him not to be so pathetic.

My mother, initially delighted that her husband was, for once, wanting to spend time with his children, was not so thrilled when we got back. That was the last time Dad took us anywhere on his own over the Christmas holidays.

*     *     *

As well as 'the move' to Park House, 1979 was a big year because Andrew went away. At the age of seven, with his freshly cut blond hair and his chubby cheeks, he was deemed old enough for boarding school. He looked so smart in his jumper and tie, with his cap pulled firmly on his head and his socks so high they nearly met his shorts.

When he said goodbye, I'm not sure either of us realized that he wouldn't be back for weeks. He wasn't just going to a new school—he was going to prep school, where he would board full-time.

'He needs the discipline,' I heard my father say. 'It'll make a man of him. It didn't do me any harm.'

'He's only seven.' I heard the warm baritone of Dad's American cousin Uncle David, his voice fluffy round the edges because of his beard. 'I'd hang on to this bit as long as you can. He'll be a man long enough, and you might find you liked him better as a little boy.'

Grandma thought sending Andrew away was a fine idea and couldn't understand why I hadn't been packed off to boarding school yet. The truth was that my parents weren't at all sure any good school would take me. I had had a bit of trouble, you see.

The school for 'nice children' had decided that I didn't really fit in. I was a bit rough around the edges, a bit loud and a bit too inclined to get into a fight. Having been taken away from there hastily, to keep it quiet from my grandmother, I was sent to Kingsclere Primary School. Keeping it quiet didn't work.

'She's a tomboy,' my grandmother said, as she dropped two sweeteners into her cup of coffee. (Never sugar, always sweeteners, carried in a little gold pot she kept in her bag.)

'That's the trouble,' she continued. 'She needs to learn a little decorum. Some manners. How to behave like a lady.'

She would never sit down when she popped round for a chat. She always stood and kept her coat on, as if she were too busy to stay. Or as if she would rather be somewhere else.

'I can hear, you know,' I mumbled under my breath as I sat in the corner with Flossy, curling my arms around her and burying my face in her neck.

'She'll be trouble all her life, I can tell.' Grandma was in full flow now, and my mother knew better than to try to defend me.

'A proper little urchin. No wonder they couldn't handle her. Well, they'll sort her out at the village school. Make or break, I'd say, and at least it's not costing you anything.'

Grandma sighed and glanced at me in the dog bed.

'Bloody waste of money educating girls,' she said. 'I mean, beyond reading and writing, what exactly is the point?'

I caught my mother's eye as she raised her eyebrows.

'Right you are'—this was Grandma's favourite phrase, a catch-all for any situation—'Right you are. I'm off. Let her hair grow a bit, will you?'

She patted Flossy and me on the head as she strode out of the kitchen. As she shut the door, I noticed that my mother stopped grinding her teeth.

So I started mid-term at the local primary school. I thought it would be fine, because my best friend, Heather Cox, went there too. Her father worked in the yard and her mother worked for my mother with the ponies and the hunters. We were pretty much the same age and had known each other since we were tiny.

I walked in that first day with Heather by my side, and everyone stared. I smiled and said, generally, to the air around me, 'Good morning. How are you?'

There were titters. Snorts of derision.

A girl with earrings bumped into me. I don't think it was an accident.

'Think you're better 'n us?' A big boy called Darren was cracking his knuckles.

'Not at all,' I said, as politely as I could. 'I am delighted to make your acquaintance. Most certainly I am.'

My mother had always taught me that good manners would get you out of a sticky situation. For some reason, in this instance, the politest voice I could summon had the opposite effect.

There was a ring of them now, all around me. Heather tried to say something but was pushed out of the way. I motioned to her to get out while she could. They were pulling at my jumper, ruffling my

110

hair, spitting at my shoes. When one girl tried to pull my satchel away, it was as if the pin had been pulled out of my hand grenade. I lost it.

'You bitch,' I shouted. I kicked, I hit, I bit and I took the storm of punches coming back my way without a whimper. I was just beginning to get the situation under control when Mrs Cook came into the playground.

'And what on earth is going on here?' Her voice did not need a megaphone. She was a human trumpet.

I froze, my fist just above my right ear. The girl with the earrings, who was now on the concrete of the playground on her back, me sitting astride her with my left hand round her throat, started to scream.

'Miss, Miss, she's trying to kill me,' she said. 'I did nuffink. She's a mentalist.'

The evidence was against me. The crowd had dissipated. There was just me, the girl with the earrings and a boy with a nosebleed, saying, 'Miss, she punched me. Look, Miss, blood.'

I could see Heather a few feet away. She tried to stick up for me, but there wasn't much point. I said nothing. The last time I had tried to be polite it had worked against me.

'You, come with me,' said Mrs Cook, pointing at me. 'Let Joanne get up. Brian, you'll be fine. It's just a bit of blood. The rest of you get into class. Now.'

She took me to the headmistress's office, where she sat me down and gave me a glass of water.

'It's your first day,' she said. 'It will get better, I promise, but fighting is not the answer. Really, it's not.'

111

I didn't trust myself to speak.

'I'll be keeping an eye on you. Now, go to your first class and try to keep out of trouble. At least for the rest of the day.'

'Thank you,' I whispered, as I crept out of the room.

As I walked into the classroom, late on that first morning, thirty pairs of eyes turned to look at me. I searched for a desk that was free and saw Heather waving at me. She had saved me a place.

As it turned out, the fact that I could punch a boy and make his nose bleed and that I wasn't frightened of Joanne Jones worked in my favour. My stock had risen considerably that morning. The tough boys avoided me at break time and the girls looked a little wary.

Heather and I sat on the concrete tube in the school yard while younger children climbed through beneath us, eating our chocolate biscuits. I didn't really care if the rest of the school didn't want to talk to me, as long as they weren't trying to rip my satchel off my back.

The evenings and the weekends were hard. I got back from school, and Andrew wasn't there. We may have had our fights, but he was my partner in crime. We didn't have to explain things to each other, or apologize, or feel awkward. Andrew was the only person in front of whom I didn't feel the need for a disguise. Our life wasn't odd to him, because he'd lived it alongside me. Now, I didn't have him and, worse than that, he was having a set of experiences of which I was no part. Meanwhile, I was having a very different set, from which he could not save me.

I took Barney for long walks under the hill and

My parents' wedding—Grandma talks to dad;
mum talks to the dog

Candy, my protector

Me and Dad

Me (aged eighteen months) with Mill Reef

Riding Mill Reef at two years old

Valkyrie was part of the family

I was sure that Andrew, like me, would rather sleep with the dogs

I never really wanted to share Valkyrie

Me on Percy with Andrew, looking cold

My favourite jacket and Andrew's best hat

'Do you like my dog collar?'

Andrew and I riding shotgun on Valkyrie, with Mum and
Dad smiling on

With my friend Flossy

Dad with Bertie upsides in the snow

Kenneth Bright Photography

Dad jumps Bechers Brook right where he should on
Ross Poldark

Grandma sitting in state with the *Sporting Life*

Grandma holding Noon with Andrew on Triley Rosette;
me on Volcano

Andrew and I were mad for sport

The aloof
killing
machine,
Bertie

Me with Grandma's whippet, Dusk

Mum with Ellie May, Stuart and beautiful black
lurcher Barney

Volcano

Frank understood me

Lily

Making it into the lacrosse team (I'm in the back row,
2nd from right)

Andrew on Raffles; me on my beloved Frank

Park House Stables, Kingsclere

down the Far Hedge. As we came back across the Starting Gate field he jumped up at my arm and ran rings round me, going 'loopy-loo', as Dad called it. Some dogs are far more sensitive to human moods—I wonder if they can smell sadness—and Barney seemed to know that I needed him. When I came home from school, he was the one who came running to greet me; in the evenings, I curled up in his bed with him to watch TV or read a book.

He was such a fine-looking animal that Dad decided Barney should follow his father, Bertie, into breeding. This was a good idea in theory— Barney had a beautiful temperament to go with his looks. In practice, it was a non-starter. Barney wasn't interested in sex.

'Come on, boy,' my father would say encouragingly. 'It's really not difficult.'

Barney was in the covered lunging school to give him and Willow plenty of space. She was a pretty brindle lurcher, smaller than Barney and keen as mustard to win his attention. Barney didn't know what to do. He sniffed her and made as if to play, but it was clear that Willow was not interested in games. She wanted sex, and she wanted it now.

My father moved outside to allow them privacy, but was watching through the gaps in the wooden sleepers that made up the circular wall of the lunging ring. From there, he saw Barney start to shake, then saw him walk to the far side of the school, where he was violently sick.

'Bloody dog,' my father muttered. 'Spends so much time playing with those children that he doesn't realize he's a man.'

Bertie was drafted in to 'see to' Willow, and Barney came back to the house in shame. I hugged him tight and stroked his head. Much as I would have liked to see baby Barneys, I was on his side. Willow looked a bit too desperate to me.

*      *      *

Back at school, they had some sort of trading market going on. They all brought pencils, pens, sweets and badges and swapped them, or bought each other's things with money.

Money. Now there's something I didn't have. I was given £1 pocket money per week and, frankly, even in 1979 that was not enough. Andrew didn't have to worry because, at his prep school, there was a tuck shop where you could buy 'on account' and it was put on the school bill at the end of term. At Kingsclere Primary School, all deals were done in cash. This was going to be a problem.

Not only were there things I wanted, there were things I needed if I was to be a part of the gang.

I remembered that I had seen money somewhere, lots of notes and coins. They were sitting on the shelf in my father's dressing room. Money could buy me out of trouble, money could buy me friends, and money was sitting there, just waiting to be used.

That evening, I snuck into my parents' bedroom, through the far door and into their bathroom. On the right was the dark walk-in wardrobe that served as my father's dressing room. There were suits hanging from the rail and ten open shelves with folded-up shirts, polo shirts, jumpers and, in one section, all of his riding gear. On the other side were two long, open shelves. There were hundreds of socks, piles of underpants and a tray with cufflinks on it and a few watches. On this tray was the money.

I took a few coins at first, stuffing them into my pocket. Just a few pounds in fifty-pence pieces. After a few weeks, I started taking the odd pound note, and then it seemed sensible to go in there less often but take a bit more—maybe a five-pound note to see me through the week. Then I got worried that Dad might notice his sterling deposits disappearing, so I decided to get clever. There were piles of American dollars and French francs that he used only when he went abroad and therefore never counted. So I started to take them. He'd never notice.

'Half a pound of toffee bonbons and half a pound of pear drops, please.' I had been a regular customer at the village sweet shop for some time now.

Norton, who had been Grandma's chauffeur, was spending his retirement taking me to school. He had got used to the daily detour and was waiting for me out on Swan Street.

'I'm sorry, love,' said Mrs Carpenter from behind the counter, 'we don't accept foreign notes.'

'Really?' I replied. 'But two dollars are equal to one pound, and I'm giving you five dollars there instead of two pounds. You're doing well out of it.'

'It's no good to me, love,' responded Mrs Carpenter. 'I can't spend it, can I? When am *I* going to be going to America? I'm sorry, I can't take it.'

'Right, not a problem,' I said efficiently. I was not to be beaten. 'Just hold those for me, will you?' I pointed at the paper bag on the scales. 'I'll be back in a tick.'

The Kingsclere branch of Lloyds Bank was right

115

next to the sweet shop, so I dashed out on to the street, signalled to Norton that I'd just be a few minutes and ran in. There was a queue and when I got to the front I had to stand on tiptoes to see over the counter.

'Can I change these into pounds, please?' I asked.

'Minimum transaction $50' came the clipped reply. 'And you'll need your passport.'

'But I just need this note changed. Really, it's quite important, you see, and I'm in a hurry and I just need some pounds. Please.'

'Sorry. I can't help you,' she said.

Damn. Damn and blast. As if my money wasn't as good as anyone else's. Technically, of course, it wasn't my money, but that's not the point. I stomped out of the bank and got back in the car. Norton drove me to school. I was still fuming when he picked me up that evening.

'Clare, a word,' said my mother as I walked into the kitchen.

'What?' I said sullenly.

'It's not "What?", it's "Pardon?". Now Mrs Jessop tells me she saw you in the bank this morning.'

Mrs Jessop was our housekeeper, a sweet, kind, slightly stooped lady of about sixty who reminded me of Madame Cholet in *The Wombles*. She did the crossword every day and collected used stamps. I loved Mrs Jessop. I couldn't bear that she'd seen me. Oh God. This was terrible.

'She said she didn't want to confront you in the bank, as it would have embarrassed you.' My mother fixed me with her direct gaze. 'So, what were you doing there?'

116

'I was opening an account.' I said it with so much confidence that I almost believed myself.

'That's funny,' said my mother. 'You already have an account with Lloyds. I have been putting money into that account since you were born and, one day, when you are old enough and trustworthy enough, you will be able to use it. It seems that day is some way off.'

Oh God. I let out a big sigh and slumped back on the window bench.

'I talked to Norton,' my mother continued. 'And he told me that you have been going to the sweet shop in the village every morning for the past month. Where have you been getting the money to spend on sweets?'

Silence.

'I give you pocket money every week, and that is all you have to spend, so you must be getting more from somewhere. Where are you getting the money?'

I could feel my cheeks going red. It was so annoying the way they did that. I felt as if I was being backed into a corner. I could say I was earning the money, but my mother would know that was a lie. I could say Grandma had given it to me, but we both knew that was pretty unlikely. I could say I found it.

My mother was still looking into my eyes. This was horrible. She took my satchel and started rummaging through it while I objected. When I tried to grab it back she slapped my hand.

'Watch it, young lady,' she hissed. 'Just watch it.'

Then she found the dollars.

'This is why you were in the bank, is it? You were trying to change these? You little thief! What the

117

hell is wrong with you?'

I had my head in my hands now, rocking back and forth. There was so much I wanted to explain. How £1 a week pocket money just wasn't enough, how money was the only way I could have any status at school, how I hated being taunted for being posh, how I missed Andrew, how everything was just awful. But instead I just bit my bottom lip so hard it bled.

'I'll tell your father,' my mother was saying. 'I'll tell him.'

A chill went through my body, and it wasn't just because of the threat of telling my father. Something awful had happened. I could feel it. I ran out of the kitchen and locked myself in my room. Half an hour later, I heard the truck my father used pulling up outside the back door. There were voices in the kitchen.

I snuck down the stairs and out of the side of the house, coming round to the truck without going through the kitchen. The back flap was down, and I could see a black head, the mouth slightly open and the tongue lolling out. It was Barney.

I ran towards him and cradled his head in my arms. He had been coursing a hare and run straight into a fence post. The impact had cracked his skull. He was unconscious and, as I held him, I felt his breathing stop. I buried my face into his neck and started crying, my whole body heaving and my throat burning. This was all my fault. This was my punishment because I was a thief.

'I'm so sorry, please don't die. Don't die. Don't die. I won't do it again, I promise. Oh God, don't let him die.'

Dad came out and put his hand on my shoulder.

He put his other hand by Barney's nose and then closed his eyes.

'He's gone,' he said. 'He wouldn't have felt a thing. I promise you.'

Barney had died because I had done a bad thing.

'I'm sorry you had to see this,' my father was telling me. 'Your mother will be upset you've seen him, but this is what happens, I'm afraid. If you have dogs, you will see dogs die.'

We buried Barney in the orchard, with a cross and flowers. Andrew came back from prep school and we stood by the grave together, holding hands as we cried. The one thing I couldn't tell Andrew was that I thought it was my fault. He would hate me if he knew that.

I never went into my father's dressing room again.

## 8
## Frank

'Your father's busy.'

'But he's always busy,' I said. 'What's he doing?'

'He's busy and he'll be busy all day. Now try not to disturb him. Go and play, go and read a book, go and do something.'

My mother was standing in front of the door to the sitting room with her arms crossed. I knew the television was on, I could hear it. My father was clearly watching sport, and I didn't think that qualified as 'being busy'.

It's amazing how many hours my father spent watching sport. If only I could one day have a job where I could get away with that—now that would be cool. Dad was watching cricket and, when I eventually snuck in, quietly as I could, he explained the game to me.

I can't pretend I grasped it first time, and I made him draw me a diagram of the fielding positions, which I then had to hold upside down for alternate overs. But I did believe him when he said: 'This is an historic event.'

Dad played the shots that the batsman should be playing and imitated the spin bowler's wrist action. He marvelled at the grace and the speed of the West Indian bowlers—this was the great side of the eighties captained by Clive Lloyd, backed up by the likes of Viv Richards, Michael Holding, Joel Garner and Malcolm Marshall. After telling me who everyone was and what they should be doing, he growled or grunted after each ball, and then he was quiet.

'Out!' I said, loudly, ten minutes later.

'What?' My father woke with a start. He was apt to sleep a lot when he was watching history in the making.

'Boycott,' I said. 'He's out. No great shame as he was scoring so slowly.'

I could feel my father's eyes on me, so I looked at him. His mouth was open slightly and then he nodded. 'That's probably true.'

'Gooch is still there. I like him. But you're right about that Whispering Death fellow. He shifts the ball, he really does,' I said, folding my arms.

121

'Good girl,' my father said.

Well, I didn't think it was that difficult, frankly, to have an opinion that seemed to be right. You just had to listen to the commentators, watch what was going on, know who was who, and away you go. It's hardly rocket science. When rain stopped play at the Oval, I wandered off to see Frank.

Frank was the ugliest pony I ever had. When he arrived, he was called Prince, but that seemed inappropriate, so we named him after Frank the Box Driver.

He had a short, spiky mane, rubbed raw in places, a pink nose, pink eyelids, brown ears and a grey body with brown splodges down his neck. His bottom and his sheath were pale pink. He suffered from sunburn, so had to have liberal applications of sunblock on his nose in the summer. He was what they call a 'Heinz 57'. That's not a can of soup, it's a mixture of various different breeds. Frank was nothing, and he was everything.

His mouth was as sensitive as a block of wood, and he frequently took hold, putting his head slightly on one side and galloping off in whichever direction took his fancy. He was not straight-forward, he was not handsome and he was not even affectionate, but I *adored* him.

Frank understood me.

Fine, he trod on my feet and barged me out of the way when he wanted to get out of his box. Yes, he never looked clean and we were the laughing stock of the Pony Club. Yes, I wasn't allowed near the racehorses with him because they all spooked and whipped round because he was 'a freak'.

I loved him with a passion of which I had no idea I was capable. I loved him partly to defend him

122

against the world and partly because I genuinely believed we were soul mates. If I had ever thought it was likely that my mother might sanction me having a tattoo, it would have read 'Frank'. Instead, I carved it into the bark of the Hollow Tree at the top of the Downs:

### CLARE LOVES FRANK, 1/8/80

In the years to come, I figured, people would see that inscription and know how much I cared.

Where other girls my age had posters of tennis players or pop stars on their walls, I had photos of Frank. I had long, long conversations with him about life at school and how much Andrew annoyed me; I told him England had drawn the Fourth Test and I admitted to him that I suspected my grandmother hated me.

I was allowed to ride on my own now, as long as I told someone where I was going. The trouble was, there were so many options, it was hard to say exactly where I might end up. I could ride on the farm, up to the Downs, over the hill to Hannington, go through the water at Gaily Mill and hack over to Ecchinswell, trespass just a bit on the edge of the Lloyd Webber estate or stay close to home and use the all-weather gallop just before Jonna harrowed away the hoof prints, to make it fresh and fluffy for Second Lot. Wherever I went there were jumps, built for the drag hunt, so I could fine-tune my eye, seeing a stride from further and further away.

The Berks & Bucks Drag Hunt had been established by a group of adrenalin junkies keen to gallop and jump, happy to ride to hounds but wanting to avoid the unpredictability of fox hunting.

Three or four 'lines' were pre-planned, with fences built or hedges trimmed to allow a field of up to eighty riders to gallop and jump across country. A runner with a sock soaked in aniseed marked out the line by laying a scent trail, which the hounds followed.

For my father, the drag hunt was the ideal option. It happened on a Sunday, so he was unlikely to be racing; it guaranteed him a rush from jumping at pace and it rarely took longer than three hours from beginning to end.

'Dad, when can I come drag hunting?'

My plea became ever more persistent. I had been out to watch my father on his big chestnut, Paintbox, and my mother on her rather plain hunter, Ellie May, and I so wanted to join in. I knew Frank would love it.

'There's a children's meet in the spring. You can come then,' my father conceded eventually.

He was the Field Master, which meant he wore a bright-red coat, confusingly referred to as a 'pink' jacket, and he led the field. The rule was that you had to stay behind him and you had to listen to what he said. Dad had never been in the army but this was the closest he ever came to being a general, barking orders, leading his troops and generally enjoying the authority.

My father was a fearless rider. He liked to do everything at racing pace, and he rode short, even in a hunting saddle. If you could stay upsides my father and jump what he jumped, you earned his respect for ever. This was my ambition.

Our ponies were now being kept at the stud, where the mares and foals lived. It was a short walk away from the yard and from the house, with

124

a different team of people running it, and all of it was fiercely protected by my mother. This was her territory—she had bought the stud from Grandma, and it was up to her who worked there and which horses were kept there.

The stud had two yards, and the one on the left, where our ponies lived, was built in red brick in the same style as the John Porter racing yard, but was more compact and much friendlier. Horses and people walked through an arch into a small quadrangle with ten boxes in total: four on either side and one at each end. The tack room was on the left of the top arch and the feed room to the left of the bottom arch. The horses all looked out into a central square, laid with red clay, with a large pot, planted with marigolds, sitting in the middle. The stable doors were painted green, the boxes spacious and solid. It was, and still is, the perfect yard—quiet, functional, warm and fine-looking.

It was also a great place to keep two tearaways out of trouble. Andrew had a dappled iron-grey pony called Raffles who did everything at 100 mph. Raffles could jump a house if he had to, but he was always on the limit. To be totally accurate, he was always out of control, except when he was show-jumping. Andrew had been studying the great show jumpers of the time—Eddie Macken, Harvey Smith and Paul Schockemöhle—and had developed a rising canter, which he liked to use in the arena. He would move up and down, as if in trot, while Raffles cantered along.

For a while, Andrew wanted to be a show jumper—but he had also wanted to be a fireman, an astronaut and a Jedi knight, so we took his career choices with a pinch of salt. It was when, at the age of eight, he announced that he wanted to be a racehorse trainer that something happened. It was as if the wind had changed direction, or that smell there is when it's about to rain had come.

My father began to have serious conversations with him about the horses, and my grandmother started sentences with the words 'When Andrew's in charge . . .' or 'When Andrew lives here . . .' It wasn't that my brother became someone else—he was still motivated by pizza, chips and chocolate—it's just that everyone else seemed to change their attitude to him. It was as if he mattered now.

I caught snippets of whispered conversations about Andrew's future as the master of Park House.

'Well, thank God he wants to do it,' my mother said.

'Of course he wants to do it. What kind of idiot wouldn't want to do it?' was my father's clipped response.

Any suggestion of a life other than the one my father had led perplexed him. Being a racehorse trainer was surely the most valuable, important and respectable job on the planet.

Women were allowed to hold a training licence by now, thanks to the efforts of Florence Nagle, who had fought hard to persuade the Jockey Club that, even though she didn't wear trousers, she could still train a racehorse. There were a few female trainers around—Jenny Pitman started training in 1975 and won the Grand National in 1983 with Corbiere; Mercy Rimell took over from her husband, Fred; and Mary Reveley had consistent success over many decades. But, in our household, training was a man's job.

Andrew read the *Sporting Life* and the *Racing Post* every day. He could work out fractions if it was computing his winnings from a five-pound bet at 6–4; he knew how many lengths to a pound over a mile and how it differed over a mile and a half; he remembered the effect of the draw at Chester or Doncaster; he understood weight for age and weight allowances for fillies. He could suddenly speak a language that allowed him to communicate with my parents and with Grandma. I listened to them all and nodded occasionally, saying things like, 'Makes sense to me.'

But none of it did. I just didn't get it, and I hated it because I didn't understand what they were all going on about and why it was all so important. I resented that every conversation was about which horse was running where, who was riding it and which one of them was going to saddle it. No one read a proper newspaper or watched the news. Nuclear war could've broken out—we were near enough to Greenham Common for it to be all too real a prospect—and none of them would have noticed unless it meant that Royal Ascot was cancelled. The world revolved around racing and, if I wasn't in, I was out.

Once Andrew had decided he wanted to train at Park House, it was clear that I was going to have to find something else to do with my life. I was ten.

I talked it through with Frank. Well, I talked. He listened, brown ears flickering back and forth.

'I'll show them,' I vowed.

I was riding on the farm, where twenty or so drag-hunt fences had been trimmed up, ready for the children's meet. I squeezed him in the belly and we sailed over the tyres, the timber and the barrels by the side of the Range Road. I patted Frank on the neck and slowed down to a trot, then let him open up into a stronger canter on the grass of Long Meadow. This is where I felt alive—with the wind in my face, galloping and jumping with Frank.

My beloved Frank devoured solid cross-country fences, but show jumps were a trickier prospect. He wasn't at all sure about coloured poles. For our first Pony Club event, Liz, who was working at the stud, had helped me wash Frank with soapy water. We had attempted to plait his spiky mane and make the best of his dreadful tail. Poor Frank looked like a farmer forced into a morning suit—it wasn't him at all. Nevertheless, we trotted into the show-jumping arena.

'Next into the ring,' said the announcer, 'we have Clare Balding riding Prince Frank.'

Mum and I had decided that we ought to at least give a nod in recognition of Frank's former name, just in case it really was unlucky to change it.

I sat into the saddle, took a strong contact on the reins and squeezed Frank into a collected canter. The bell went. We found a lovely rhythm and cantered into the first—red- and white-striped poles. I thought we met it on the perfect stride, but Frank didn't really take off and crashed straight through it. Thrown off balance, I nearly fell off but picked his head up off the floor and on we went.

The next was a rustic brown fence and he sailed over, then a blue and white oxer—crash, the back pole came down. Into the green and white double and Frank brought the first part down with his hind legs, the second with his front legs, the pole coming with us for two more strides.

I didn't know what to do apart from keep going.

128

The plain white or rustic fences were fine, but the coloured ones he smashed to pieces. We finally finished; I patted Frank on the neck and the announcer said, 'An interesting round there for Clare Balding and Prince Frank. Thirty-two faults. Don't think we'll be winning any prizes with that.'

My face turned bright red as we trotted out of the ring. I could tell from looking at my mother that she was in shock.

'I just don't know what happened,' I said. 'He jumps so well at home and he was fine in the collecting ring. Something must have scared him.'

'Never mind,' my mother was saying. 'Poor old Frank, maybe show-jumping's not for you.'

From across the horsebox park, I had just caught sight of a woman running. She was making a strange sound, like a goat bleating.

'Oooh, ooh, ooh. It's Prince. It's my beloved Prince.'

She had flung her arms round Frank and was kissing him on the neck. He looked bemused and I felt a pang of something I would later identify as jealousy.

'Hello,' said my mother, as politely as she could. She didn't do well in the face of public displays of affection. 'Can we help you?'

'I heard the clattering,' said the woman, 'and I thought—I only know one pony who could knock down that many show jumps.'

She stroked him gently as her words came tumbling out.

'Oh, I thought he'd died. I thought I'd never see him again. Where did you find him? How is he? Where's he been? Did you know about the animal-testing place? You do know he needs

129

sunblock, don't you?'

The questions came so fast I couldn't take them in, but it emerged that this woman, Sarah, had ridden Frank when she was a little girl. When she grew out of him, her father promised he would find him a nice home but, in fact, the pony had been earmarked by some scientists who had noticed his extra-sensitive skin. They wanted to test creams and potions on him and offered £1,000 for him to go to an animal-testing unit near Newmarket. Her father had accepted. When Sarah found out, they had a huge row and she left home. She had not since spoken to her father.

Frank—or Prince, as she called him—had been rescued from the animal-testing place by a trainer called Frankie Durr, had gone through various racing families and had ended up at Swindon market, where my mother had bought him for £500.

'It's the colours,' she was saying. 'He's scared of the coloured poles. You'll find he's fine with plain ones, but stripes and all that—he hates them. Oh, I'm so pleased you've got him. You will keep in touch, won't you?'

Sarah scribbled her address and phone number on the show programme and thrust it into my mother's hand. She kissed Frank on the nose and she was gone.

'Well, that was an experience,' my mother said, as she filled a bucket with water. 'An animal-testing unit? Poor old Frank.'

Mum sent Sarah a letter every few months with a photo of Frank to let her know what we were up to. I tried to accept the fact that I was not the first to love him, and I hoped that Sarah would keep her distance. Over time, I realized that, as Frank couldn't read her letters, she was not a threat.

*      *      *

The day of the children's meet was upon us. This was the one day of the year when children were actively encouraged to go drag hunting. The fences were smaller than usual and you could go round them all if you had to. Dad had given Andrew and me a stern talking to. We were to listen to him and to stay right behind him.

I was so excited I had barely slept the night before, and I arrived at breakfast dressed in my beige jodhpurs, my shirt and my Pony Club tie. I had, however, learned my lesson. They were covered by a scruffy pair of jeans and a sweatshirt so I could get as dirty as I needed to, peel off the top layer and be spotless underneath.

Andrew didn't mind so much, nor did he intend to do much in the way of preparation for Raffles. If he was nervous, he didn't show it. I couldn't stop chattering on about what we were going to jump, who would be coming, which lines we were doing and how much I thought Frank would enjoy it. Andrew sat there, stuffing toast into his mouth, grunting.

Dad was out putting up signs directing people where to park and trying to make sure they didn't turn their horseboxes into the main entrance of the yard. He kept running back into the house, slamming the back door and shouting, *'Emma!'* at the top of his voice.

He had left something behind, or lost something, or forgotten someone's name. This needed to be solved, immediately, by my mother. Mum was getting Andrew's things together, so I headed off to the stud to start preparing Frank for the big day.

Liz, our supersonic groom, had already done most of the work. Liz did things very fast. She even walked fast, like Patrick Swayze in *Dirty Dancing*, or Andre Agassi, with short steps. She had curly brown hair and a round face. She never seemed to lose her temper and was so happy every day just to be paid to be working with horses. Liz had cleaned our tack and groomed our ponies, so all I had to do was put on Frank's tack while I told him who was coming, and paint on his hoof oil. I stood back to admire my wonderful pony in all his glory.

'Ah, well, you can't polish a turd.' My father had arrived in the yard. I had no idea what he meant, so I just sighed and said, 'Doesn't he look smart?'

'I suppose that's one way of describing him. Now where's your lazy brother?'

Dad was wearing his bright-red jacket with gold buttons, white breeches and gleaming black boots. He carried a hunting crop and there was a horn in a leather pouch to the side of his saddle. Paintbox, with his white face and his shiny chestnut coat, looked magnificent. And huge. He was a big horse who pulled so hard no one but my father could hold him.

I got on Frank, but there was still no sign of Andrew. Raffles was all ready in his box, so I suggested we lead him up to the house to save time. As we headed up the path, my mother appeared, dragging my brother behind her. His shirt was hanging out, his tie had egg on it and his jodhpurs were too tight. He had spilt butter and Marmite on his smart jodhpurs so was now wearing brown ones. They would at least hide the dirt.

132

'He went back to bed,' Mum explained as my father made a low, growling sound, the same sound he made when a puppy peed in the house.

We rode together to the meet, in the field behind our house. There were loads of children on ponies, their parents on foot looking rather anxious. Andrew and I stood either side of Dad for a photo and then he hollered at the assembled masses, 'Gather round!' I always thought it was a good thing my father had a loud voice, because he seemed to do a lot of shouting.

'Welcome to the children's meet here at Kingsclere. It's lovely to see so many of you. We have four lines today and there is an alternative route round every jump so, please, if your pony decides it doesn't like the look of something, just go round it. There are certain rules that we all need to follow for safety, so listen carefully while I take you through them . . .'

As Dad listed all the things we couldn't do, Frank and Raffles both started to get edgy. They wouldn't stand still, so Andrew and I peeled off from the gathering and took them for a trot round the field.

'There's no point us listening,' said Andrew. 'We've heard it all before.'

Raffles had a Balding gag in his mouth, a gag invented by our great-great-grandfather. It's a bit with holes in the rings on either side and a piece of rope going through them which pulls down on the poll so that the horse lowers its head when the rider pulls on the reins, in theory making it easy to slow the horse down.

Dad had finished shouting, for now, and the hounds moved off with the Master, Roger Palmer, in his red coat at the head of them, and four more people around the hounds. They were 'whipping in', so it was their job to make sure the hounds were following the scent and staying on track.

The first line started on the farm, went down the Range Road, left up Long Meadow, through Smith's Bushes and finished at the end of a long climb at the top of the Downs. My father thought it would take the sting out of the ponies who were too fresh and pulling hard. This was a good plan, but what he hadn't foreseen was the downhill end to the Range Road and the sharp left turn. With fifty ponies all charging together, this turned into a Grand Prix-type chicane and hairpin bend.

Dad let the hounds get well ahead and then, with one last holler at everyone to stay behind him, he set off. I was right behind him and heading towards the first set of tyres in relative control. I thought Andrew was with me but Raffles started dancing on the spot as he heard the horn of the Master. He was rearing slightly and jumping up and down, so Andrew gave him a kick in the belly and loosened his reins a notch. That was an invitation Raffles could not refuse.

The round-bellied little monster took off. As we jumped the second fence I could hear Andrew screaming as he flew past me. He took the third fence upsides Dad, who shouted, '*Do not* go past me, I said, "Do not—"' he realized who it was '—Andrew, pull him up, pull him up. Turn left, *left!*'

Andrew had never really got the hang of left and right, so he went one way and then the other and ended up going straight on. At the bottom of the Range Road is a double-width six-bar white gate. It's for the tractors and combine harvesters to come into the farm from the Sydmonton road. It's over five feet tall and made of iron. Andrew and Raffles were heading straight for it.

Raffles cleared the gate in style but, as they landed the other side, Andrew fell off—more out of shock than anything else. My father put his hand in the air to signal to the rest of the field to stop and called over the gate, 'Are you all right?' Andrew nodded and bit his lip. 'Right, catch that damn pony and stay at the back. Clare, you look after him. The rest of you, follow me.'

With that, the Field Master, our father, took the field and headed up Long Meadow. I opened a small wooden gate to the side, told Andrew to wait there and went trotting off towards the village. I found Raffles not far away, munching grass at the side of the road.

Andrew and I could see the field disappearing up the hill to the Downs, so we hacked along together, jumping all the fences up Long Meadow. By the time we'd caught them up, Mum was anxiously looking for us. Despite much hurrumphing from Dad that 'the boy should carry on—it'll be good for him,' she decided to take Andrew and Raffles home.

Over the next three lines, I stuck right behind my father. Frank was brilliant. He put in short strides, saw long ones, met most of the fences just right and didn't even pull. When we got to the Team Chase fences, Dad said, 'Come on then, girl, get right upsides me.'

We raced the whole way up to the top ring, Frank and Paintbox side by side, the one tall and handsome, the other squat and ugly. Dad turned to me as we pulled up, and grinned.

'Handsome is as handsome does, I suppose. You're quite some pony.' He was smiling at Frank.

I felt so proud as we headed home. I was flushed with excitement; Frank was still high on adrenalin so refused to walk but jig-jogged the whole way back. We were covered in mud, flecks of sweat and froth, but we were happy.

My Frank wasn't born to jump coloured poles in smart show-jumping rings. He was born for this.

\*     \*     \*

Grandma was not a fan of Frank's. By way of introduction, he had stood on her toe and butted her hard in her considerable bosom.

'That pony is unattractive and ill mannered,' I heard her say to my mother. 'I suppose they'll suit each other well.'

I had been reading enough adventure books to think that it would take just one act of heroism for both Frank and me to turn Grandma in our favour. We just needed the opportunity.

That chance came on a murky evening in 1980, right at the end of the summer holidays. Grandma's favourite dog was called Dusk. She was a small, fine-boned black whippet and a law unto herself. She would take herself off hunting for hours on end and, on this particular evening, she had been gone for longer than ever. Grandma had walked to every spot she could think, she had whistled and called, but there was no sign of Dusk.

Seeing my chance to be the hero of the hour, I said, 'Don't worry, Grandma. Frank and I will find her.'

Grandma was standing in our kitchen with her

husky jacket on. Andrew was forcing cake into an already full mouth. My father was out in the yard and my mother was chopping vegetables she had picked from the garden. None of them seemed to hear me as I waved a cheery goodbye and headed off to tack up Frank.

We rode over to Grandma's side of the road, along the boundary hedgerows, through Smith's Bushes and up to the Downs, back down the chalk track, through the farm and over to the avenues, under the hill and down the Far Hedge, me calling all the way, 'Dusk! Dusk, where are you?'

After an hour, it started to rain. Then it began to pour. It was getting so dark I could only just make out the white furlong-marker poles on the gallop to our left. There was no sign of Dusk and, even in my fervent desire to be a hero, I could tell we were doing ourselves no favours. We were only going to get wetter and colder. The dog had disappeared.

Frank was supposed to be turned out at night. He was allergic to straw and all the boxes at the stud were full, so I took him up to the row of four stables by the tennis court. He had been such a good boy and I couldn't bear to turn him out in such filthy rain. The least he deserved, I reasoned, was a warm, dry bed for the night.

The boxes were empty and had no bedding at all. I left him standing while I carried his saddle and bridle to the tack room and then I set about my work. Andrew and I hardly did any mucking out because Liz did it all for us, so neither of us were particularly good at it, but I did know how to lay a decent bed and I was determined to do so for Frank that night. Evening stables had long since finished and there was no one around. The lads were back in their houses or watching TV in the Hostel.

In the barn at the end of the row of boxes were some paper bales wrapped tight in black plastic. They were for racehorses with respiratory problems, because there is less dust in paper than in straw, so I figured one of those would be perfect for Frank. I split open the bag with a knife, placed it carefully back on the windowsill and picked the sharpest, shiniest pitchfork leaning against the wall.

I raised it high above my head and speared downwards through the paper bale. It felt as if it had got slightly stuck and I thought it must've gone right through to the ground, so I pulled it back out, with some difficulty, and then scooped under the paper to carry it to Frank's box.

As I started walking, I felt an odd sensation in my left foot. It was really itchy. When I got to the stable door, I put down the chunk of paper, leant the pitchfork against the wall and reached down. I had to pull my boot off, because my foot felt really odd. Something was wrong. I can't remember if I saw the blood on my sock first, or the blood on the blade of the pitchfork but, either way, it made me feel sick. Like a tap being turned on, pain suddenly coursed through my body, and I collapsed against the frame of the door.

Frank came over to nuzzle me and butt me in the ribs.

My foot hurt so much I had to stifle a scream. I couldn't put my boot back on, so I hopped to the nearest dwelling, which was the mobile home on blocks of concrete where Spider, the Travelling Head Lad, lived. Luckily, he answered the thud on his door.

'Oh dear,' he said. 'What have you been up to,

young Clare?'

'I've had an accident,' I replied, as calmly as I could. 'I was out with Frank, trying to find Grandma's whippet.' I was whispering, but I thought it was important he knew the context. 'He was so good. So good. Didn't want to turn him out in the rain. Not fair. Was making him a bed. Pitchfork. Foot . . .'

My voice trailed off and I was falling backwards, sliding out of consciousness. I felt an arm behind my head and another one under my knees. Spider had caught me and the next thing I realized was that we were heading down the gravel path by the runner beans. He was carrying me back to the house.

My mother answered the front door to see Spider standing in the rain with me in his arms.

'Oh God—what's happened?' said my mother. I was coming back into the world to see Grandma over her shoulder, standing in the hall.

'What's she done now?' said my grandmother. 'Honestly, such a drama queen.'

'I couldn't find her, Grandma. We looked everywhere, but I couldn't find her.' My voice was small. I felt as if I was removed from the scene, looking on from above.

'She's stuck a pitchfork through her foot,' Spider told my mother as he carried me into the house. 'There's a lot of blood, but I don't think it's broken. She'll probably need a tetanus jab.'

'Thank you so much,' said my mother. 'I'm sorry she disturbed you.'

'What do you want doing with the pony?' said Spider, laying me down on the sofa and backing out of the sitting room. 'The ugly one—Frank?'

'Turn him out in the paddock at the back,' said my mother.

'*No!*' I thought I had shouted it, but no one seemed to hear.

Mum sighed; a big, deep exhalation of air. A 'why?' without words.

'You silly girl. We'd better get you to the hospital.' My mother was in practical mode now. There was to be no fussing. I had done a stupid thing and it would have to be dealt with. There were people coming for dinner and it was damned inconvenient.

Luckily, the prong of the pitchfork had slid between my second and third toes and missed the main chunk of pedal bone. The curved blade meant that it came out the other side further down my foot than it went in. I still have scars top and bottom as a reminder.

Dusk was never found. Grandma is convinced she got caught in a trap or stuck in a rabbit warren. The next day she brought over a packet of Polos for Frank to say thank you.

*       *       *

My funny-coloured Heinz 57 got over his fear of coloured poles and became quite a good show jumper. We went to Pony Club camp together, where we won the Thelwell Prize for pony and rider most like a Thelwell cartoon. I was thrilled. (Andrew won it the following two years.)

Frank and I had a 100 per cent clear round record in hunter trials. I took him drag hunting whenever I was allowed and Andrew and I rode in pairs competitions together. Mum said she could

140

hear us shouting at each other from two fields away as we argued about who should be leading.

When I got too tall for Frank, Andrew rode him for a year, but then he got into polo and the day I dreaded had come. I cried all week leading up to it. We were giving Frank to a sweet little girl who I knew would look after him and remember to put sunblock on his nose, but I couldn't bear to see him go. He trod on my toes, just for old times' sake, as he was loaded on to their horsebox. Then he backed up against their sparkling-clean wall and did the runniest, greenest dropping all down it and down his legs.

Despite his propensity to make himself look his worst, despite the fact that he had no manners and no particular affection for me, I worshipped that pony. I still don't really understand why—perhaps because he didn't care, perhaps because I needed an ally or perhaps because I identified with him always getting it wrong and always being the outsider. Something clicked, and I loved him more because other people did not. He was tough, he didn't care what anyone thought—mainly because he was a pony and he didn't understand what they were saying—but he understood me and I think I understood him.

Only a few years ago I was asked to contribute a story about my first love for a book. Who or what had I first fallen head over heels in love with? Most people chose film stars, fictional characters or real-life boyfriends or girlfriends. For me, it was an obvious choice: I wrote about Frank.

# 9

## Hattie

At the age of ten, I had taken a Common Entrance exam. Despite a woeful score of 13 per cent in maths, I had been accepted by a boarding school called Downe House. It was the same school my mother had been to twenty years earlier. It sat high on a hill on the outskirts of Newbury, less than twenty minutes from home. The buildings were all white, with red-tiled roofs. The girls wore long, dark-green cloaks, which made them look as if they were skating or moving on wheels as they swept through the arched cloisters or ran down the outdoor amphitheatre known as the Greek Steps.

On the first day of the first term we arrived late. It was just getting dark and in the murky half-light all I could make out were the tennis courts and the big white walls that protected the school from the outside world.

Andrew had told me that boarding school was fun. He seemed to have made lots of friends and he was in the rugby team, but Andrew was quite easy to please. When he made a mistake, everyone laughed. Early on at Caldicott, his class were asked if they could name the seasons of the year. Andrew's hand shot up.

'Flat and National Hunt,' he said, with confidence.

'I'm sorry?' His teacher had no idea what he was talking about.

'In racing,' Andrew explained, 'there are two seasons. The flat season, which runs roughly from the beginning of April until November. And the jumps season, also known as the National Hunt season, which runs from October to the end of April.'

Technically, my brother was correct. But it was not the answer his teacher had expected.

'That's excellent, Andrew. A very original and detailed answer. Anyone else?'

On the way to Downe House, I hugged Flossy tight in the back of my mother's Citroën Dyane. She was getting on a bit by now—her teeth were rotting, she had cysts between her toes, she was overweight and her bottom burps had got even

143

worse—but I had begged my mother to let her come with us. Flossy snuffled at me, and I'm pretty sure she said, 'Be strong. Be yourself. You'll be fine.'

My mother helped me with my case and came with me to the door of Darwin, a new house that had been recently opened for the Remove year. It was named after Charles Darwin, who had lived at Down House in Kent, where in 1907 Olive Willis had founded a girls' boarding school. By 1921, the number of pupils had outgrown the surroundings and the school was moved to a former nunnery called the Cloisters in Cold Ash, Berkshire.

There were six houses in total—four for the senior girls and two for the first year. Hill House was bigger and was set down in the woods, at the end of a long path. I always thought it was rather spooky. Darwin was less architecturally impressive, but it was functional and convenient, being closer to the classrooms and the dining room.

A tall woman with a beaked nose, hair scraped off her face and glasses on a chain answered the door.

'You are late.' She glared at my mother, who retreated without saying a word.

'You must be Clare. I am Mrs Berwick,' she said, her words precise and trimmed at the edges. She would train us to write with our letters sloping forwards, as that reflected an eager mind; sloping backwards denoted laziness. 'Follow me,' she continued, the heels of her sensible shoes clacking on the floor of the corridor. I trotted after her.

I realized I had forgotten to say goodbye to my mother but, by the time I turned round, she had gone. I waved at the empty space she had left

144

behind and followed the daunting Mrs Berwick into a room where twelve other girls were sitting on squishy sofas and beanbags. I sat cross-legged on the floor, as we used to do in assembly at Kingsclere Primary School.

'What's that pong?' I heard one girl with long hair scooped up in a scrunchie say to another, also with long, tumbling hair.

'I think it's coming from over thar.' The other girl pointed towards me.

I sniffed at my clothes and realized that I did smell of Flossy. I tried to tuck myself into as tight a ball as I could, hoping I would disappear. Mrs Berwick looked down her beaky nose and told us all what we could and, mainly, what we couldn't do.

I was sharing a room with two other girls who were much older than me. Everyone was older than me by nearly a year and they all seemed to have been to boarding school before.

'What does your father do?' a girl asked me, as she wound her long blond hair round her index finger.

'My dad's a racehorse trainer,' I answered.

There was a snort from one corner, giggles from another. I heard the word 'Dad' being uttered with incredulity.

'You mean your father's a stable boy?' the blond girl said.

'No, he's a trainer. He trained Mill Reef.' Usually, that was my get-out-of-jail card.

'Huh,' said a girl whose father was a colonel in the army. 'Mill Reef? Never heard of him. But if you were born in a barnful of horses, that explains why you stink of manure!'

The other girls started laughing hysterically,

145

rolling around on the floor together. I got up and silently left the room.

'I can ride. I can ride,' I said to myself.

It was the one thing I knew I could do better than anyone else at this school.

We were straight into lessons the next day, which meant wearing the uniform of green and white striped shirts, green skirt, red or green jumper and green blazer with red stripes. I chose to wear the red jumper as it was new, whereas my green one was second-hand. Everyone else had chosen green. My skirt needed to be rolled over a few times, as it was on the big side.

'You'll grow into it,' my mother had promised me.

Mum had refused to buy me the burgundy penny loafers that were on the school uniform list because they were 'ridiculously expensive'. Instead, I had orthopaedic shoes that would support my arches. I hated them.

The dining room, large enough to seat nearly three hundred girls, had a wooden floor with timber posts around the side that supported a gallery above. There was a store up there of second-hand uniforms, and my mother had instructed me to go there as soon as I could to get a cloak. Beneath the red-lined hood, underneath the chain with which I could hang the cloak, were the nametapes of girls who had owned it before me. There were five previous owners, which meant that this cloak was at least twenty-five years old. It felt like an historic object and, as I wrapped it round me, I decided that my cloak would have magic powers. I could be invisible, indestructible. That cloak would be my saviour. What I did not yet know was that the cloak

146

would also be my downfall.

I was not stupid and rapidly realized that I needed to work on my language and my accent. Where I said 'Yes', they said 'Yah'. When I said 'Year', they said 'Yar'. Where I said 'No', they said 'I don't think so.' When I said 'I beg your pardon?', they said 'Sorry?' Everything you liked was 'cool', everything you didn't was 'gross'.

My challenge was to break the code and, although there were some things I knew not to do or not to say—'serviette', for example—there were other things that flummoxed me: I had no idea that black wellington boots with yellow soles and a waterproof anorak were off limits as wet-weather gear. Hunter boots and Barbour jackets were the only acceptable outdoor attire. I was better off getting wet than wearing what my mother and I had packed for the winter months.

Through the course of that first week, my accent duly modified, I started to make friends, and my brand-new best, best friend was called Jenny. We sat next to each other in class, I saved her a place at lunch, she laughed at my jokes and we talked about our ponies together. She invited me to stay with her in Jersey during the holidays. I was amazed. If it was this easy to make friends at boarding school, I was going to have a ball. I would have cut my finger and mixed it with the blood of her finger if she had asked me to be a blood sister.

The weekend came and, after Saturday-morning lessons, for the first time we changed out of our uniforms into 'mufti'. That's what we called our own clothes. I had packed a sparse mufti collection, just my favourite things and a couple of new shirts with flowers on them that my mother had bought me. This was 1981—one of the greatest racing years ever. Aldaniti won the Grand National with Bob Champion, recently recovered from cancer, in the saddle. Shergar won the Derby by a record-breaking ten lengths. In second place was a horse trained by my father called Glint of Gold. His jockey, John Matthias, who had breakfast with us every morning, hadn't been able to see Shergar because he was so far in front. John genuinely thought he had won.

Unfortunately for me, I may have known which horses finished first in the Derby and the Grand National in 1981, but I was way off the pace as a clotheshorse. My wardrobe was firmly stuck in 1975.

Had I known anything about fashion, I would've known this was the era of drainpipe trousers. Jenny had a pair of bright-yellow, skin-tight jeans and a baggy, collarless shirt hanging out underneath an oversize cashmere jumper she had 'borrowed' from her father. I emerged from my three-bed dorm wearing my usual kit.

Jenny looked me up and down and said, with thinly veiled disgust, 'What the hell are you wearing?'

'These are my favourite trousers,' I explained, smiling.

They were blue cord flares, slightly worn at the knees, with creases down the front ironed in by Mrs Jessop. I wore them with the black polo neck with the gold hoop on it that I wore when I was pretending to be a jockey—the one Grandma had knitted me. It was a little tight these days, but it kept me warm.

'Well, you're not coming anywhere near me.

Not dressed like that.' Jenny turned on her winkle-picker heels and marched off.

I saw her later with a gang from Hill House, all of them in drainpipes and baggy cashmere or lambswool jumpers pulled over their hands. They were just hanging out, not doing anything special, but they clearly knew that they were 'in' and I was 'out'. They knew the rules for mufti were even stricter than those for school uniform.

Jenny looked at me with an expression that smacked not of hatred but of something much more dangerous—pity. Such a tough thing to fight. You can fight outright prejudice, you can shout back at someone who offends you, but pity is utterly draining. There is no way to respond, no way to defend yourself and there is no coming back because pity says you will never be equals.

Human beings are tribal. Despite our supposed superiority to other animals, we are remarkably herd-like. As children, we are more willing to discover our own character, plough our own furrow, but as society impacts upon us—in other words, the knowledge that the opinion of others has influence—we retreat to a position of safety. We hit puberty and suddenly we need to fit in, we require safety in numbers. Some people grow out of this fear of being different, this reluctance to swim against the tide. Others do not.

Right then, at ten years old and in my first week at boarding school, I did not want to stand out. I wanted to be just like Jenny and her friends. I wanted to look the same, sound the same, think the same.

I spent the afternoon in my room, with a needle and thread, taking in the lower legs of my cords. I

149

was thrilled with the outcome—the lower legs were tight and sort of straight. When I emerged, Mrs Berwick was standing outside her flat at the end of the corridor.

'Are we impersonating a frog, my dear? How very o-rig-i-nal.' She separated the syllables and peered at me over her glasses and her beak.

I spent most subsequent weekends pretending I was either going to or coming back from lacrosse practice—that meant I could wear tracksuit bottoms and my green games jumper and get away with it.

After a month, we were allowed a long weekend away from school. It was called the Short Exeat. Most of the other girls seemed to be meeting up in Sloane Square near somewhere called the King's Road in London. I watched them greet their parents. A kiss on both cheeks, a bear hug from their fathers—it was physical. We didn't do that in our family. My mother's idea of a public display of affection was a wave, from a distance. As for my grandmother, even a wave was pushing it.

I stood outside waiting for my mother. Annabel's parents had come down from Scotland to take her out for the weekend. I stared at Jenny's divorced parents, watching how they each hugged her in turn, hanging on for a long, long time before backing away and allowing the other one to come forward. I had never before met anyone whose parents were divorced, so I was fascinated. I probably stared a bit too intently, because Jenny gave me a dirty look as she climbed into the front seat of her father's Mercedes. Her mother followed them in a Range Rover. They kept cars in the UK as well as at home in Jersey, so that they didn't have to hire one. Or two.

I looked at my watch and wasn't surprised that my parents were late. It was a Saturday—work morning on the gallops. Dad would be busy. Too busy to come and pick me up, I supposed. My mother would have been making sure everyone had breakfast. She'd be here soon. It was eleven o'clock.

The next time I looked it was twelve o'clock and all the other girls had long gone. Mrs Berwick came out and saw me sitting on the concrete step, a small bag at my feet.

'Who's picking you up?' she asked.

'My mother, I think,' I replied.

'Have you called her? Is everything all right? Could she have been called away on an emergency? Could she be ill? You cannot sit here all weekend, my dear.'

I found a ten-pence coin and headed off to the phone box in the corner of the Darwin common room. I think my mother said, 'Oh shit,' or words to that effect. She had forgotten. Clean forgotten her daughter's first Short Exeat from her boarding school. Of course I didn't tell Mrs Berwick that—I said she'd had a car crash and was waiting for the AA but would be here as soon as she could. Half an hour later, my mother came racing through the gates of Downe House in her blue Citroën Dyane, which had clearly not been in a crash.

'I do hope you're all right,' said Mrs Berwick, looking as concerned as I'd ever seen her. 'Such a terrible thing to happen. I had a crash only last year. Very disturbing. You may find you'll be suffering from shock for days to come.'

'I don't know what you m—' My mother was interrupted from whatever she was about to say

151

by me, flinging myself at her like a koala bear, my arms wrapping around her stomach.

'Mummy,' I cried. 'I'm so glad you're all right. Thank God for that. Thank God.'

As I hugged her, I pushed her towards the driver's door and forced her into the car.

'Best to get straight back in the saddle,' I said as I slammed the door and gave Mrs Berwick a knowing glance. 'That's what Daddy always says when you have a fall. "Get straight back in the saddle."'

I waved Mrs Berwick goodbye and headed off home to see Frank and Flossy.

*       *       *

We had many nannies. There had been Jane the nurse, who looked after Andrew when he was a baby; Liz the Irish nanny, who found us when we had run away from home—we had only got to the bottom of the hill before Andrew realized he'd forgotten to pack his pyjamas; Jackie Knee; and then Annie the Nanny, who was the sister of John the Jockey; Elaine, who crashed my mother's car; Emma, who told tales about triangular aliens and took us swimming in Basingstoke; and Geraldine, who left when Andrew walked in on her having a bath for the third time.

Once I went to boarding school as well as Andrew, we didn't need a full-time nanny so we had an au pair over the summer. One of the French ones pointed at a bowl of cherries and asked my father what they were called in English. 'Nipples,' he replied. He kept a totally straight face as she asked if she could have another nipple. For one reason or another, none of the au pairs came back for a second summer.

I was reading *Black Beauty* by Anna Sewell—again—when the front-door bell rang.

'I'll get it,' I shouted and ran through the hall, across the white and black marble tiles, skidding to a stop by the heavy door. The glass in it was thick, distorting the shapes on either side. I stood there for a few seconds, eyeing up the silhouette on the outside.

I opened it.

'Hello, I am Clare Balding. Who are you?'

I looked at him from the floor up. The shiny, expensive shoes, the impeccably cut suit, the round tortoiseshell glasses perched on a prominent nose, the receding grey hairline. This man had the aura of importance.

'Well, well,' he said slowly, examining me with as much care as I had bestowed upon him. 'You look a little like your father, a little like your mother and, most of all, you look a lot like *you*.'

'Good,' I said. 'I want to be me.'

He handed me his hat as I held open the door and then crouched down so that he was eye level with me.

'Never forget that, my dear. Whatever the world throws at you, you must be your own person, responsible for your own decisions and your own destiny.

'I am Arnold Weinstock, by the way, and I am here to see your father, but it has been my pleasure to see you.'

'Ah, Lord Weinstock.' My father was charging through the house. 'I'm so sorry, sir. I hope my daughter has been behaving.'

Dad's hand was gripping my shoulder now, just a

153

little more tightly than I would've liked.

'She has been quite delightful,' said Lord Weinstock. 'She has spirit.'

They started to walk together towards the drawing room, and I heard Lord Weinstock say, 'If that girl ever needs a job, you just let me know.'

I did not realize it then but Arnold Weinstock was one of the most respected businessmen of the twentieth century. As managing director of the General Electric Company, he had masterminded its development into a firm with an annual turnover of £11 billion. As far as my father was concerned, he was a hugely knowledgeable owner and breeder of racehorses, including the 1979 Derby winner, Troy.

\*     \*     \*

That winter and over the spring, I had a growth spurt. All of a sudden, I was not just too tall for Frank, I was too tall for ponies, so my mother and I went in search of my first proper horse. Most people think the difference between horses and ponies is purely a size issue and, to some extent, it is. Ponies generally go up to fourteen hands two inches in height, and a horse is anything above that, but just as a tall child is still a child, there are some tall ponies and some small horses.

The other differences are in attitude and in looks. Ponies tend to be—how to put this politely— slightly dumpy in their proportions. They have a bushy mane and tail, thick-set necks, stumpy legs and round tummies. Horses are rather finer in their hair, their bones and their skin. But where the ponies have the upper hand is in intelligence. You

154

will rarely find a pony who is not the equal of or superior to their rider in terms of how fast they can learn.

This does not always work in a rider's favour, as a clever pony is not necessarily a good pony. They work out what they like doing and also what they don't like doing. They will test your patience and your willpower, your skill and your strength.

All in all, I have always thought that ponies are harder to ride than horses, so a child that rides well at eight or ten years old will always ride well.

My mother had seen an advert in *Horse & Hound* for a bay mare. She was sixteen hands high, twelve years old, and she was called Hattie. We went to try her in Ashampstead, a village about twenty miles from Kingsclere.

'She's beautiful,' I said, patting her on the neck. I could not quite believe I was going to ride something so beautiful. I got a leg-up—it was a long way into the saddle—and rode her into the field. Even though Hattie was big, she felt as though she fitted. We trotted and cantered around the field and then popped over a few show jumps. She was lovely.

'Do you like her?' my mother asked as I came towards her and Hattie's owner, Mrs Williams.

'She does flying changes! Did you see? And she goes from walk to canter! Wow, she's amazing.' I was buzzing. This was like tasting wine or eating smoked salmon—it felt so grown up.

My mother smiled and started talking to Mrs Williams in her 'money' voice. I gave Hattie a pat and walked her back to the stables. I had never really ridden a mare before. I didn't think there would be much difference. It's funny how wrong you can be.

Hattie came home with us that day. The first time I rode her up through the yard, I felt so proud. Spider whistled as I walked by with Hattie's head down and her neck arched, like a proper dressage horse.

'My word, young Clare, that's a good-looking mare you've got there.'

I sat a few feet taller and squeezed slightly with my legs so that her hind legs came up underneath her and she walked even more elegantly.

One of the three-year-old colts came out of the top yard, with a young blond boy called Danny Harrap riding. I liked Danny. He was only a few years older than me and he wanted to be a jockey. Nearly all the young boys who joined our yard came with the ambition of being a jockey. Many of them would get the chance to ride in 'apprentice' races, a few of them would do well, and maybe one or two would make it and become fully fledged professional jockeys.

Those who didn't make it—and they were the majority—did not fail because they weren't good enough, they failed because they were built too big. They were too tall or too heavy, or enjoyed food and drink too much to keep their body weight below eight stone. Racing is a tough master for a jockey. You can be as talented as the next person, but you have to be light, or there is no future.

Danny was a beautiful rider. He was kind and sympathetic, he never lost his temper with a horse and my father often used him on difficult animals and to break in yearlings—teaching them to accept a saddle, a bridle and a rider on their back. Danny rode into the Straight Mile, and I was just ahead of

156

him.

I still have no idea how Hattie knew it was a colt behind her. She must have smelt him. Her tail suddenly shot up over her back and she started prancing on the spot. She was making a strange noise and started backing up towards the young colt.

'Bloody hell, watch out,' shouted Danny.

I was trying hard to watch out, but there was nothing I could do. I kicked her in the ribs, smacked her down the shoulder with my stick, but she was still racing backwards. She seemed to be spraying urine as she did so.

Spider started laughing. 'She's a madam, all right. You've got your hands full there,' he said. 'Just trot on by, Danny. Go on, that's a lad. On you go. She's only winking at you, that's all. Ha ha!'

I was so ashamed. My beautiful bay mare was an out-and-out tart. She was at her worst when she was in season and so I had to learn about the oestrous cycle of horses. Mares come into season (i.e., are sexually receptive) from the spring to the autumn about every three weeks. Their hormones are triggered by the lengthening of the days and, as the gestation period of a horse is eleven months, in the wild they naturally avoid getting pregnant during the winter months, as that would mean giving birth in the winter as well, when a foal in the wild would have little chance of surviving.

Hattie seemed to be in season from March to November, pretty much all the time. She would shove her backside under the nose of any male horse—colt or gelding—within a hundred yards. She wanted it so badly that I had to keep her well away from the racehorses and any other horse at a one-day event or a show-jumping competition. It may have been a valuable biology lesson but, to me, it was mortifying.

My father had trained many tricky fillies and showed more interest in Hattie's development than he ever had in mine. He told me to keep her busy and to make sure she was as fit as she could be.

'She'll be better if she's busy, but you can't force a mare,' he said. 'They're funny like that.'

I now realize that, although my father trained many good fillies, he never rode a mare. They were too fickle for him. He preferred a big, brave gelding who wouldn't question his desire to jump everything in sight at speed.

As for owners, Dad was direct and honest with them. He may have been born into a horse-dealing family, but he lacked the persuasive qualities of a salesman. He thought it much better to tell owners whether their horses were any good or not, rather than allow them to dream of the Derby if a donkey derby was the only thing their precious colt or filly was likely to win.

Some owners are happy with phone calls about the progress of their horses; others like to see their physical and mental development for themselves. The latter group tend to be those who know what they are looking at and are less driven by results, more by achieving a greater understanding of the equine bloodlines they are developing.

My father rang his owners each Sunday to discuss the likely running plans for their horses. If he had shown any interest in current affairs or life outside Park House Stables, he would have had interesting conversations, as his owners had influence over a broad range of businesses and countries. Occasionally, if something so big had happened that even he couldn't miss it, he might stray off the topic of racing. There was betting on the General Election, with prices offered on who would be prime minister, what the majority would be and which individual seats would be won. It was therefore covered in the *Sporting Life*.

When he rang Buckingham Palace, he was put through to the Queen immediately.

In May 1979, he started their conversation thus:

'Your Majesty.'

'Ian, how are you?'

'Fine. All well here. The horses are in good shape and I think we'll have runners at Royal Ascot.'

He went into more detail about which horses were being aimed at which races and told the Queen about the one or two who had had slight setbacks and would need time to recover. She took it all in, made the odd comment and, as he reached the end of his update, the Queen said, 'By the way, what do you think of the election result?'

The Conservatives had won the election and Margaret Thatcher had become the country's first female prime minister. Dad was vaguely aware that this event had occurred, but as it did not affect his daily life, he had not given it an awful lot of thought. My father is not a stupid man, but he does sometimes lack intelligence and that is the only way I can explain his reply.

'Well, it's going to take a while to get used to a woman running the country.'

Honestly, that's what he said. *To the Queen.*

I have always thought it is entirely to her credit that the Queen did not remove her horses straight

159

away. Maybe she thought my father was a 'card', an oddity, a bit of a loose cannon. Maybe he amused her. Or maybe she just concentrated on his ability to train racehorses and ignored the rest.

The Queen liked to track the behaviour of her horses from birth onwards—which ones were being difficult, which were showing promise, who liked to lead on the gallops, who might pull and who might show reluctance. Whenever she came to see her horses, my father would make sure Andrew and I were prepped well in advance:

- 'Your Majesty' on first greeting. 'Ma'am' (as in 'spam' or 'jam', not as in 'farm' or 'palm') from then on.
- Don't grip the hand, touch it lightly, and curtsey or bow. Left leg behind right, or right behind left, Dad wasn't clear. Consequently, I have never been sure.
- Don't speak unless you're spoken to, and look the Queen in the eye.
- Don't swear—you might think this was obvious, but I had been developing an impressive array of profanities and anything could happen.

On this April day in the early 1980s, my father had neglected to tell us that the Queen was coming to Kingsclere. So it was that I came charging in from riding Hattie to find two men wearing suits sitting at the kitchen table. I thought perhaps someone had been murdered and these two charlies were in charge of the investigation. I had been watching *Bergerac* and that was just the sort of thing that was always happening in Jersey.

160

'Wotcha,' I shouted through the door, as I tugged off my jodhpur boots in the dogs' room. 'Where's everyone else?'

'Next door in the dining room,' said the one who looked like the chief inspector.

Skidding along the cork floor in my socks into the kitchen, I saw Mrs Jessop carefully placing bacon and sausages on to one of the smart china serving dishes.

'Oh great, cooked breakfast!' I said excitedly. As I ran out of the kitchen I thought I heard Mrs Jessop saying something about someone feeling queasy or queer—it started with a Q.

I flung open the dining-room door and, in my haste, fell into the room. I was wearing my green-cord riding jodhpurs, with stains from two weeks of wear, one red sock and one blue, my favourite rugby shirt and a spotted handkerchief around my neck.

The Queen, who was sitting at the head of our dining-room table, was dressed rather more soberly in a navy-blue dress coat. My entrance had caused a break in the conversation, one of those uncomfortable silences you always hope will not happen because of you. And then it does, and there's not a lot you can do except say, 'Sausages. Yummy!'

My father made that growling noise that I thought must make his throat feel a bit sore as I headed for the table in the corner where there was a hotplate with my mother's best china dishes, laden with scrambled eggs, bacon, sausages and mushrooms.

I had rather missed my moment to curtsey and say 'Your Majesty,' so I just carried on with

161

breakfast, as if nothing was any different. Keep your line and kick on—that's what Dad always said about riding. I figured it was the same in life.

The Queen drank tea, not coffee. She liked it weak and without milk. Only one slice of toast, and none of the eggs, sausages, bacon, hash browns, mushrooms or tomatoes that were on offer. Her gloves were to the side of her plate, and on her feet were black court shoes. She seemed very small and rather quiet—not at all as she was on the television when my father made us watch her Christmas speech.

My father glared at me, but it was too late to say anything now. So I concentrated hard on buttering my toast, smothering it with marmalade and cutting my sausage long-ways. It was an American delicacy—sausage on toast with marmalade—and I had decided that this would be part of what made me 'interesting' and 'different'. Sausages on toast with marmalade would form part of my statement to the world.

The trouble with concentrating hard on cutting a sausage long-ways is that, if you press too hard, it's a bit like squeezing a bar of soap. The sausage can shoot out of your grasp. I know this; I know this only too well. I can still recall in slow motion the way my sausage shot across the table towards the Queen as she sipped her tea.

Quick as a flash, I tried to grab it. I knocked over the milk jug. My mother yelped. My father growled again. The Queen glanced at me and raised an eyebrow.

I froze, wishing I could crawl under the table and pretend I was a dog. My brother seized the sausage and shoved it back on my plate. My mother

162

mopped up the milk with that look in her eye that said, 'I am not even going to count to ten. You are in so much trouble.'

I knew my parents couldn't actually say or do anything until the Queen had left. That gave me time. Time to escape. My father escorted the Queen out of the front door and took her to the stables to watch Second Lot 'pulling out' of the yard. The horses walked around the huge flowerpot as my father identified each one and told Her Majesty about their breeding and their achievements.

The Queen's knowledge of racing is extraordinarily detailed. She remembers all sorts of facts and behavioural quirks of horses from previous generations and can spot inherited traits in her own horses and those of other people. As the horses left the yard to begin their trek up to the Downs, my father jumped in his Subaru truck and told the Queen's chauffeur to follow him in the royal Range Rover.

The Queen's racing manager and great friend, Lord Carnarvon, was with her as they headed up to the gallops. The Queen never said very much when watching her horses. She asked questions and absorbed the answers, fascinated by the detail and diversity of equine behaviour.

I was not on hand to witness any of this, as I had disappeared to the stud to sit in the corner of a field and talk to the foals. It was something my mother liked me to do, as it familiarized the foals with human contact. I would just read a book and wait for them to come up and nudge me.

The timid ones would take a while but, as they realized I wasn't a threat and that I was more a curiosity, they came closer and started to take an interest. It was a game of patience but, in moments like this, it was a useful one to play. I did not want to go back to the house and, at least if I was here with the foals, I was doing something useful.

In my absence, the Queen watched through binoculars as her horses galloped, she talked to the lads riding them and discussed options with my father and Lord Carnarvon. An hour or so later, with the detectives in tow, she was driven back through the village and headed off to Newbury Races.

I calculated that, if I was gone for three hours, Dad would have already left for the races and my mother might, if I was lucky, have gone with him. I was right on the first count, wrong on the second.

As I crept back up the drive and silently opened the back door, Flossy and Bertie jumped up to say hello. Flossy came towards me, waggling her hips, Bertie peeled back his lips in a trademark grin/grimace. Cindy stayed in her bed, the lazy cow. My mother came into the kitchen and looked at me without saying a word. She just shook her head.

I went up to my room and stayed there for the rest of the day, reading *Frankenstein* and wishing I was a scientist so that I could create an alternative form of human life.

When she started talking to me again, Mum drove the horsebox to competitions the length and breadth of the country, where Hattie and I would perform, with some success. We weren't world-beaters, but she could do a decent dressage test and jumped well enough that we usually came home with a rosette of one colour or another. My father would say the same thing every time.

'Did you win?'

If the answer was no, he wasn't interested. I tried to explain to him that at most one-day events you have a field of around seventy competitors. It is statistically hard to win. A top-ten finish is outstanding. My father, however, was a man whose life depended on results. If you weren't first past the post, you were a loser.

My mother would share my delight at finishing tenth or seventh or fifth, knowing that we had performed well and that I was enjoying myself. We understood how it worked and, as far as we were concerned, Dad just didn't get it.

# 10

## Ellie May

It would be too easy to think that snobbery is a trait restricted to human beings. Horses can also be arrogant, and thoroughbreds, bred for beauty and speed, tend to be the most self-admiring and superior of all. Then there are horses who are slightly less refined, whose bones are thicker and whose coat does not gleam like mahogany, however much it is brushed and polished. They look like grown-up ponies. These horses are referred to, even by people who would hesitate to define themselves as snobs, as 'common'.

Ellie May was as common as you like. She had a deep girth, a thick-haired mane and tail, an enormous backside and a head that was pretty only to those who believe boxer dogs beautiful. Consequently, my mother adored her. Ellie May was Mum's hunter and, a bit like my beloved Frank, her mouth had all the sensitivity of a block of concrete.

Ellie May may have had a bit of Irish Draught in her and a bit of cob. She was chunky and strong, with an ankle sock of white on her hind legs, a tiny line of white above her near-fore hoof and a small white star at the centre of her head. She was officially 'bay', meaning she had a black mane and tail and a deep-brown body, neck, face and upper legs. She was fifteen hands three inches high and about seventeen hands round: to ride her, my mother's legs went out sideways before they dropped downwards.

Ellie May was no beauty, but she was safe and reliable. She would never fall, never refuse, and although she could pull she wasn't fast enough to run away with her rider. She would plod along at the same pace, see a fence and shorten her stride accordingly, finding a place to put down her hooves where no space looked available. If two fences were five strides apart, Ellie May could fit in seven.

'She looks like a carthorse,' my father would say from his tall, handsome thoroughbred.

'Well,' said my mother at the opening meet of the Berks & Bucks Draghounds, 'let's just see who comes home in one piece, shall we?'

My father duly fell off three times as his fancy horse jammed on the brakes at the last minute, once sending him flying over a hedge on his own,

167

while my mother took the sensible options and returned without a hiccup. She and Ellie May knew their limits and preferred to remain within them.

My mother was firmly of the belief that there is no point looking the part if you can't do the job.

Unfortunately for me, Mum's lack of interest in physical appearance meant that she had no truck with 'fashion'. My growth spurt meant that I needed a new set of clothes and, while she relented enough to buy me blue-suede ankle-boots and purple- and white-striped leg warmers, she stopped short at collarless shirts and oversized cashmere jumpers. She also refused to buy me white jeans because they were 'impractical'. I managed to catch my father at a weak moment and persuaded him to give me a few old shirts and jumpers that had shrunk in the wash. With a pair of scissors and a bit of uneven sewing, the shirts were transformed into collarless ones, while the jumpers were stretched over the back of an armchair until they hung loose and shapeless, just how I wanted them.

*      *      *

My year in the Removes at Downe House had come to an end and we were allocated what would be our senior accommodation. A house was more than a place to live, it was also the team for which you would play, the group you would represent, and it would form the basis of the friendships you'd make. There were four houses at Downe House, and each had a different character. Tedworth was known as being quite academic, Aisholt was sporty, Holcombe was laid back and Ancren Gate (known as AG) had a reputation for being anarchic.

We were all moving from a tight-knit, tiny cluster of sixteen girls in Darwin to be divided up into random groups with the Hill House girls and then flung into one of those four houses, where we mixed with all of the girls up to the age of sixteen. It was pot luck.

The Removes sat together as Mrs Berwick called out the names and which house they had been assigned. There were cheers as girls who were friends discovered they would be in the same house for the next five years. These were nascent friendships that would become cemented into unbreakable bonds.

'Clare Balding,' announced Mrs Berwick, 'Ancren Gate.'

There were no cheers. If anything, there was a sigh. None of those already selected for AG particularly wanted me there, and all the friends I had made in Darwin and through lacrosse—Becks, Toe, Heidi, Char, Katherine, Cass and Shorty— were going into Aisholt or Tedworth.

The AG gang were confident, casual and detached. They seemed older than their years, and infinitely more sophisticated. I longed to be able to flick my hair from one side of my head to another, I dreamt of having a leather jacket, an older brother and a chalet in Switzerland. I so wanted to belong to this gang and yet I knew it was impossible— unless I changed.

I would have to impress them by being even cooler, even more daring, than they were. I would have to be the wildest child of the lot.

Some lessons in life, you learn the hard way.

AG was separated from the rest of the school. It was half a mile down a tarmac drive, surrounded by

169

pine trees. We would cycle or walk up to the main school, our cloaks billowing out behind us like trainee witches'. It felt like an exclusive world, a closed environment where we could live and behave differently. Perhaps it was that degree of separation that encouraged those who felt they could write their own rules.

I was in a four-bed dorm with three other girls known as Bear, Pickle and Snorter (this was a girls' school—we all had nicknames). They had all been in Hill House together and were firm friends. Bear was tall, with long, dark hair and a voice so deep you'd swear she'd been smoking since the day she was born. Pickle was thin as a rake and had scruffy blond hair permanently tied back into a scrunchie, with wisps carefully pulled out to fall around her face, which was drawn and worried. She bit her fingernails and had patches of dry skin on her arms, which she scratched when she was fretting. Snorter was always snorting. She would snort her food, snort out her words and snort when she was laughing. Her job was to laugh at everything Bear said, whether it was funny or not. She was a one-woman show reel of canned laughter.

As I unpacked my trunk on the first day of Michaelmas term 1982, I had a strange sense of foreboding. This was not going to end well.

Lessons were fine. I really loved learning. Having been a long way behind the others in subjects that hadn't been covered at my primary school, particularly in French, Latin, maths (I just didn't get it), religious studies and chemistry, I was slowly catching up. My saviour was English. I couldn't get enough of reading, and I could use a book as a shield. I could disappear into my own little world,

170

where the fact that I wasn't included in the AG gang didn't matter any more.

I was fascinated by Greek and Roman myths. (I particularly noticed Golden Fleece winning the Derby that year, with Pat Eddery in the saddle, because of Jason and the Argonauts.) I enjoyed the impossible challenges thrown down to humans, the tragedy of vanity—Narcissus falling in love with his own reflection or Echo's mournful cry haunting remote, rocky places. I loved the story of Pandora opening the box she had been told to leave closed. Out flew pestilence, war, disease and a myriad of evils. She shut the box and heard a knocking. The last thing remaining in the box was hope, without which none of us would be able to cope with life. I would remind myself of this tale when things went wrong—which they did.

The girls in my dorm largely ignored me. So I decided it was time to do something attention-grabbing. We were on a school outing to Oxford, all of us wearing our skirts, blazers and long green cloaks. A small group, including me, took a detour into W. H. Smith.

'Time for some fun,' said Bear. 'The one who comes out with most free gear is the winner.'

Snorter snorted her approval. Pickle looked nervous but nodded enthusiastically.

'Come on, Balders,' Bear said to me. 'Stop being such a square.'

So the gauntlet was laid down. In my head, I would be Hercules. I would fulfil the impossible task and become a hero in the process. My magic cloak would protect me. So I started to scan the shelves, accidently knocking off five bags of Opal Fruits. I bent down to pick them up, my cloak

171

covering the ground beneath me. Four of the bags made it back on to the shelf, one went invisibly into my blazer pocket. Sherbet Dip Dabs were next, followed by strawberry Chewits and a packet of green- and white-striped Pacer mints.

Underneath my cloak, my pockets were bulging. I could see Snorter and Pickle slipping smaller but more valuable items into their pockets—a fountain pen, ink cartridges, a Dennis the Menace ruler and even a cassette of *Thriller*. I could hear my heart thudding against my chest as I turned for the door. The rush of adrenalin made me feel faint.

Outwardly, I remained calm and cool. I even smiled at the assistant as I walked out, and said, 'Thank you so much.'

We had agreed to meet up in a side street around the corner from Smith's. I got there first and waited nervously for the other three to appear. Pickle came sprinting round the corner, her face flushed. She was giggling hysterically as she showed me some of the booty in her pockets.

'Wow, that was awesome. But so scary too. I sooo thought I was going to get caught.' Pickle was almost crying with relief.

Snorter appeared at a rapid rate a few minutes later. 'Ohmygod, ohmygod,' she snorted. 'The security bloke came in. With a walkie-talkie and everything. And Bear's still in there. Ohmygod, ohmygod! What if she gets caught? What will we do?'

We looked at each other in shock, and then Pickle said, with tears in her eyes, 'If my parents find out, I'm dead meat.'

She put her arms around Snorter and me. Together we formed a tight ring, chanting together,

'Bring back Bear! Bring back Bear!'

For the first time, I had been allowed into the group. Adversity—well, crime—had united us. Then came a deep, raspy voice.

'What the hell are you lot up to? You haven't gone soft on me, have you?'

I looked through the sliver of a gap between Pickle and Snorter's bodies to see the familiar swagger of our gang leader.

'The Bear!' we said in unison. 'The Bear is back.'

We were all talking at the same time, all asking the same questions as fast as we could. None of it made any sense, but the sentiment was genuine. If you could smell relief, we stank of it.

We started to count the goods and to divide them equally between us. We were like the Four Musketeers or the Famous Five minus Timmy the dog, and I was high on love, laughter and adrenalin. We developed our own terms: 'What did you buy?' covered goods you paid for, whereas 'What did you get?' meant 'What did you steal?'

Bear was the undisputed shoplifting queen. She came back from Newbury once wearing a brand-new leather jacket.

'Wow, how much did that cost?' I asked, still envious of anything that resembled a fashionable item of clothing.

'Nothing,' said Bear laconically. 'Well, it would have cost over a hundred quid if I'd paid for it,' she said, running her right hand through her hair. 'But I didn't, did I? I tried it on, liked it and walked out with it on.'

I gasped. I was staggered at the daring. Pickle and Snorter were told of the Bear's latest achievement, but it was strictly a dorm secret. No

173

one outside those four beds was to know about it.

*    *    *

It is a Downe House tradition that, when it is someone's birthday, a collection is made in a litter bin. The bin fills up with Hunkydory coloured writing paper, purple Sailor pen cartridges, sweets, stickers, felt-tip pens and the like. If the birthday girl is really popular, the bin will overflow with goodies. If she is not, it will be a rather measly offering. The deal is that you only ask for gifts from your year and the years below; you never ask an older girl for presents.

As the youngest year in AG, we were constantly getting a knock on the door and the call of 'Whacky-bee!' That's what the birthday bin was called—a whacky-bee. Our dorm, obviously, had a huge collection of gifts, so we would happily pass on our stolen goods throughout the house. That way I could tell myself that, in fact, we were robbing from the rich to give to the poor.

This, of course, was a ludicrous defence. 1. No girl at Downe House was poor, and 2. Stealing from shops was not the same as robbing taxes back from draconian landowners to divide among the poor who paid them in the first place.

I had backed off the whole shoplifting season for a month or so, opting out of trips or insisting that I had to go to another shop without Bear or Pickle or Snorter, where I wouldn't find anything I liked enough to steal.

'Oh, Balders, you just don't get it,' said Pickle, chewing the sides of her already raw fingers. 'You don't have to like it or want it to nick it. You just do

174

it for the thrill, you div.'

I was being edged out of the gang, I could feel the foundations of our dorm starting to tremble beneath my feet. I needed them. I needed to feel that I was part of the team.

So, one Saturday, after the three forty-minute lessons that took up the morning, we all hopped on our bicycles to head off to the Cold Ash village store, Foxgroves. It was about a mile down the road, and we were only allowed to go there at weekends. It was December, a week before the end of term, and we had decided to give each other a special Christmas whacky-bee—a bit like a stocking, only with stuff we actually liked.

I had saved up my pocket money so that I could buy some proper presents for the others. All our money was kept in a safe, and you had to be supervised by the housemistress if you took any of it out, signing in a book to confirm the amount.

I didn't want to steal stuff, because this was a show of mutual respect and affection—you couldn't just pass on 'hot property'. I was in the far-right corner of the shop, inspecting the furry toys, when Snorter came up behind me.

'Look at these,' she whispered. She had in her hand three sets of tiny plastic mechanical feet. When you twisted the button on the side, like winding up a watch, they marched forward. They looked like brightly coloured Doc Marten boots, and Snorter thought Bear and Pickle would love them.

'Cool,' I said, as this was the stock response.

'The thing is,' said Snorter, 'I haven't got any money and I haven't got the right clothes on to, you know, "get" them . . .'

175

Her voice trailed off and she looked at me with baleful eyes.

'I can buy them for you,' I said. I pulled out a ten-pound note from my pocket. 'Look!'

'Don't buy them, Balders. Christ, you div. Don't buy them. *Get* them for me.' Her voice was urgent.

Snorter left the mechanical feet on the shelf beside me and walked to the till to chat to the shopkeeper. I could hear them laughing and realized that she was trying to distract Mr Fell for me. So I took the three mechanical pairs of feet and slipped them into the enormous square pockets of my very square jacket.

I walked up to the till to pay for the other presents I had found, and Mr Fell looked at me strangely.

'Is that all?' he said.

'Yes,' I smiled. 'I think it is for now.'

'Are you sure?' He seemed to look straight into my soul as he asked.

I had been here before, so I knew that I could get away with it. We were invincible. Besides, they were only mechanical feet—it wasn't a leather jacket.

'Thank you so much.' I smiled at him again as I paid and turned to go. 'You have lovely things in here.'

If I had looked back, I would have seen the sadness in Mr Fell's face. I would have seen him shaking his head as he picked up the phone.

I gave Snorter the feet as soon as we got back to our dorm, and she hugged me.

'Cheers, Balders. You're a rock. The others thought you'd lost your nerve, but I knew better.'

She patted me on the back. I sank into a beanbag to read my book, *An Amateur Cracksman* by E. W.

176

Hornung. It was about a gentleman thief called Raffles. An hour or so later, there was a heavy knock on the door.

'Come in,' I shouted from my beanbag. Raffles was climbing over the rooftops with a diamond necklace in his dinner-jacket pocket. I kept reading. I looked up when I heard a clearing of the throat.

Mrs Hamilton, the housemistress of Ancren Gate, was standing just inside the door. I had always thought she looked a bit like a rabbit, with buck teeth, fluffy hair and an edgy way about her. She seemed to be hopping from one foot to another.

'Clare, Miss Farr wants to see you.' She sounded terrified. 'I really don't know what it can be about on a Saturday but you are to go to her drawing room. Immediately.'

I closed my book. I really was calm, considering my little world was about to explode in the most unfortunate way. I patted the blanket on top of my bed as I left the room.

My legs carried me downstairs and on to my bicycle, but my brain had gone into neutral. I knew disaster awaited me, and I was flatlining. Don't look into Medusa's eyes, I thought. You will turn to stone.

Miss Farr was our headmistress. She was a jolly sort, round-faced, pale-blond hair scraped back into a sort of a do that none of us could work out. It wasn't a bun, but it all folded in on itself and seemed magically to stay in place, except when she played lacrosse, when it would escape from the pins and stray down her head. Miss Farr had been an England lacrosse player, and she personally coached the first team.

I carefully opened the fragile wood and glass double doors that led to the headmistress's drawing room and walked up the green-carpeted stairs. I knocked at Miss Farr's door and sat to wait.

'Enter!' said the voice.

My hands were clammy. This didn't feel good.

'Ah, Clare. Sit down, would you please?' Miss Farr was behind her desk, writing in a large leather-bound book.

I swallowed hard and sat. I looked out of her windows. There were so many of them. There was glass all down the south side of the room and beyond the windows was a stone-flagged balcony that connected the two sides of Aisholt, the house that was as near to the centre of the school as possible. As I stared out of the window, I saw two of my year walk across the balcony. They looked in, and I quickly sank into the chair, hoping they wouldn't see me.

Miss Farr looked up. She did not smile. Her eyes were kind, but I looked away, not wanting to hold her gaze.

'Now, Clare, you have a chance here. A chance I would like you to take. I had high hopes for you, very high hopes indeed.'

She sighed and her shoulders shuddered with the effort.

'I need you to tell me whether you were acting alone,' she said, and then stopped.

'Sorry?' I replied. 'What do you mean?'

'There is a video camera at Foxgroves. They had it installed a few years ago, when we had an unfortunate incident. Mr Fell informs me that you were in the shop this morning and that you left without paying for certain items.'

178

She paused, and I felt her gaze upon me. I was looking at my hands, which were gripped together in my lap. The rug, I remember, looked Persian.

'That,' continued Miss Farr, 'is beyond dispute. It is captured on film. You will be suspended immediately. I am not going to expel you, although I certainly could. What I would like to know is this—were you acting alone or were you told to steal the items?'

'No,' I said immediately. 'No, it was just me. No one else. It was all me.'

I thought this is what Hercules would do. He wouldn't let his friends go down with him.

'I see,' said Miss Farr. 'It just strikes me that you are not the strongest character at Ancren Gate and I fear you may have been led astray by other, more daring girls. Are you telling me that this is the first incident of its kind and that you are the only guilty party?'

'Yes. Yes, I am.'

They would really love me now. I would come back a hero.

'Right,' said Miss Farr. 'Well, that is a shame. I have rung your mother already, and she is on her way here to collect you. You are suspended with immediate effect and, as we are only a week from the end of term, you will not be coming back to Downe House until January. By which time, young lady, I hope you will realize the error of your ways.

'I do not wish you to return to Ancren Gate,' she continued. 'You will come here, to Aisholt, where I can keep an eye on you. I think you will find a more suitable set of friends here. Now go.'

Miss Farr picked up her pen and started writing again in her leather-bound book. She did not look

179

up as I left the room. I felt as if I had been in a boxing match and, although bruised and beaten, I had upheld the honour of the noble sport of pugilism. I just needed someone to pass me a towel and raise my arm above my head.

I cycled back to AG and went up to our dorm. There was no sign of Pickle, Bear or Snorter. I started packing and, as I folded my clothes, a tear trickled down my cheek. I organized the three Christmas whacky-bees for my roommates and hid them in the cupboard where I knew they would eventually find them before the end of term. I left a note on top of the dressing table.

'Have a great Christmas. You guys are the best. Love, Balders. xxxx'

As I dragged my trunk down the stairs, I saw Bear appear in the hallway.

'Hey,' I said. 'Looks like I got caught, but don't worry, I didn't say a word.'

Bear walked straight past me and went up the stairs, without even looking at me. So much for our special bond, our proper friendship. So much for loyalty. I was more hurt by this than anything that had happened that day.

I sat on my trunk at the bottom of that long tarmac road to AG hoping my mother would arrive before the rest of the house came back from watching and playing in matches. I heard the chugging of the Citroën Dyane before I saw it and saw my mother sitting behind the steering wheel, her hair in a ponytail. She was chewing her lip.

'I don't know what the hell you've been up to,' she said, as she lifted one side of the trunk and we lugged it into the boot and across the back seats, which were pushed down. 'But you've got a bloody decent headmistress there. Why on earth she didn't expel you, I do not know.

'You'd better have those bloody feet with you as well, because we're taking them back.'

'I can't, I don't,' I stammered. 'They're not mine to take back, you see.'

I stopped. To say anything more would be to give the game away, so I fell back on another solution.

'I have this, though.' I pulled out the change that was left from my pocket money. It was nearly eight pounds.

'Well, why the hell didn't you pay for the things you wanted if you had the money? Honestly, even now we've given you the money you're still stealing. *What is your problem?*'

My mother slammed the boot and walked to the driver's side. She stopped at Foxgroves and pointed at the door. I got out, went inside to apologize to Mr Fell and gave him the money for three pairs of mechanical feet. We drove home in a heavy fog of silence.

My father wanted to know exactly what had happened. He knew I was lying, and he told my mother so. It didn't stop him being cross, knowing that I had been part of a gang—he was livid—but it did help explain why I had got into such trouble. My father was a blow-up, blow-out kind of man: one big eruption and then he would forget about it. Mum was a stewer, and her anger simmered on for weeks, months, even years.

Mum erased any benefit I may have thought I was getting by being on holiday early by banning me from riding. I wasn't even allowed down to the stud to see Ellie May or Hattie. I offered to help muck out and groom, but Mum wouldn't have it. She

181

made me work every day in the dining room, as if I was still at school.

I felt as if the oxygen had been turned off at the valve. I was plodding through each day with no joy, no comfort. Please let me off the hook before Christmas Day, I repeated to myself. Please.

Andrew came back from prep school, and the glow around him shone brighter than ever. Grandma came over for tea to hear his stories and to ask him what he wanted for Christmas. She only looked at me once, and said: 'I think you can do without a Christmas present this year, don't you?'

I told Andrew what had happened to me—he was shocked but defended me whenever he thought I was being unfairly blamed for something else. He was my little brother, and he would fight for me.

Once Andrew was home, it was harder for my mother to keep me locked in the dining room all day, so I was partially freed and allowed to ride. Hattie was having the first part of the winter off so, if I wanted to ride something that jumped, it would have to be Ellie May. In my ridiculous Downe House way, I had been a bit of a snob about the heavy-footed, bushy-tailed Ellie May. She was not as fine as Hattie and I had felt faintly embarrassed as I rode through the yard on her.

I decided to take Ellie over on to the farm to jump the drag-hunt fences, just to give myself a thrill. I was still feeling full of self-loathing and my head was dull, as if I was recovering from concussion. As I turned down Long Meadow, Ellie took it upon herself to wake me up.

She broke into a canter and then picked up the pace, her stride not altering in length but multiplying at a faster rate. I had her on a line towards the first of the fences, a heavy log over red barrels. As we came towards it, I started to lose my nerve and tried to steer her round it, but Ellie wouldn't hear of it. She ignored my tugging on the reins and attempts to pull her sideways, and set herself like a large ship on a Channel crossing.

I could only sit tight and try to go with her. We sailed over the barrels and, as the tempo increased, we came to the Tiger Trap, then the tractor tyres and the row of straw bales. There were three sizes to this last set—nine jumps in all, the biggest of which were about three feet six. Sizeable enough for an eleven-year-old riding an unfamiliar horse. I attempted to angle Ellie towards the smaller option, but it was pretty clear by now that she was in charge, and I was too tired to fight. I sat into the saddle, squeezed my legs round her belly and felt her soar off the ground. Once, twice, three times she flew over the big straw bales, which had a thick black telegraph pole on top of them.

It was the first time I had ever jumped the biggest bales at the end of Long Meadow. Ellie May pulled herself up to a trot after she had jumped the last one, then to a walk, puffing at the effort of it all. We had covered a mile in distance, jumped nine large cross-country fences, and all of it had been at her insistence. She turned her head to the left, looking straight at me with her left eye, and then nodded, as if to say, 'That'll teach you, you stuck-up little posh girl.'

As we walked down the chalk path that ran below Smith's Bushes back towards the farm, I thought about where I had gone wrong so far at Downe House. I had been sucked into valuing appearance and possessions above all else. I had lost my respect for honesty, for kindness and for hard work. Ellie May was the proof I needed that I should not judge anyone on looks alone.

## 11

# Lily

A life without a boxer dog is a life without laughter. I know this because, after Candy died at kennels and age had finally caught up with Flossy, my mother stopped laughing.

She still smiled, she still enjoyed life, but she didn't laugh the way she used to. She didn't come home to waggling hips and a slobbering, smiling mouth. We now had two lurcher bitches called Jenny and Polly. Jenny was wild and rough-haired,

Polly was timid and smooth. They were graceful and beautiful, like the racehorses, but they weren't funny, they weren't cuddly and they wouldn't jump out of a top-floor window if they thought you were being abducted.

After a period of mourning and due respect for Candy and Flossy, my mother finally felt ready to have another boxer. She took me with her to inspect a litter of puppies in Kent, and I chose the one who sucked my pointy chin with her tiny little mouth. She was dark brindle with a white map of Africa across half her neck and down one side, a tiny line of white in the middle of her face and white around her nose. We called her Lily.

We had to wait a few more weeks before she could have all her injections, but my mother smiled all the way home and kept chuckling to herself. She had Lily to look forward to, while I had the beginning of Lent term to dread.

Going back to Downe House in January 1983 was singularly the most difficult thing I have ever done. I was terrified. A new house, a new group of girls, a new housemistress and the shame that all the teachers knew I was a thief. The one thing I could rely on was that Bear, Snorter and Pickle would stand by me. I was sure that Bear had ignored me on the stairs only because she was annoyed with me for being caught. Now they knew I hadn't dobbed them in, I would be a hero.

My mother took me back to school and helped me carry my trunk up to my new room in Aisholt Middle East. It was the closest room to the balcony that ran past Miss Farr's drawing room. I would have to walk in front of her windows at least twice every day, possibly more often. She was true to her word—she would be keeping an eye on me all right.

The housemistress of Aisholt was called Miss Houghton. She had the biggest bosom I had ever seen in my life, bigger even than Grandma's. Her breasts sat horizontally out of her chest like a tray. She could have balanced a plate and eaten her lunch off them. Quite often, she *was* eating her lunch or her supper in her study while she held meetings with her girls. I had been brought up not to talk with my mouth full but I was fascinated by the tactic deployed by Miss Houghton. She stored her food in her cheeks like a hamster, pushing it out of the way while she conducted her half of the conversation and then retrieving bits of food and chewing on them while she listened to the answer or the explanation.

Miss Houghton was a kindly soul, but I found it hard to concentrate on what she was saying while I wondered which stop her food was at in its journey from plate to stomach.

'Sit down, please.' She ushered my mother and me into her tiny ground-floor sitting room, right next to the staff room.

'Now, Mrs Balding,' she said, 'I would like you to rest assured that we will keep a close eye, as it were, on young Clare.'

She nodded towards me as she spoke, in case my mother had forgotten who I was.

'She will be well looked after here at Aisholt, and we will ensure that she has a chance to regain the ground that she has . . . that she has lost, as it were.'

She dropped her voice a notch and said conspiratorially to my mother, 'We both know that all Clare needs is a slightly different group, as it were, around her, and she will flourish. I will make sure of it. Abssso-lutely sure of it.'

As my mother thanked her for her thoughtfulness, Miss Houghton pushed her tongue into the gap between her teeth and lower lip to find a piece of potato. She chewed and swallowed as she pushed herself up from her high-backed armchair. She took her glasses off her nose, leaving them hanging from a chain on her chest. My mother and I leapt to our feet.

'Thank you, Miss Houghton,' my mother said, behaving as if she too were coming back for Lent term.

It was less than twenty years since my mother herself had been a pupil at Downe House—some of the teachers who had taught her were still there, so it must have been a bit weird.

I kept my head bowed as I climbed the wooden staircase and crossed over the balcony to my new room. I was sharing with Henrietta Short, known as Shorty, a matter-of-fact girl who didn't stand for any nonsense—or any snoring, as I found out on my first night, when she threw a shoe at me.

We had a whispered conversation after lights out.

'So, what happened?' Shorty asked.

I told her the full story, right down to leaving the mechanical feet for Pickle to give the others in their Christmas whacky-bees. Shorty tutted. Then she sighed. Then she propped herself up on her elbow. I could see her outline in the half-light.

'We've got some work to do, Clare.'

'What do you mean?' I replied.

'The thing is'—Shorty sounded a bit angry now—'that is not exactly the story that Snorter has been telling. She said that she gave you money to buy her some things at Foxgroves and that you stole the toys and then pocketed the money.'

'She what?' I said. I was sitting bolt upright now. 'But you can check the pocket-money book—she didn't have any money left, that's why I offered to pay for them, but she told me to steal them . . .'

I stopped. I had broken my own code, but I was so outraged—not only had Snorter not told the truth, she had invented a whole new lie that made me look even worse.

'Hmm,' said Shorty. 'Well, that makes a bit more sense. I wondered why Miss Farr hadn't expelled you. She must have seen it on the video footage. Did Snorter tell you to take them and then walk away?'

'Yes,' I said. 'Yes, she did, but I didn't tell Miss Farr any of this. I said it was all me on my own, all of it.'

The next morning, another girl in Aisholt, called Antonia Kingsland (known as Toe) walked into breakfast with me.

'You can sit with me, Balders,' she said.

'Oh. Great. Thanks.' I followed her with relief, as walking into that dining room with every girl in the whole school looking at me was making me feel a bit sick.

Toe's mother was a science teacher at the school. I later found out that Miss Farr had briefed the teachers not to be hard on me and that Mrs Kingsland had told her daughter to look out for me. Toe knew not to question her mother and just carried out her instructions.

When the gang of Bear, Pickle and Snorter arrived, Shorty and Toe moved their chairs closer to me, acting as a human shield. They glared at the three girls, and Snorter blushed as she walked by. None of them acknowledged me, but I realized that I didn't care. I no longer wanted to impress them, I just wanted to avoid them.

It took time but, gradually, I felt a little more confident, a little stronger, and I threw myself into the things all girls do at school—mainly recording the Top 40 on Radio 1 on my cassette player, making sure to press Pause to cut out the inane chatter of Tony Blackburn and letting it go back into Record as the next song started. If you mistakenly got a bit of the chat, you went back, timed it and recorded blank noise to cover it, leaving a short gap before the next song. It was a tricky art, but one which I think I can say I mastered. I was the Top 40 recording queen.

The chosen winter game at Downe House was lacrosse. We all wore gum shields, because too many girls had had their teeth knocked out and, in the age of orthodontic renaissance, that could be an expensive injury.

I wasn't the best lacrosse player on the planet, but I learned the art of contributing even when you didn't have the ball, of trusting your teammates, of anticipating what might happen. I also found that regular exercise made me concentrate better in class and less angry at the injustice of my 'situation'.

We were allowed to watch television at weekends and the whole house gathered around the TV in the top common room. Char lay on her front as close to the screen as possible because she said she couldn't see otherwise. I squashed on to a sofa with broken springs between Shorty and Toe, or with Heidi and Cass. *Dynasty* and *Dallas* were unmissable— we knew every character, every twist, every eyebrow-lift of Krystle Carrington or pout of Alexis Carrington Colby. The whole house hummed as the closing credits rolled, the more musical girls adding harmonies of their own.

On the rare night that we were allowed to stay up late, I liked *Cagney & Lacey*, because it was the first time I had seen two female leads who weren't at the forefront of a show just because they were 'sexy'. I would play Cagney and Heidi played Lacey:

'Ready, Christine?'

'Ready, Mary Beth,' I would reply, before we charged round the corner of the corridor, imaginary guns at the ready.

Each term, we changed dorm. Aisholt had lots of small rooms so, more often than not, just two girls would share. There were a few three-bed rooms and one four-bed room, known as Top Central, which was bang next to the main common room, where the TV was. Consequently, Top Central was only for girls in Upper Fifth, as they were always the last to have to put their lights out.

As my confidence grew, so I made proper friends—friends I still have today.

\*       \*       \*

In the second week of February that year—1983—Cass Donner came running into my room and turned on the radio.

'You've got to listen to this,' she said.

There was a reporter talking about a kidnapping in Ireland. The kidnap victim was not a child, it was a horse—Shergar. I remember sitting down on the bed, shocked. Why would they take a horse? How would they manage a stallion like Shergar? Would they hurt him? Who would pay the ransom?

Shergar was never found. It is assumed that he was shot four days after he was taken, either because the kidnappers could not handle him or realized the ransom would not be paid.

A month later, when I came home, I noticed security cameras in the top and bottom yards. There were cameras in four of the boxes as well, so my father could keep an eye on the most valuable horses. He had a small TV screen in the sitting room, which would flick between the various cameras all night long. The locks were all changed and the lads were given a lecture about security.

Shergar was one of the few flat horses to which I had really paid any attention. Andrew always told me that I knew absolutely nothing about racing and, while he would stand alongside my father naming every horse and its breeding, I was really only interested in riding and jumping. I liked watching them run and I loved to see them work at home, but I wasn't a form student, I didn't know which races they should go for next and, once, at the kitchen table over breakfast, my brother mocked me mercilessly when I suggested a horse called Free Press, who had won his last three starts, might run in the Derby.

'Don't be stupid,' Andrew jumped down my throat, as my father laughed. 'He's a gelding and he's four years old.'

'So?' I said, hurt by his tone.

'The Derby's for three-year-old colts. Surely even you know that?'

If anyone showed a tiny hole in their knowledge, the rest of the family would sneer. It was like a constant game of Mastermind as they battled over handicap marks, race conditions, jockey statistics and ground preferences. Grandma would come over for a cup of coffee—standing, of course—and have the most incomprehensible conversation with my brother about the horses in the yard.

She read the *Sporting Life* from cover to cover every morning. There was nothing she did not know about what was running where or how it ran yesterday or whether or not John Matthias, our stable jockey, had given it a decent ride. Often, in her opinion, he had not.

I was a bit lost, so I opted out. The only thing that got me really excited was the Grand National. I adored it. Andrew and I got so worked up in the weeks leading up to Aintree that my mother decided we had 'Grand National Fever' and took our temperature.

On Grand National day itself, we turned the telly on at midday to make sure we caught each second of the *Grandstand* coverage on the BBC. I loved the features in the yards with horses looking relaxed and being allowed to show their character. I preferred jump racing to the flat because the horses stayed around for longer and I could get to know them better. I also thought the jockeys were unbelievably brave and I watched them seeing a stride at speed, wondering how they did it over fences as big as Becher's Brook or the Chair.

Every year, we picked two horses each and my mother phoned up to have bets for all of us. The horses selected by Andrew or me would also be 'ridden' by us. This involved us both wearing our knitted jumpers in racing colours, our hats and our goggles. We sat on each arm of the sofa, a whip in hand, and rode 'our horse' for the whole race. If he fell, we had to fall off the arm of the sofa, rolling around on the floor until we miraculously mounted our second-choice horse and rode a finish on him instead.

1983 was different because, for the first time, we actually went to Aintree. My father was in a spectacularly grumpy mood. This often happened during the winter, when he was on a permanent diet to be light enough to ride in point-to-points, but this particular year he had also decided to ride in the Fox Hunter's Chase at Aintree.

Dad had an outstanding point-to-pointer called Ross Poldark with whom he had run up a string of successes that winter at Tweseldown, Larkhill, Hackwood Park and Lockinge. Poldark was something of a superstar and Dad had decided, at the age of forty-five, that this was the horse who could fulfil his lifetime's ambition.

Despite all his success as a flat trainer, had he been given the choice, my father would have been a jump jockey. In his early twenties, he had been a decent amateur rider and had ridden in the Fox Hunter's at Aintree twice, finishing fourth once and falling off the other time. Now, twenty years later, he had in Poldark a horse who could jump like a stag, gallop for up to three miles and was clever enough to negotiate the particular challenges of the Grand National course at Aintree.

The Fox Hunter's was restricted to amateur riders. If you were a professional jump jockey, you wanted to win the Grand National. For an amateur, the Fox Hunter's was the ultimate prize.

My father's diet of fruit, no alcohol and Lean Cuisine ready-made meals had gone on many months longer than usual, to make sure that he was light enough to make the weight of twelve stone with a decent saddle. He went for runs wearing a plastic sweat suit, and even insisted on having a wooden sauna built into the bathroom that Andrew and I shared. He could lose four or five pounds, sometimes more, in a day, but would put it back on again as soon as he drank any liquid. He looked pale and drawn, and his temper was shorter than ever on the long drive to Liverpool.

When we got there, Dad was in no mood to hang about.

'Right, come on, you two, we're going to walk the course.' He bustled off towards the wide, bright-green strip of grass beyond the white rails.

Later I took in the covered winner's enclosure and the old-fashioned weighing room that I had seen so often on the TV. But for now I was staggered at how flat the course was. I had been to Newbury, Sandown, Ascot and Cheltenham—all of which had contours of varying degrees, but this racecourse had been rolled out like a big grass pancake. On the inside of the racecourse was a smooth tarmac road. Mum told me that it used to be a Grand Prix circuit.

The course we were examining was equally smooth, the lush green grass thick at the roots with plenty of 'cover', ensuring that even if there was no rain and the ground was good to firm, the cushion of grass would dispel the concussion effect on a horse's hooves.

The Fox Hunter's is run over two miles, five furlongs—just over one circuit of the Grand National course. It starts at the top of the straight with the Chair as the third fence, the water as the fourth and then past the Grand National start to the line of fences that includes Becher's Brook.

I could not believe how big the fences were, all of them at least four feet six inches high, with the Chair standing at a whopping five feet two, with a ditch on the take-off side giving it a width of eleven feet. They looked so much bigger up close than they ever had on the TV, but my father kept telling us that they used to be even more frightening.

'See all this spruce on top?' he said, picking up bits of the greenery. 'It never used to be this thick. And all this padding at the front? They used to be just straight up, with no apron on the front, nothing to help a horse stand off. Just like vertical walls, they were.'

He placed his right foot on the lower part of the fence, where it stuck out like a swollen belly, and pressed up and down.

'Much better now.'

I have no idea whether my father was saying all this to make himself feel better or to make us less nervous but, as we came to Becher's Brook, I had a rush of genuine fear. The hedge on either side of it always let you know that the runners were approaching the most fearsome fence on the course, and I knew from watching on TV that the horses galloped towards the fence so fast that it became a blur.

So far, my father had been walking on the inside of the course but, as we approached Becher's Brook, he started to angle off the inside towards the middle. He walked right up to the fence. It was as big as he was. He patted the spruce on top.

'Go round to the other side,' he instructed.

Andrew and I ran round to the landing side of Becher's Brook, from where we could barely see my

196

father's head above the mound of green.

'Walk along that landing side and tell me what you see.'

'There's a big ditch,' I said, staring at the murky water running through it. That'll be the Brook, I thought, where Captain Becher got a ducking in 1839.

'It's got a bigger drop here,' said my brother, who had walked right across to the inside rail. 'You don't want to land here.'

He pointed to the ground, where the turf clearly sloped back towards the ditch. Even if a horse jumped it well, it would be caught out by the camber and crumple to the ground.

'That's why I will jump it right in the middle,' Dad said, coming round to join us on the landing side.

My mother, who had said little thus far, marked a line on the fence and said, 'Jump it here or wider, Ian. No further in than this.' She said nothing else to my father the whole way round.

Dad talked us through the angle he would take at the Canal Turn, where the field has to swing through ninety degrees sharp left, how he would 'take a pull' as they crossed the Melling Road back on to the racecourse proper so that Poldark could fill his lungs with air, ready for the final two fences, and how he would jump the last upsides the leader but not ride a finish until he reached the elbow. There was still about a furlong to the winning post from there and, as we knew from watching Crisp get caught by Red Rum in 1973, it was a long, long way on a tiring horse.

Dad started to jog up the home straight, and we ran with him, all three of us racing to the line. Dad still wouldn't let us win a race unless we had earned it, so he dipped for the line to make sure of victory.

The next day, my mother kept Andrew and me out of the way as Dad studied the other runners in the *Sporting Life*, making sure he knew which ones jumped well and which ones to avoid getting stuck behind. We were worse than an irrelevance—we were a hindrance.

It was my first insight into the psychology and utter self-absorption of the committed athlete. It doesn't really matter whether you are an amateur, doing it for the love of it, or a professional earning money from sport, you are either completely committed or you're not.

We watched from the grandstand, the white-sheepskin noseband making it easy to pick out Ross Poldark and my father. They made most of the running, jumping Becher's Brook exactly on the line my mother had marked. Dad sat back on landing, then gathered up his reins—he always told me that learning to slip the reins through your hands and then take them up again was one of the most important riding skills—and they galloped on towards the Foinavon fence together. He saw the line he wanted to take at the Canal Turn and stuck to it. As the field crossed the Melling Road, I could see Dad trying to give Poldark a breather, but there were three other horses going just as well as him.

Andrew and I started to shout, 'Come on, Dad, keep going,' as he jumped the last two fences, but the writing was on the wall and although he got round, Poldark could only finish fourth. It was the same placing as my father had attained twenty years earlier on a horse called Christmas Robin. At least that meant they got to come back under the roof of the winner's enclosure. Andrew and I cheered, Liz was beaming as she led in Poldark and my mother allowed herself to breathe again. Dad was the only one who didn't look happy. Fourth was not good enough.

Had he been younger and not a full-time flat trainer, I suspect my father would have had many more attempts at winning the Fox Hunter's. As it was, he tried once more and was unseated at Becher's Brook, jumping too close to the inside. He didn't pay any attention to my mother advising him to stop, but he did finally listen when his owners pointed out that they were paying good money to have him train their horses and it would be preferable if he wasn't trying to kill himself at Aintree every spring.

We were home by Saturday, in time to watch the 1983 Grand National on the telly as Jenny Pitman became the first female trainer to win it with Corbiere. I may not have thought much about racing or been at all interested in the ninety inmates of Park House Stables who provided a living for my father and his employees, but I had felt the buzz of a big sporting event. One day, however far away it may be, I wanted to be involved in the Grand National.

*     *     *

Lily the boxer puppy arrived later that spring. You could spend hours just watching her wobble about on her rubbery legs. As she strengthened up, she started to bounce around the garden like a lamb, taking off on all four feet and twisting her body in the air. She wagged her whole bottom when she was happy and she smiled like a demented clown. Mum was laughing again. We all were.

Sleeping late is a crime nearly as disgraceful as shoplifting in my family. To sleep past nine o'clock was anathema to my father, who was always up and about as dawn was breaking. For my brother and me, growing as we were, sleep became more and more attractive. Andrew was particularly grumpy in the mornings, but both of us found waking up easier if it wasn't our parents getting us out of bed.

As my father raged downstairs—'How long are those bloody children going to stay in bed?'—my mother would slip upstairs with Lily, open my door to let her in and close it again. Lily was a hands-on alarm clock, jumping on top of me and licking my face until I eventually got out of bed. It was my favourite way to start the day.

# 12

# Querk and Stuart

With every horse or dog you love comes 'the deal'. You will get hours and hours of pleasure, years of fun, education and love. In many ways, you will become more human—certainly more humane— because of the relationship you develop. Then comes the hard part. The animal will die before you. Sometimes it will die right in front of you. If you are unlucky, as I was with Ellie May, it will die right underneath you.

It was a beautiful day. Crisp spring air, a blue sky, the pale sun giving light but little warmth. The buds on the trees were starting to burst forth and I was filled with that feeling of expectation that I got every spring. All around me there was evidence of new beginnings and the chance to develop and grow.

There was a big field for the Berks & Bucks Drag Hunt at Highclere. We parked by the Temple of Diana, my favourite Roman goddess. Diana was goddess of the moon and the chase. She was the sister of Apollo and she was an out-and-out tomboy, wearing hunting gear all the time and carrying her bow and arrows on her shoulder. Diana was my first feminist pin-up, a strong woman who could hunt for her own food and didn't need a man to provide for her or to define her.

I was chatting away about Diana as I pulled the tail bandage off Ellie May and checked her boots hadn't slipped during the short journey from Kingsclere. There was a holler from another horsebox and Ellie May started whinnying back. It was Ben—the giant gelding who had come over from Ireland on the same ship as her some ten years earlier. Ben had been our Uncle David's hunter and, when Uncle David returned to America to set up a circus, Ben was sold to another Berks & Bucks member.

Ben was infatuated with Ellie May. He charged down the ramp of his horsebox and dragged his new owner, Peregrine, towards our box. No person, however strong, could stop Ben in full flow. He nuzzled up to Ellie May and seemed to kiss her. Only after he had finished his romantic greeting did he agree to be led back to his own horsebox.

202

Ellie May had looked after me on so many days' drag hunting that I had lost count and, even if she wasn't the finest-looking hunter on show, I had a real soft spot for her. Highclere was a highlight of the whole season because one of the lines took us on the cross-country course that was used for the BHS (that's British Horse Society, not British Home Stores) one-day event. I loved the chance to jump the beautifully built fences; they were technically more challenging than the galloping courses I was used to at home. At Highclere, it wasn't just a case of kick on and be brave—you had to be accurate, measure your distances and get your line right.

I wanted to ride at the Olympics and at Badminton like my heroine Lucinda Green. In our first year at school, Mrs Berwick had asked us all what careers we would like to pursue. My hand shot up.

'I would like to be an eventer,' I said, with the utmost sincerity.

'Really?' replied Mrs Berwick. 'What would you like to invent?'

I think she was rather disappointed when I clarified my position.

\*　　　\*　　　\*

Back at Highclere, Dad was climbing aboard Poldark. To qualify for point-to-points and hunter chases, the horse had to get a certificate to say he had been out drag hunting. This was no problem, as my father loved to ride him and knew that, as Field Master, he could stay ahead of the whole field while barely out of a hack canter. Poldark looked down his nose at Ellie May, who stood helpfully next to the ramp so that I could use it to clamber on board.

We headed off to the meet behind the Carnarvon Arms in Highclere and I let her stand next to Ben, where she was happiest. I followed Ben for the first line, with Ellie May jumping everything that he jumped. The bright-scarlet jackets of the Master and the Whipper-ins streaked away behind the hounds, who had their noses down on the ground as they followed the strong scent. Once in a while, the poor runner who had laid the scent would not be far enough ahead, and the hounds would catch him. Although it's never much fun to be hunted down by a pack of hounds, there was no danger of them doing anything worse than licking him to death.

As always with the drag hunt, a line covered about four miles, after which the hounds got some meat, and the horses and riders had a chance to catch their breath. As I pulled up Ellie May after the first line, she was breathing heavily and I remember worrying that she'd lost her fitness rather quickly. My mother was on foot, and I asked her to have a look to check Ellie was OK.

We both agreed that I would take it steady on the second line and bring her back if there was any sign of tiredness. She was about seventeen years old by now, getting on a bit, but not ancient.

At the very beginning of the second line, down in the valley with trees all around, we were cantering towards a small post and rails. It was no more than two feet six inches and just needed popping over. I asked Ellie to shorten her stride by pulling gently on the reins. There was no response. I asked again, more urgently, but instead of coming back to me, her head became heavy and her mouth was set.

She didn't take off at all. She just crashed straight through and, even though the top rail snapped, the impact was enough to turn her sideways and thudding to the ground. I was thrown clear and, as I scrambled back towards her, I could see her sides heaving.

Luckily, the rest of the field had steadied up enough that they did not jump into us. My father was too far ahead to know what was going on, but Ben had pulled himself up and was charging back towards us, whether Peregrine wanted him to or not. He was whinnying frantically. Ellie May tried to nicker back at him.

After half an hour or so, she recovered enough to get to her feet, and I led her back up the hill towards the horsebox park. We stopped frequently to allow her to find the strength to put one foot in front of the other. I was shouting out for my mother, who came running down towards me.

'I don't know what happened.' My voice was panicked. 'She just didn't take off. I was trying to get her back but she wouldn't listen.'

I was terrified. This was my mother's horse, her trusted companion, and I had put her on the deck. I had hurt her. It was my fault.

My mother took the reins and stroked the side of Ellie's head. 'There must be something wrong.'

There *was* something—horribly—wrong. As she reached the horsebox, Ellie staggered and collapsed. Her ribcage rose up with one last heave and then stopped. She was dead.

I have no idea how she made it back up the hill, how she even recovered enough to stand up after the fall. Mum said she hadn't wanted to die in a place that would be inconvenient.

Ben had refused to carry on without her and, moments later, we saw him trotting towards us, a confused Peregrine shaking his head. Ben slowed to a walk and then stopped as he came close. He lowered his head to Ellie and sniffed at her face. Then he let out a deep, guttural noise, like a strangled cry of pain, and turned away.

They say that horses and donkeys need to see the dead body of their companion to be able to grieve. Ben needed to see Ellie May for himself, otherwise he would have spent the rest of his days hollering out for her with no reply.

The vet said Ellie May had had a massive haemorrhage as she approached the jump. I was lucky she didn't trap me underneath her as she fell. Awful does not begin to cover the feeling of driving home in the horsebox with just one horse instead of two and walking back into the yard with an empty bridle. Liz was there, bustling towards us and taking Poldark from my father. She saw my eyes, red from crying all the way home, and she knew that something terrible had happened.

A few days later I had to go back to school and I was still in shock. How did you explain what had happened to anyone who didn't ride? So I kept it to myself and carried on as normal, distraction being the chosen method of medication in my family.

\*       \*       \*

Ellie May had, during the course of her life with us, been mated twice with thoroughbred stallions in the hope of producing offspring with her honesty and cleverness but with the quality injection of blood that might give them a little more class. The first foal, by the successful jumps stallion Idiot's Delight, was called Quirk and the second, by a stallion called Turnpike, was a chestnut colt called Stuart.

Both of them were gelded while they were still young, and they were turned out until they would be old enough to be broken in. The vast majority of non-thoroughbred male horses have their testicles removed when they are still foals. Being 'gelded' makes them more manageable, lighter in weight and altogether less alpha male. Racehorses are broken in before they are two years old, but other horses, who will be carrying heavier loads than seven-stone stable lads, are broken in when they are about four.

Quirk resisted being led, he bucked when he was mounted and he dug his toes in when he was being asked to go forward. He was like a gifted but reluctant child. He hated to be made to do anything but, if you let him think he was doing it on his terms, it was a different story. He was clever. Too clever sometimes.

When Quirk was six, I started riding him, and we got along pretty well. I had time, during the holidays, to hack him for hours and, if we went up on the Downs to school over the hunter-trial fences, I could practise again and again until he jumped the table, or the railway sleepers, or the coffin, with confidence. Mum thought it would be a good idea if I took him to Pony Club camp, because he would get a year's experience all in one week.

The Craven Pony Club held its summer camp at Englefield Park near Pangbourne. There was the most beautiful walled estate within, where over a hundred children on ponies could get into all sorts of trouble. Quirk would be ridden for up to six hours a day and would do dressage, show-jumping, be ridden bareback and schooled in cross-country. The stimulation would be constant.

First things first: he had to learn to stand still. The Pony Club erected temporary stables for all the ponies. They were wooden structures forming rows of boxes with canvas roofs. They were perfectly safe and solid unless you had a strong little horse intent on pulling the whole row down. A horse like Quirk.

'What is that racket?'

I heard the voice of Mrs Gardiner, our ride's instructor, as I filled a bucket of water. She sounded a little shriller than usual. I had left Quirk for all of five minutes. As I looked back towards my stable row, I could see it rocking from side to side. There were now lots of voices, all of them shouting.

A cloud of panic gathered around the far end of the row, the end where Quirk was stabled. I left the bucket of water and ran back, to find him swaying from side to side and pulling backwards on his rope.

'Quirk, stop it. Stop it right now,' I said, as firmly as a girl not yet turned thirteen can say anything.

He looked round at me, and I could see that he wasn't scared, he was just being naughty. Like a small child desperate for attention, he was making a fuss because I'd left him on his own. We compromised. I didn't leave him tied up, and he didn't pull the stable block down around our ears.

By the end of the week, when he was exhausted from constant lessons and was learning manners from the horses around him as much as from our instructor, I tried it again. I tied him up and hid round the corner, near enough that if he started rocking and pulling again, I could step in before he did any damage. He stood quiet as a lamb for half an hour.

Quirk embraced Pony Club camp. He loved the different lessons, he enjoyed meeting other horses and he particularly liked getting more food to reward his hard work.

Ellie May's other son, Stuart, was two years younger than Quirk and about a hand bigger. In personality, they could not have been more different. They were chalk and cheese, tomato and pineapple, *Dynasty* and *Tenko*. Both of them were fairly chunky and could put on weight easily but, when they were fit, they scrubbed up pretty well.

Stuart was broken in gently by Spider and Danny Harrap. The trick to educating a young horse is to be consistent and firm, while always being kind. There is no point getting involved in a tug of war with a horse who has half a ton of weight to pull with—you're going to lose. So Danny took it gently with Stuart, who responded with a degree of timidity. He was a little bit scared of his own shadow in those early days.

My mother banned my father from going near either Stuart or Quirk. They were her horses and 'off limits' to him. She said he had enough on his hands with all the horses he had to ride and, also, she didn't want him galloping them all over the place jumping things they weren't ready to jump. When she went away, my father snuck down to the stud and asked Carol, who had joined the stud to work alongside Liz, to saddle up Quirk for him.

'But Guv'nor,' said a confused Carol, blushing bright red, 'Mrs B said you're not to ride him. She told me that explicitly.'

'Well, she's changed her mind and told me this morning that she wanted me to,' Dad lied.

Half an hour later, Quirk came trotting back to the stud on his own. He had bucked my father off, farted and left him sitting on the grass. Dad was furious, and decided that Quirk was a useless, temperamental, undisciplined individual. If that's what Dad wanted to think, my mother was perfectly happy. At least it meant he wouldn't try to ride him.

Years later, when Quirk and my father had both mellowed with age, they struck up a most unlikely partnership. My father needed something he could ride with the string that would hack about, lead difficult horses or just stand and eat grass if he got off to inspect the racehorses. I suggested he try Quirk, who was as biddable as a polo pony and greedy enough never to move if he had the chance to munch on fresh grass.

Although initially reluctant, my father was won round by the romance that blossomed between Quirk and his most talented racehorse of the early nineties, a sprinter called Lochsong. She was the fastest animal Dad had ever trained, but she was also one of the trickiest and would plant herself in the Starting Gate field, refusing to take a single step towards the four-furlong all-weather gallop, which had been resurfaced with a mixture of sand, rubber and oil. As she grew more successful (Lochsong won the Prix de l'Abbaye at Longchamp twice, the Nunthorpe, the King's Stand and a host of top-class sprint handicaps), she became more and more truculent at home.

Lochsong would not budge unless Quirk came up alongside her and led her to the gallop. Once there, she would leave him for dead as she tore off at 100 mph, with Francis Arrowsmith, known as Scully, trying desperately to maintain some sort of

210

control. Lochsong was an all-or-nothing filly—she would either win a Group 1 like the Abbaye in Paris without seeing another horse, or she would run away going down to the start, as she did with both Willie Carson and Frankie Dettori, and then finish stone last.

Dad enjoyed the challenge of training Lochsong and, because she loved Quirk, he grew to love him too.

As for Stuart, well, they never got along. Again, Dad ignored the ban (he was worse when you told him he couldn't do something) and rode Stuart up Cottington Hill to do a recce on what would be the second line of the drag hunt. They came to a tiny post and rails in the fence line with no way round it, and Stuart refused.

Dad smacked him with his whip. Stuart refused again and absolutely would not budge. Whatever Dad did, however hard he kicked or growled, Stuart was having none of it. They say you can't make a horse do what he doesn't want to do, and Stuart was out to prove it to my father. He reared and went into reverse. Dad had to come home and admit defeat.

I took Stuart up to the same little post and rails the next day and he popped over it with no trouble at all. He wasn't scared, he wasn't incapable of jumping it—he just didn't want to be strong-armed. They had attitude, these sons of Ellie May.

Stuart was not a man's man. He was a gentle soul, and Mum and I were very protective of him. He was bigger than Quirk and much more cuddly, a soft, mild-mannered boy, with a permanently concerned look on his face. He would take Polo mints out of my mouth, the whiskers on his muzzle lightly brushing my face. I could lean right into him and he'd put his head over my shoulder to give me a hug like a teddy bear. He loved to stop and look at a view or watch as a roe deer hopped across the field in front of him. Our rides always took time, because he didn't like to rush anything.

My favourite time of year was when the wheat had just been cut. Early in the morning, there was a slight haze and the fields looked as if they had been sepia-tinted, the Downs rising like an enormous blue whale behind them. I loved the colours and the quiet of the early morning. I liked to disappear on my own to the farm or up on to the Downs.

One morning, I rode up through Smith's Bushes, intent on schooling Stuart over the hunter-trial fences. When I got to the top of the Downs and Stuart was fully warmed up, I reached down to tighten the girths a notch. One of them snapped in half, so I took off the saddle and left it on the fence. Stuart was a wide-backed horse and pretty comfortable, and I had done plenty of bareback riding at Pony Club camp. We didn't need a saddle.

We jumped ten or fifteen fences up through the fields and, although I can see why saddles were invented, riding bareback is a superb way of really feeling what your horse is doing and of improving your own balance. As we cantered back through the paddocks (trotting was not an option—far too uncomfortable), I saw Jonna who, having climbed out of his red tractor, was inspecting my saddle.

'Or'right, Miss B?' he said, chewing a long piece of grass. 'Broke yer tack, 'ave you?'

'I did, Jonna, yes. But I didn't want to disappoint Stuart by not letting him jump!'

'Di'nt wanna disappoint yer'self, more like!' he

212

replied. 'I never saw a girl so into jumping as you, Miss B. Just like yer pa. Now, d'yer want me to take this saddle back fer yer?'

'That would be most kind. Thank you, Jonna.'

Jonna would always keep an eye out for me, especially when I was teaching a young horse to jump. He never once told my parents if I'd been doing something I shouldn't.

His face was battered by the elements, his clothes always stained by grass and sheep dung, his gait a little arthritic as he plodded up and down the gallops, treading in the divots made by the horses. But he had an innate peace that many of us spend our lives trying to attain.

One morning when the stubble was cut and the hedges had all been trimmed, I decided to take Stuart down to the end of Long Meadow. We did a bit of flat schooling, we popped over every size of straw bale and then I took him to have a look at the big hedge that ran down the side of the bales.

I don't know to this day what possessed me, but I felt an urgent need to jump that hedge. It was huge—as big as Becher's Brook—and I was on my own, a mile away from the yard. I was not out drag hunting, when your blood is up and you go with the crowd, jumping fences you'd never consider in cold blood.

I let Stuart have a good look at the landing side then took him round the other side, where the stubble field would let us have a slightly downhill run at the hedge. I had to pick my spot carefully so that the landing would be safe and I wouldn't frighten him unfairly. Then I cantered him round in a circle, collected him up into a short, bouncy stride so that he could get power from his quarters, and

213

cantered towards the hedge. I kept my legs strong and, when my brain started to doubt the sense of what we were doing, I tried not to let it transmit to my body.

Stuart took off. He sailed over that hedge and landed effortlessly the other side. A horse who wouldn't jump a post and rails of two feet six with my father had just jumped a hedge which I later measured at five feet two inches high. I reached down and hugged him, kissing the side of his neck. What a saint.

Stuart was so eager to please and, with a bit of help from our French assistant trainer, Erwan Charpy, he became pretty good at dressage as well as cross-country. Erwan had grown up being taught the French skills of equitation, and he was a fine horseman. I watched his lower leg—so strong and steady as Stuart lengthened into an extended trot or smoothly transitioned from walk into canter.

'You see, Clare, it's all about confidence,' Erwan shouted at me, as I sat on the fence watching him go round in circles on Stuart. ''E must feel that you are confident in what you are doing. Keep your leg on; 'e will give.'

Stuart was black with sweat, every ounce of him making the effort to give Erwan what he wanted. When he did something right, there was a pat and a murmur in French that Stuart seemed to understand; when he did something wrong, a patient repetition of the command until he understood what was being asked of him.

I watched Erwan carefully, his face etched with concentration. He was thinking like a horse, talking to Stuart all the time, and underneath him the timid, fearful young horse was growing in stature

214

and self-belief.

'You take this horse. 'E now thinks 'e is a better horse, because I have made 'im feel that way. Life, you see,' said Erwan, 'it is all—'ow you say?—a con trick.'

'Really?' I replied.

'I mean "con" as in "confidence". The more confident you are, the more people will believe in you; and the more they believe in you, the more confident you will actually become.'

At Downe House, I tried to put into practice what I had learned from Erwan. Be confident, and others will be confident in you. Be consistent. Be fair and be honest. I had a lot of ground to make up, but it helped if I wasn't always trying to impress people.

# 13

## Henry

Occasionally, you come across a horse with no natural sense of self-preservation, a loose cannon, a nutter. Meet Henry.

Mum and I went to try him at Wylye near Salisbury. We were on the estate owned by Lord and Lady Hugh Russell, where the British event team used to train before major competitions. Lady Hugh Russell would spray paint spots on cross-country fences at the exact point she wished them to be jumped and bark from her electric buggy at any rider who strayed left or right.

Henry was almost black, with a paler brown muzzle, dark-brown eyes and the smallest trace of a white star in the centre of his face. His ears curved into sharp points, like Mr Spock. His coat was smooth and shiny like a racehorse, his body so fine compared to that of Quirk or Stuart, and he was alert to everything going on around him, reacting to any sound or sight.

With all this space around, it surprised me that I was trying Henry in an indoor school. He had a short, bouncy canter and needed plenty of restraint, but he jumped brilliantly. I asked if I could take him outside for a gallop.

'Oh, I wouldn't do that,' said the girl who was selling him. She paused, and then said rapidly, 'The sheep are being moved today, and we're not allowed on the cross-country course. It's best we stay in here.'

Mum and I looked at each other, and I shrugged. I was dreadful at buying horses, because I liked them all. Even if they were difficult, I was convinced I could improve them; and if they were affectionate, I was hooked. My mother was more savvy but, in this instance, both of us were hoodwinked. Not just for saying yes, we'd take Henry, but for failing to add the condition of a week's trial at home.

He was fine in an indoor school or in a field with a fence around it, but when Henry saw open spaces there was no stopping him. There were racehorses trained by my father that couldn't keep pace with Henry in full flight. And full flight was what you got if you wanted to canter in a straight line. Round and round in circles—he would do that nicely; but across a field or up the Far Hedge—that would be full pelt.

I foolishly thought that, if I pointed him at some decent-sized fences, he would have to slow down. Henry thought otherwise. We once covered a cross-country course at Tweseldown so fast that the fence judge at the water didn't even see us arriving before we were through the other side. Henry was not a horse my mother, or anyone else, wanted to ride.

I saw him as a challenge and rode him at Hickstead in the Downe House show-jumping team for the school championships. We entered that arena in trot and, as I halted and saluted the judges, it hit me that I was riding in the same arena as show-jumping legends like Eddie Macken and Harvey Smith, jumping the same jumps as Nick Skelton.

The Hickstead arena is the biggest in the world. As I asked Henry to move from halt straight into a fiery but controlled canter, it felt as if we were on a cross-country course rather than in a show-jumping arena. I kept him turning so that he wouldn't realize how big a space it was. As I heard the bell, I circled round and through the timing beam that ran across the start.

Henry flew over the oxer, the planks and the white gate. He shortened up for the double and stretched again for a big parallel. He gathered pace as he came to the last—a brown upright with panels rather than rails—and it took all my strength to contain him. He rattled the centre post where I had aimed him, but the panels stayed put. Henry had jumped a clear round, and at the home of

British show-jumping, and as I took my hand off the reins to acknowledge the applause, he zoomed forward as if I'd pressed a booster button. He took off at 100 mph round the outside of the ring. I tried to pretend I had intended an impromptu lap of honour while I struggled to get him back under control.

Our Downe House team, which included Daisy Dick (later a top-class international eventer), finished third and I won an award for 'Best Style' from Dougie Bunn, who owned Hickstead. He had clearly been fooled by the lap of honour.

We tried a variety of bits on Henry—the solid ones, like a Pelham and a Kimblewick; the jointed ones, like a Dr Bristol and a Waterford; the various types of gag—American and Balding—that lowered his head as well as restrained him. None of them worked. Henry was officially uncontrollable. His competing was restricted to cross-country courses with lots of turns or just dressage and show-jumping. He certainly couldn't go out drag hunting or team chasing, which rather spoiled my fun.

I enjoyed my holidays, because I could ride two or three horses a day, and I was never bored, but other girls at school seemed less enamoured of their time at home.

'Oh ya, we went to the south of France and it was really dull.'

Or: 'Daddy had a yacht on the Med this summer, but he had to keep going back to work so it was just me and my stepmother. A bit, you know . . . boring.'

Their holidays had been a whirl of beaches, parties and shopping. I envied the glamorous lifestyle and couldn't understand why they never seemed to have enjoyed it much. During the winter, my parents had decided—rather late in life—to take up skiing.

My father's approach to skiing was the same as his approach to everything. He went as fast as he could and was afraid of nothing. Style was not something that bothered him, which was lucky, as he had none at all. He was like a demented cowboy tearing down the slopes, turning once in a while straight across the path of an unsuspecting skier, wiping out children at will, and falling often. He once tumbled the whole way from the top of a black run to the bottom, losing both skis and one boot on the way.

'I did it,' he said as he picked himself up at the bottom, brushing the snow from his trousers, his arms and his face. He was smiling, and his eyes looked glazed. Andrew and I didn't have the heart to point out that falling down a black run did not mean that you had skied it.

My mother was more cautious. Her main objective was to avoid my father. The best way of doing this was to ski on a different mountain.

Family skiing holidays gave me something to share with the other girls when I returned for the Michaelmas term, although most of them went in the spring, when it was much warmer and the snow was softer. Dad, of course, was busy in the spring, so we went in January when it was freezing and the snow was icy. Not that I'm complaining, just explaining how Andrew and I got frostbite on a T-bar in Zermatt.

I had grown used to feeling as if I wanted to vomit as my mother drove me through Thatcham towards Cold Ash at the start of each term.

Sometimes I thought I was going to faint and maybe, hopefully, I would end up in hospital and wouldn't have to go back to school at all. I can't remember exactly when I stopped feeling sick and actually started feeling excited at the beginning of term, but it must have been around the end of my Lower V/start of Upper V year.

I was playing lacrosse regularly and, because I was younger than my classmates I could play under-fourteens when the rest of the year were under-fifteens, and so on. It meant that I was the senior player on the team, instead of being the most junior in my own year. I worked hard on trying to read the game, intercepting the ball or stopping an opponent from making an attacking move. I practised my cradling and got much better at picking up a loose ball from the ground. My fitness improved. The team were bonded by sweat, effort and mutual honour. That worked as a pretty good glue.

My mother came to watch whenever she could. She whistled at me from the sidelines so that I knew she was there. Whenever Andrew or I were in a crowd, my mother didn't shout, she whistled, as she did for the dogs. It was a two-note whistle, like a wolf whistle in reverse. My father wasn't interested. He didn't understand lacrosse.

'No boundaries?' he said, when I tried to explain. 'How the hell do you control the game if there are no boundaries? You mean you can run right into the crowd?'

'Well,' I said, reasonably, 'the referee would probably blow the whistle if you did that but, yes, you can go behind the crowd or behind the goal if you want. It's a really good game, Dad. You have to come.'

He made a noise like a kettle when it's boiling.

'Sounds stupid,' he said. 'Anyway, I don't like women's sport.'

I persisted. 'But you've only been to my school once, and you were really embarrassing. You told my Latin teacher she had good legs. So, don't do that again, but you have to come to a match. Please.'

'I'll come when you're in the first team.'

I did eventually make the first team but I only played in three matches. In the third, I twisted my leg, ripping the cartilage and pulling the ligaments in my left knee. I hobbled off the pitch and was driven back to the main school by Miss Farr, who sent me up to the San—the school hospital on the second floor of Tedworth. Sister prescribed ice packs and a heavy dose of painkillers, but it was still agony when I went home for the Short Exeat.

I tried to ride. It hurt when I got on, it felt sore in walk and, as I tried to trot Henry up the main avenue, the pain was excruciating. I turned round and went back to the stud in tears.

'I can't ride,' I said. For me, this was akin to saying, 'I can't breathe.'

My confidence was shattered. If I couldn't ride— if I could *never* ride again—what would I do? What would I be any good at? What would I say to myself when things were going wrong?

I had surgery in Oxford and spent the next month on crutches. I wasn't allowed to ride for eight weeks. My first-team career was over, and Dad never did see me play lacrosse.

So it was that I headed towards my sixteenth birthday on crutches and, thanks to orthodontic work, metal tracks on my top and bottom teeth and a head brace to wear at night: how to make a girl feel special. Despite the clear sign on my face that spelt out 'Do not kiss' in metal, a boy had actually kissed me at the school ball. Well, he was either kissing me or trying to eat me—it was hard to tell—but he was sweet, and we exchanged letters for months. We never saw each other again, of course, but I liked the way he wrote the name 'Hugo'.

For years, every other girl had opened Valentine's cards—probably sent by their parents in the name of the hamster—but my pigeon hole was empty.

'Commercial claptrap. Just an excuse to make you buy cards' was my mother's attitude.

When I got my first Valentine's card in writing that looked like Hugo's, I felt that I was finally on track. I was one of the team, just like everyone else. I ignored the nagging doubts in my head and concentrated on the relief that I was fitting in at last.

The school ball was a huge success for our year. Everyone 'got off' with someone, and some girls were virtually engaged by the end of the night. On the minus side, quite a lot of girls got caught smoking—half our year had to come back the following weekend to pick chewing gum off the bottoms of chairs and tables. It took them two days. I did not get caught smoking, because I did not smoke. I say this for my father's benefit, as he insisted that my taffeta dress of red, purple and green smelt of smoke. This was because Hugo had been smoking, but I couldn't tell him that so I just said, 'It wasn't me.'

'Don't lie to me, Clare. I can smell smoke. I know you've been smoking and, given your track record, I do not feel inclined to believe you just because you tell me you haven't.'

My father had given up smoking at the age of twelve. He told me this as if it was quite normal. His parents, like everyone else in the 1940s, kept wooden boxes of cigarettes around the house, to which guests or family members helped themselves. So Dad helped himself from the age of six to twelve, when he decided smoking ten Philip Morris full-tar cigarettes a day made him feel sick. He spent the following decades lecturing everyone else on the ills of smoking from the position of being a convert. In this instance, I was innocent, but try telling that to a born-again non-smoker with a penchant for delivering lectures.

\*          \*          \*

Dad, once he'd got the smoking thing out of his head, promised me that, when I was sixteen, I could ride in my first point-to-point. This was assuming that I would be able to ride again and that my knee would take the pressure of having my stirrups short, as jockeys had to. It also assumed that I wanted to ride in a point-to-point. I knew my father's idea of fun—tying a sledge to the back of a truck and flinging two young children about in the snow, flying headlong down a black run with no skis on and riding round Aintree. He said point-to-point riding was the biggest thrill in the world but, on the evidence I had, this wasn't a great recommendation.

When I came off crutches and started to walk again, my father told me that I needed to lose weight. My mother had been making the odd comment about clothes looking tight, but my father

224

just said it outright.

'You'll need to ride at eleven stone with a saddle in a point-to-point,' he told me, 'which should be fine, but I want you to have a really decent saddle, and you need to be fit. Much fitter than you are now. You've got very porky. Lose it.'

My knee was bearing up pretty well. I had to do exercises every day, lifting weights draped around my ankle, to strengthen the muscles on either side. I had a long scar where the surgeon had cut in to remove the folded-over, distorted cartilage that had caused all the trouble. The ligaments were damaged, but not torn—they would recover, with time.

Riding would be the real test. I chose Stuart because I knew he was the kindest. I led him out to the concrete mounting block so that getting into the saddle would be as easy as possible. He stood stock still, his ears pricked. I climbed gingerly into the saddle and adjusted my stirrups to be a little longer than usual. So far, so good.

We walked up through the yard, and it felt wonderful just to be on a horse again. I was nervous, worried that I would have lost my touch or that, once I started to trot, my knee would send sharp arrows of pain to my brain. We walked up the main avenue, straight on up Christmas Tree Avenue, and turned right at the top. I wanted to take my time, to savour the smell of the trees, the sight of a deer running across the fields or a buzzard hovering overhead.

We headed up the side of Cottington Hill and, once on the track that led steeply uphill, I asked Stuart to move into trot. This would be the big test. I sat up and down, up and down, my knees bending and my calves squeezing the sides of his big tummy. It didn't hurt. It felt strange, but it didn't hurt.

I could do it! I screamed in delight and punched the air. Stuart pricked his ears and quickened up his pace. We rode through the White Horse car park, crossed the main road and went through the gap by the side of the five-bar gate on to the Downs.

We cantered, with me sitting down into the saddle. We jumped on to the side of the Downs that looked over the farm. I let Stuart go a little quicker and sat up in the saddle like a jockey. I was going to be OK.

That evening, I needed a bag of frozen peas on my knee to take down the swelling. Mum said I must have overdone it. I denied it, but the next morning I was aching all over. Inside my thighs, up my bottom, my back and my arms were screaming. Dad pronounced that the only way to deal with it was to ride through the pain. My muscles had got out of the habit and I must make them learn how to do it all over again. I was a little less demanding on my limbs for the next few days and the knee seemed to be bearing up.

\*      \*      \*

At the end of our 'O' levels, my year went to the Lake District on an 'Outward Bound' course. It was meant to be a year-end release, a reward for finishing our exams and a chance for us to bond in different groups than our tightly formed cliques. I was fairly unfit after a summer of exams and limited exercise, but my knee was mending and I was determined not to shirk on the physical side of things. We headed off to Penrith on the train and then across to Ullswater, where we would sleep in a Georgian mansion with dormitories for the first night.

We were woken even earlier than my father got up and told to put on our swimming costumes. As the sun rose, a large group of shivering, yawning public-school girls ran down to the lake's edge.

'In you get, then!' shouted the main Outward Bound organizer.

We looked at each other. Surely we weren't expected to get in the freezing water?

'Come on, you bunch of overprivileged wimps!' he continued. 'You're not expecting a nice warm shower and a bar of frothy soap, are you? This is how you'd do it in the wild, so come on, get in.'

'This is a bloody sick joke,' said my friend KT. 'I thought this was meant to be a treat. Not a boot camp.'

'Put your heads under. It doesn't count unless you put your heads right under the water!'

There was a younger guide there. He could only have been about twenty-two. He whispered towards where I was standing with my friends KT, Toe and Gerry.

'It's only water. It's fresh, it's clean, and it's the best way in the world to wake up. Go on, get in. I promise you you'll never forget the feeling.'

I decided to get it over with as fast as I could. I pulled off my dressing gown and broke ranks, running towards the water's edge in my swimming costume. It was a glacial shock to the system, but I kept running, splashing and then diving under the dark surface. The nerves in my body tingled, my brain stopped for a second and then started to transmit at a thousand volts. It was the boost that I

227

needed to recharge my aching brain.

The shores of Ullswater are deceptively welcoming—the water lapping over rounded boulders, inviting you in—but the depth of the lake means it is freezing cold even in the height of summer.

I bobbed up to the surface and shouted back to the shore, 'Come on, it's incredible!'

Mike, the younger instructor, gave me a thumbs-up from the shore. The others started to follow, one by one and then all in a rush. High-pitched screams sped across the water and bounced back from the hills the other side. The air was filled with a storm of shrieking and nervous laughter. I swam until I was numb and then headed back. Mike was right—I did not forget the feeling.

The second evening, we slept out on the side of the lake in bivouacs. They were makeshift shelters which, as we discovered, were not watertight. It rained hard that night, the drips coming through the 'roof' and making the bedding wet. As the ground around us became increasingly sodden, some of the bivouacs started to slip towards the water's edge. I awoke to screams from Heidi and Char, whose bivouac had slid right into the lake.

I ran in my pyjamas to help pull them out, while Mike rescued their rucksacks and sleeping bags. Char never recovered, and even Heidi, who was habitually happy, was a shadow of herself until the fell run on the final day, when she took out her frustration by beating everyone to the finish. Never a natural runner and wary of my fragile knee, I hobbled along at the back with the stragglers, telling silly stories to take our minds off the agony of the cross-country run.

Apart from that hellish end to the week, we had a wonderful time—building rafts, abseiling, rock climbing, making our way round an agility course built high in the trees.

'Come on, Gerry, you can do it.' I was on a platform ten feet up a tree, trying to coax my friend along the wire. 'Take it steady, don't look down. That's it.'

'I can't do it. I can't do it. Don't make me do it.' Gerry was terrified of heights.

'It's fine,' I said. 'It's fine, really, just look at me. Look me in the eye and keep walking.'

Gerry started swearing at me, said she hated everyone, hated the Outward Bound and particularly me but, as she shouted obscenities, she was making progress, so I kept talking and put out my arm for her to grab as she got close. She threw herself at the platform, both of us nearly falling off it with the impact.

'You've done it!' I shouted as I held on to her. 'Well done, you've done it!'

'I hate you. I absolutely hate you!'

She continued to swear at me, but I told myself it was just the fear talking.

Mike Evans was our group leader and, if he had told me to fling myself over a cliff, I would happily have done so. I knew he would always make sure I had a rope attached to me. I trusted him completely and, as I abseiled down the side of a cliff, I had fantasies of being in an action film. I held the rope out behind me with one hand, gripping lightly with the other above my head, and bounced off the cliff sides. It was fabulous.

Away from the narrow, Z-shaped lake, we climbed towards Helvellyn and, within an hour, were further away from any sign of civilization than I had ever been before. After about two hours of walking, my brain stopped being cluttered with worries or daft thoughts and flicked on to a calmer setting. All I could think about was the path we were taking and the vast emptiness around us. The schoolgirl chatter had dissipated, and there was just the quiet scraping of boots and the puffing of exercising teenagers. It's what they call 'passive thinking time'—that place where your brain goes when it stops being distracted by the ephemera of life. I can only achieve it through walking or riding for a decent stretch.

We had huge adrenalin rushes that week, but we also had moments of absolute calm and the utter exhaustion that comes only from outdoor exertion. In Mike, we had a leader who knew how to make us find our core strength. He gently coaxed each girl through the start to any challenge—the moment when you go over the cliff edge or the tentative search for a new foothold as you climb up it—and then kept asking for more effort. He would not tolerate whinging or bitching and, as he sat by the fire in his khaki cargo shorts, he demonstrated how few possessions were necessary in the hunt for happiness. All he needed was a torch, a penknife, a map and a compass.

Mike knew how to challenge us enough to push us beyond our limits without snapping us in half. Unlike the boys of our age we had all met, he was not impressed by long, wavy hair or short skirts— he was only interested in how we might broaden our experience by losing ourselves in the landscape, and in testing our initiative as well as our physical ability. I dangled from his every word because, as far as I was concerned, Mike was delivering the gospel of true living. He wasn't a fictional figure or a film star, he was real and he was my hero.

Two years later, in 1988, I heard that Mike Evans had been killed in a climbing accident in New Zealand. I sobbed for the loss of a free spirit. I cried again when, only a few years ago, I was recording BBC Radio 4's *Ramblings* on a section of the coast-to-coast path near Patterdale and came across a plaque in his memory. It was outside a remote hut that walkers use for shelter. I had to stop the recording, because my throat had constricted. In just one week he had helped me understand that the world was so much bigger and more interesting than anything I had yet experienced and that, somehow, I would find my place in it.

*       *       *

Miss Houghton had written a notice in her swirly handwriting and pinned it on the board outside her ground-floor flat. It asked to see every girl in our year individually and gave us a timetable to fill in. I put my name in the last box, thinking that I could at least ask the others what it was all about before I had to go in.

Toe came out and told us that Miss Houghton had asked her to be a house prefect. Heidi said she had been appointed Games Captain, and Shorty was also a house prefect. We were all a little confused, as we had assumed that one of those three would be Head of House and that Miss Houghton would make that announcement later in the evening, when we were all together.

I knocked on the door.

'Come!' Miss Houghton's voice tinkled.

'Ah, Clare. Please sit down.' She took her glasses off and let them rest on her bosom, dangling from their gold chain. There was a plate on her desk of half-finished steak and kidney pie with peas and new potatoes.

'Now, first of all, my dear, can I say, "Well done." Well done, indeed! I have never, in all my years, read such a glowing report, as it were, from the Outward Bound. You really did find your feet, didn't you?'

'Well,' I replied, sitting back, crossing my legs and watching Miss Houghton retrieve bits of pastry from her cavernous cheeks, 'I really did enjoy it. I think I was lucky—I found some things much easier than other people did, and I'm not scared of heights.'

Miss Houghton swallowed her masticated food, folded her hands in her lap and leant forward.

'My dear, you may think that you did well, as it were, because of your own achievements, but it's not that which impressed your group leader. Oh no. It's how you were with those who were struggling that caught his eye.'

'Oh,' I said. I hadn't realized we were being watched so carefully, nor had I been aware that Miss Houghton would be sent a detailed report.

'Now, as you know,' Miss Houghton continued, about to say something that I definitely did not know, 'I make some of my most important decisions after my girls return from the Outward Bound, as it is my experience that it can be the making, as it were, or the breaking of some.

'Clare, it has been the making of you.' She

232

Andrew
and me in
jump-jockey
colours
knitted by
Grandma

Quirk and
I grew up
together

Me on Stuart with Mum

Andrew thought if he pouted he'd look thinner

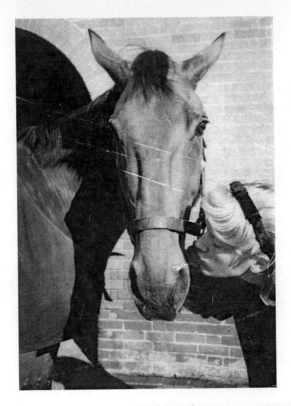

Me kissing a
reluctant
Pot Luck

Mad Henry

Lochsong (Scully) and Quirk (Dad) were inseparable

Quirk could fly, when he felt like it

I had a few fans when Respectable Jones
won at Chepstow.
Well, two fans

The Queen Mother at lunch in our dining room

My first ride in a race—beaten in a photo finish

Interview
in the
*Racing
Post*
(1989)

**FATHER AND DAUGHTER**  **IAN AND CLARE BALDING**

The first of an occasional series by Marcus Armytage

## Life of sport in the fast lane

Grinning after first ride on Mailman

Laughing with surprise as Knock Knock (25–1) wins
at Kempton

Knock Knock was a pretty boy and he knew it

Me riding Waterlow Park at Goodwood (left)

Song of
Sixpence

Winning the magic Mini, my first car

Who could
ever say boxers
aren't the most
beautiful dogs in
the world?

Attempting to build bridges with Princess Anne

Winning my weight in champagne. For once, the scales are tipped in my favour

At my skinniest to ride at Ascot

Respectable
Jones: relief
in victory

Andrew walks the course at Chepstow with me

I finally
get to
Cambridge

The beautiful
grounds of
Newnham
College

paused to savour another saliva-softened morsel of food and then delivered the line I never expected to hear: 'I would like to ask you if you would be my Head of House for next year.'

I sat up and coughed.

'You're joking?'

'I most certainly am not,' said Miss Houghton, offended that I could question her judgement.

How could I be Head of House? I had been suspended and de-housed, I had spent most of the Lower and Upper IV in tears, I had never had any responsibility and there were about ten people in my year more deserving of the accolade.

'I'm so sorry,' I finally spluttered. 'I didn't mean to suggest that you might make a joke over something so serious. Or that you might make a joke at all, about anything. I am just so . . . so surprised. Are you sure?'

'I have never been more sure of anything,' she said. 'Now if you could keep it all quiet until this evening, I would be most grateful. I will make an announcement, as it were, at our house meeting.'

She stood up and offered me her hand. I took it.

'You have come a long way, Clare. Well done. Well done indeed.'

When Miss Houghton made the revelation that evening, there was a sharp intake of breath. If we'd run a book on it, I'd have made myself a 100–1 shot and would have had no takers.

I found some change to take to the pay phone and ring home. My mother sounded as surprised as I was and was thrilled, whereas my father was matter-of-fact.

'Quite right,' he said. 'I always knew you would be.'

233

I genuinely think Dad had forgotten that I had ever been in trouble. Sometimes, it's quite useful that he never remembers a darned thing I have done.

## 14

## Ross Poldark

Ross Poldark was not a good everyday ride. He was fine in a race, when he loved to be in front of a crowd and tended to show his best side, but at home he pulled too hard and he wouldn't stand still to watch the other horses.

So Dad said I was to ride one of the racehorses called Miller's Tale. He was a son of Mill Reef, out of a mare called Canterbury Tale. It was a great name. Naming racehorses is a fun process and, for Mr Mellon, it was part of the challenge. He picked names that were memorable, clever and often funny. All racehorse names in Britain have to be registered with Weatherby's, who will ensure that names are not repeated and are not rude or offensive.

Names such as Wear the Fox Hat or Sofa King Fast have been rejected on the grounds of poor taste. Other racing authorities are sometimes not as eagle-eyed or as aware of how a name might sound when a commentator is in full flow. In South Africa, Hoof Hearted had ten runs without troubling the judge while, in France, Big Tits was similarly unsuccessful.

Much later in Mr Mellon's life, when discussions over the division of the family fortune were a little too regular for his liking, he bred a foal by Seeking the Gold out of You'd Be Surprised. He called it Wait for the Will.

The Queen has proven inventive at naming horses. She has a horse in training with my brother by Motivator out of Small Fortune—he is called Bank Bonus. Years ago, a horse of the Queen's by Young Generation was called Unknown Quantity, and one out of Contralto was called Soprano. Shaft of Light was out of Reflection. The royal names are often rather beautiful words or phrases—Zenith, Phantom Gold, Sleeping Beauty, Insular, Vitality or Tolerance (by Final Straw).

Dad got out his Dymo Maxi printing gun and typed out my name: Clare B. I was going to appear on the slate, like a proper jockey. He slotted it into a rung next to the bottom and put Miller's Tale in the gap for First Lot. I tried to persuade Dad to put Stuart's name on there too (as I would be riding him Second Lot, after breakfast), but he was a trainer—he had some pride. He didn't want to be typing out the name of a half-bred hunter who weighed over 700 kilos, or more than 110 stone. That would be plain embarrassing.

The next morning, Dad woke me up at six thirty and I headed out into the yard. I know it sounds odd, as I had spent my whole life there, but I really didn't know much about the way the yard actually worked. I had been banned from going anywhere near it for most of my childhood, and for the past four years I had been obsessed with my own ponies and horses at the stud.

My father employed around forty staff, and they all rode out until they got so old that their creaking bones wouldn't take it any more. If they still wanted to be around horses, and most of them did, they would help out around the yard, muck out, sweep up—there was always someone sweeping—or take the horses swimming. It was a job for life, and among the team was a hard core of men who had been there ever since my father had started training.

The Head Lad for nearly twenty years was Bill Palmer. He was a bow-legged ex-jump jockey whose face was weather-beaten from a life spent outdoors. He lived in brown jodhpurs, battered brown boots and a tweed cap. He used to ride in just the cap, but my father now insisted on and provided crash hats for everyone. He had seen too many head injuries. Bill was probably only a couple of years older than my father, but he seemed ancient.

'So, Miss Clare,' he said as he pulled down a saddle for me, 'going to ride a racehorse, are you? It's about time, I s'pose. Take this bridle for now,

237

and be sure to wash it after you've used it. There's a cover here for the girth that you need to put on the laundry pile afterwards. There you go.'

Bill handed me a light leather saddle that was no more than a handspan in width, two in length and absolutely flat. The lads in the yard all had their own tack and transferred it to each horse they rode. To prevent ringworm or other skin diseases being spread around the whole string, the girth was covered in a washable cotton sheath, which was cleaned after every use.

I set off to tack up Miller's Tale. He was so gentle and his skin so soft that I dared not brush it. I polished him instead, with a stable rubber. His muzzle felt like satin as he took a Polo from my hand.

One of our young apprentices, Seamus O'Gorman, was tacking up in the stable next door, so I asked him for some help. He showed me how to fold the sheet up over the top of the saddle and secure it with the surcingle, which went over the top of the girth and round the saddle, keeping it all in place. It was complicated and had to be done so fast. We pulled out at seven twenty on the dot. I made the best job I could and led Miller's Tale out in the middle of the yard.

'Forgotten the dandy brush?' Seamus was pulling bits of straw from Miller's Tale's black tail. 'And what about your hoof pick?'

Miller's Tale was spreading caked droppings all over the yard as his hooves met the tarmac and the contents were banged out. I had forgotten to pick out his feet. It was not a good start.

All the lads led their horses towards Bill, who grabbed the reins with his left hand and gave them a leg-up with his right. I watched how it was done and presented myself with my left leg sticking out.

'One, two, three,' said Bill, making a lifting motion on 'three'. Nothing happened. I stayed firmly rooted to the spot, hopping on one leg to keep up with Miller's Tale, who was walking towards the gates.

'You've got to help me,' explained Bill. 'You have to jump on "three".'

'Oh, I didn't realize. I always use the mounting block.'

I scrambled into the saddle in a rather undignified manner. Many of the younger lads just vaulted, wriggled and swung their legs in the saddle. For that, you need a little more natural spring than I possessed, and a little less dead weight.

The saddle for other equestrian pursuits is designed to help keep you in place, to allow you to sit deep and to 'feel' a horse. If a normal saddle is a chair, a racing saddle is a bar stool. You don't sit on it, you use it to perch.

Once I was on board, I gave Miller's Tale a pat and joined the crowd of chattering riders in the indoor school. My stirrups felt perilously short, but I didn't want to look as if I didn't know what I was doing.

The colts were at the front of the string, fillies at the back, and the geldings, like Miller's Tale, could go anywhere they wanted. We went right at the back. The indoor school is a big ring built of concrete breeze blocks, forming a circular corridor about eight feet wide. The outside wall is solid, the inside wall open to the elements from just above the height of a horse's head. If it rains and the wind is blowing in an unhelpful direction, the rider's face gets battered but the horse is fully protected. As was true for most things at Kingsclere, the comfort of the horses came first.

My father stood on his hack at the open gates to the indoor school. He watched each horse walk by and asked each rider if they felt OK—the horse that is, not the person. He wasn't interested in human coughs and colds, but if one of the horses had given a cough or taken a false step or felt strange for any reason, he wanted to know. I came past at the back of the string, my stirrups shorter than I had ever had them.

'All right there, Clare?' Dad called.

'Yes, I'm fine, thanks,' I replied.

'Not you, you idiot, Miller's Tale—is he all right?' he said firmly.

'Yes. Yes, I think so,' I said, not really sure what he was meant to feel like.

We walked another circuit or two, and then I heard Dad yell to Spider and John Matthias, who were at the front: 'Jog on now. Eight circuits. Come on, let's get going.'

The entire string of forty horses eased forward into trot. Some of them bucked, others snorted. The riders all sat tight, bracing themselves for the usual signs of freshness and well-being. It was then I noticed that I seemed to be the only one with my stirrups hoiked up short. The others all had a nice long length of leather, allowing their legs to wrap around their horses. I looked like a frog, hopping up and down as I did rising trot round and round in circles.

After three laps, I realized why they had their stirrups long. Doing rising trot with short stirrups is absolute agony. My thighs felt as if I had lit them

240

with a blowtorch. They were burning with pain. As we trotted past my father, still watching from the main entrance, I said, 'How many more?'

'Five.'

Good God, I wasn't sure I could last one more at this rate. It was nothing to do with my knee this time, but my muscles were protesting.

Bill was directly behind me.

'Getting a bit tired, Miss Clare?' he laughed. 'Rest your hands on his withers and just stand. He'll do the rest.'

The relief as I kept myself in the raised position was immediate. Miller's Tale plodded on, following the horse in front, and I could effectively freewheel until the cries of 'Whoah' came back through the string and we could pull up into walk. You can't do this on a fresh young two-year-old, but on a sweet old gelding like Miller's Tale the odd short cut is allowed.

'Best to wait until after you've trotted to shorten your stirrups,' said Bill as he pulled up his leathers.

Oh, what good advice. How very helpful. Thanks so much for telling me this now it's over.

We headed out of the school, round the cinder track and into the Starting Gate field. The 'round chippings' was a huge circular track of woodchip where we would have our first canter. The string stayed in exactly the same order, with the colts at the front and the fillies at the back.

Spider set the pace at the front, with every horse a length behind. Some pulled for their heads, others settled beautifully. Miller's Tale was a gent. He wouldn't dream of running away with a teenager on her first day riding a racehorse. Other horses would not be so kind.

241

Dad came trotting over to have a word.

'Let him have his head,' he said. 'You need to relax a little more. Flatten your back, keep your lower leg still—it's moving backwards and forwards all the time—and just keep a light contact on his mouth.'

He moved to the front of the string and started shouting out instructions. Nearly all of us were put into pairs, a few into a group of three, and one horse, who was particularly difficult, would canter on his own. I was paired with Bill, who was riding a horse called Mailman. The lads around me hitched their stirrups up a little bit shorter, so I did the same. It was a bit like getting into a steaming bath: I had got used to the temperature by now and could take a little more heat.

I followed Bill to the bottom of the straight four-furlong gallop, left a gap while he set off and let Miller's Tale find his stride. I sat up and rested my hands on the withers, slipping a finger under the neck strap to keep my hands still. Bill set off so fast I had to give my horse a squeeze to catch up. Then, suddenly, Miller's Tale was pulling my arms out. I could enjoy the magic of galloping at speed on an animal that has been designed to do exactly that.

The faster a horse is travelling, the more the weight of the rider needs to be positioned forward, over the shoulder. In the 1870s, Degas painted jockeys with long stirrups, their legs hanging down below a horse's stomach. This increases control and security, because it's hard to fall off, but impedes the speed of the horse.

Two American jockeys revolutionized the British jockeys' riding style. Willie Simms rode with great success in America and came to Britain in 1895, to be followed two years later by Tod Sloan. Sloan won five consecutive races at Newmarket in 1898 using the 'monkey crouch', which sealed the fate of the old British bolt-upright style.

Miller's Tale pulled himself up at the top of the hill—he had been doing this for so long he knew exactly where the gallop ended—and I patted him furiously as we walked along the path and down the hedgerow towards my father.

'Good boy. You are a good lad,' I gushed.

'All right, Bill?' my father asked.

'Yes, Guv'nor. He feels great. He'll be ready to run next week, I'd say.'

'All right, Clare?'

'Oh, he was lovely. Just lovely.' I was still patting Miller's Tale furiously.

'For Christ's sake, girl, he's not a pony. Leave him be for a second,' he snapped. 'What were you doing for the first two furlongs? Climbing all over Mailman, you were. You looked like a sack of potatoes. You need to find a bit of muscle somewhere.'

He was right. Riding racehorses was about as similar to my kind of riding as flying is to driving. I would need to start again from scratch.

Back in a normal saddle, I was still persevering with the madness of Henry. I took him up on the Downs and tried to make him jump the Team Chase course at a sensible pace. He hopped up and down on the spot and then shot forward, hot breath steaming from his nostrils like a dragon. I tried dropping my hands completely, thinking that, if I didn't resist him, he wouldn't fight for his head. That didn't work so well.

We came into the double of brush hedges that

243

separated the first paddock of jumps from the second so fast he tipped up at the second part. I crashed to the ground, cracking two ribs in the process. I didn't need to go to hospital, but it was darned uncomfortable for a while. Every time I laughed, it hurt, and when I tried to sneeze, my body would cut out just before 'atishoo'.

My point-to-point debut was put on hold.

\*      \*      \*

Most horses like attention and respond to affection. They like to be stroked, patted, kissed and cuddled. They like it almost as much as we do, but we do it for us, to make us feel better and to make us feel loved. It's why humans domesticated animals in the first place—to bring something warm and furry into our lives that needs us.

Richard Dawkins, the evolutionary biologist, argues that horses have domesticated humans as much as we have domesticated them. I believe that horses bring out the best in us. They judge us not by how we look, what we're wearing or how powerful or rich we are, they judge us in terms of sensitivity, consistency and patience. They demand standards of behaviour and levels of kindness that we, as humans, then strive to maintain.

I wonder if that's why some of the most famous and powerful people in the world—the Queen, the Aga Khan, Sheikh Mohammed, even Madonna—develop strong relationships with horses. Perhaps, surrounded by those who flatter, it's the only way they can get a true reflection of themselves. The horse will be their honest mirror.

During the First World War, the British Army

acquired over a million horses. The Great War was the last of the major cavalry encounters, because it saw the arrival of an enemy the horse could not match—the tank. The tank was stronger, but the horses provided the men with so much more than just a means of transport. For many, the only thread connecting them with sanity in the face of such despair and chaos was the daily care for their horse. Michael Morpurgo's *War Horse* tells that story through the eyes of Joey, a plough horse who is called up to fight.

In the midst of extreme inhumanity, man is given a chance to show his humanity. Respect for human life was disintegrating before their eyes, but the moral code of care for their horses held as strong as it could until the end. If only we could say that we honoured them after the end of the war but, largely speaking, we did not. Of the half-million or so horses that survived, only 62,000 were deemed worthy of being transported home. It was the largest ever loss of British horses.

I rode a horse for a while who could have been an officer's charger. Henry had run away with me once too often, Stuart wasn't ready for competition and Quirk was lame, so my mother organized for us to borrow a horse for the summer. A cartoonist called Tony Cuthbert who drag hunted with the Berks & Bucks had been trying his hand at eventing, but it wasn't working out that well. He was having particular trouble with this one horse, so he figured a break for both of them might be the answer.

Tony's horsebox was even bigger than the six-berth box that took the racehorses to all parts of the country. It didn't hold as many horses, but it had living quarters, a shower and a TV. It was too big to park at the stud, so it had to be taken up to the yard for the ramp to be let down. I had no idea what sort of a horse was coming to stay, but I hadn't expected this.

If the horsebox was enormous, so was the horse that emerged. Tony said he was over seventeen hands high, but no one had ever been able to get a measuring stick near enough to him to get an accurate reading. He was called Pot Luck and, as he came down the ramp, he was dripping with sweat.

'Hates the horsebox,' said Tony. 'He's a shocker to load and doesn't like travelling.'

I took the rope from Tony and put my hand towards Pot Luck's head to calm him. He pulled away from me and put his ears back.

'Thanks so much for having him.' Tony was talking to my mother. 'Weight off my mind, to be honest. I'm not sure he likes me much.'

I led Pots away, and we walked slowly down to the stud. He spooked at a bird in the tree, at the foals, at the tractor in its shed and, seemingly most terrifying of all, at a dandelion. Yes, a dandelion.

This giant of a horse, who weighed enough to crush a lorry and looked as if he could lead the Charge of the Light Brigade, was scared of his own shadow. He hesitated at the red-brick arch that led into the yard and started to resist me. I let the rope go slack and moved back towards him.

'Come on, you old fool,' I said, trying to sound jolly and encouraging. 'Honestly, there's nothing to be scared of. It's just an arch.'

Carol came out of the tack room at the far end carrying a head collar. Well, it might as well have been an air gun. Pots rushed backwards; the rope in my hands suddenly tugged hard, pulling me into the air with the force of it. I clung on and used all my weight to set myself against him. I didn't want to get into a tug of war so, as soon as I was close enough, I slackened the rope again and let him stand.

He was quivering like a jellyfish. He wasn't like Frank or Quirk or Hattie, who could behave like this out of naughtiness. He was genuinely terrified. I stood just under his head, and waited. I talked to him constantly, in a low voice, just nonsense but getting him used to the sound of me.

I got a packet of Polos out of my pocket and put one in my hand, not offering it to him but just letting it sit in the palm of my hand. Pots could have trampled me, he could have bitten me or pulled away and got loose, but he didn't. All horses are curious—whether they are foals or adults— and they will stay with the thing or the person that interests them.

The usual clattering of the stud carried on around us, the sounds of horses being brought in from the fields, being fed, watered and groomed. I explained to Pots who they all were and what was happening. Slowly, his head came lower and, eventually, I felt his breath behind my neck. I carried on chatting, trying not to move my hands or my head and, as his nostrils came towards my left ear, I started to breathe more deeply, through my nose, as a horse does.

He hesitated for a second and then kept coming, his head appearing over my shoulder and reaching for my hand. I raised my palm just a fraction to make it easier for him, but his head shot back and we had to start again from scratch. I have no idea how long it took, but I had time on my side and I knew that this first bonding would be crucial.

When Pot Luck finally succumbed, he took the Polo from my palm, chewed it and spat it out. His top lip curled back in disgust, and I started laughing. He looked so funny, behaving like a baby spitting out its food. He let me stroke the side of his enormous head and, as I slowly inched closer, he leant towards me.

'Here we go, big man. Do you want to see your new room?'

I started to walk steadily towards the arch, leaving the rope slack so that, if he came, he was doing it because he wanted to. Gingerly, he placed one hoof in front of the other and followed me into the yard. We turned left towards his box, where Carol had laid a deep bed of fresh straw and a big pile of sweet hay. As we got towards the door, Pots barged past me, squeezing me against the side. I let go of the rope as he charged in, and slammed the door shut before he could change his mind.

In the stable on the opposite side of the quadrangle, the noble head of Ross Poldark poked over the top of his door. He was having his summer break but, earlier that year, he had, finally, carried me in my first point-to-point.

It had been at Hackwood Park on Saturday 4 April in the Ladies' Open. I had borrowed Dad's racing breeches and boots. Both were too big, but he would not allow me to wear my eventing gear. For one thing, it was too heavy, and for another, as he said, 'You'll look like a bloody amateur.'

'But I thought this was an amateur sport? Isn't that what point-to-pointing is?' I asked.

'Yes, but there's amateur and there's *amateur*.'

It was clear I could be one but not the other. I

could take part in this sport for the love of it, as in the French or Latin translation of 'amateur', but I must not seem amateur in the British sense of 'a bit rubbish'. The point-to-point has its roots in Ireland, where, two hundred and fifty years ago, people would race on horseback from one point to another. Often, they would use the steeple of a church as a highly visible point to race towards—hence the term 'steeplechasing'.

I didn't really want to ride in a point-to-point at all. It was just one of those things that had taken on a life of its own. Dad had said it would happen, and therefore it was happening. The trouble was, I couldn't win. I could, in theory, win the actual race, but if I did it would be Poldark's victory, and if I didn't it would be my fault. I felt inadequate and nervous, so I dealt with it by being grumpy and pretending I didn't care.

Hackwood Park is on the outskirts of Basingstoke, less than half an hour from Kingsclere. I travelled in the horsebox with Mum and Liz, who would lead up Poldark. Dad and Andrew came later in the car. The weather was atrocious, so the field had been reduced to just four. As long as I stayed in the saddle, I thought, I would be placed in my very first race.

The circuit at Hackwood is a tight left-hand oval of only a mile, so you have to go three times round. I walked the course with my father, who tried to explain to me the importance of taking the inside line. With it being such a tight course, he reckoned I could save lengths if I was always on the inside at the bends. I was more worried about counting the number of times we were going round so that I didn't ride for home a circuit too early.

I headed off to the ladies' changing room, which was one section of a large tent, to get ready. My father's breeches were too loose around the waist and kept falling down at the back. His boots were made of paper-thin black leather, with brown tops; they were classical and smart, but the soles felt like cardboard. I stuffed the toes with cotton wool. I wore my back protector over a cotton T-shirt. Then a cream silk stock around my neck tied with a stock-pin that used to belong to my great-grandmother and, finally, my father's colours—turquoise with brown sleeves and a turquoise cap.

This was to be a rather public debut. There had been a piece in the *Racing Post* saying that I was making my race-riding debut. Grandma was there, along with girls from school for whom Hackwood was their local course. There were bookmakers taking actual money from people who were backing me. This was not a game any more—there were investments from people I had never met.

I emerged from the changing room in my kit, feeling distinctly uncomfortable. I hated wearing a back protector, because it made me look like a hunchback and, at sixteen, I was far more concerned about how I looked than the protection it offered my spine. Dad had the saddle ready, with racing girths and surcingle balancing on top. The weight for all ladies' races at point-to-points is eleven stone, including saddle. Some of the smaller girls needed weight cloths with lead weights to make their weight up. Suffice to say, I did not.

Dad disappeared to saddle up Poldark and I waited with the other three girls—well, women— who were riding in the race. One was Amanda Harwood, whose father, Guy, was also a trainer.

He had trained Dancing Brave, one of the most brilliant horses of all time and number one on most people's lists of 'horses that should have won the Derby'. He finished a narrow second in 1986, having won the 2000 Guineas. He would go on to win the Eclipse, the King George and the Arc.

Amanda was a year older than me and had ridden winners already. She was focussed and serious. We stood, the four of us, waiting to walk out from the tent to the rainy paddock. I think that was the worst moment of the lot. I tried to lighten the mood by chatting away, saying things I thought were funny but, for the moments before a race, were deeply inappropriate. I was getting on my own nerves, and no doubt theirs as well.

I walked out into the centre of the paddock. My father looked serious; my mother, nervous. My brother looked odd. He was wearing Dad's old leather jacket, one of my shirts hanging loose over his jeans and a grey cardigan. It wasn't the clothes I minded—I had been telling him exactly what to wear for about five years—it was the hair.

Unlike the rest of us, Andrew had curly hair. It sat on top of his head like a fluffy toupee. He had tried Brylcreem, gel, mousse, fudge and wax. He had even tried hoof oil but, despite the rain, it was still a bouffant, like Lionel Blair's.

Dad talked me through exactly what he wanted me to do. He was firm with his instructions and went on and on about sticking to the inside rail. I was distracted by the crowds of people thronging round the paddock, so I wasn't really listening. When he gave me a leg-up, I missed my timing fractionally. It wasn't the most stylish or dignified arrival in the saddle. I heard tittering in the crowd, and voices saying, 'Are you sure she knows how to ride?' and 'I know the horse is top class but even a great horse can't carry a passenger who doesn't know how to drive.'

Liz looked up at me and smiled.

'He's really well today,' she said. 'He's been pulling me round this paddock. You just sit tight and you'll be fine.'

Poldark was elegant, proud and, luckily for me, knew exactly what he was doing. We cantered down to look at the first fence, a peculiar tradition that I am sure is more for the benefit of the rider than the horse. I like it because, even in the midst of the hard-nosed industry of horse-racing, it reveals a softer side—the side that acknowledges a horse's brain and character.

Poldark didn't look that closely, he looked over the fence, his ears pricked and his gaze far into the distance, as if he saw beyond the tight turns of Hackwood. A few cameras clicked—he was, after all, extremely photogenic. My father always reckoned he had 'the look of eagles'.

We circled at the start, the four of us saying nothing to each other. I was looking at the crowd, while the other three were looking at the starter. They turned as the starter raised his flag and shouted, 'Ready?'

Amanda and the others were absolutely ready. I was away with the fairies. The starter's flag dropped, and the three of them went thundering towards the first fence. I heard my father's voice shouting at me to get a move on, realized they wouldn't be called back and pointed Poldark in the right direction.

On the plus side, we had a clear view of all our

fences and were in no danger of jumping into the back of the other runners or being brought down if one of them fell. On the minus side, we were tailed off, a fence behind Amanda and the others. As I passed the start again, I heard my father shouting, 'Give him a bloody kick! Lay up. Come on, lay up!'

I duly moved my lower leg as much as is possible when you're perched up a horse's neck like a monkey up a tree. Poldark responded and started to make ground on the others. He jumped brilliantly, seeing his own stride and adjusting accordingly if he was slightly wrong. I kept my hands in the neck strap and tried not to interfere. I lost my balance a couple of times on landing, and my reins were so slippery that I didn't have any grip, but he stayed so straight and true that I was never in danger of falling off.

He sailed over the Open Ditch, and I could hear my schoolfriends shouting their encouragement. By the time we passed the start again, I was only a few lengths behind the others. I hugged the inside rail and, as we turned into the home straight for the final time, with two fences to jump, I snuck up the inside of Amanda Harwood.

'What the hell are you doing there?' I heard her say, before she gave her horse two cracks with the whip. We jumped the last near enough together before her horse, Red Shah, picked up again and forged clear.

I let Poldark ease down (or I was so exhausted I stopped riding) as we were well clear of the others, and we finished second. The first time you race over three miles is an absolute killer. Liz ran to meet me to lead Poldark back towards the winner's enclosure, her face wreathed in smiles. She patted him and me and told us how brilliant we were.

I could see my mother having words with Dad as they stood in the place reserved for the second. I thought he was about to launch into a Grade A bollocking, but he smiled and said, 'Did you enjoy that? There's a bit we need to work on, but not bad, girl. Not bad for a first effort.'

'I got up Amanda Harwood's inner!' I said, relieved that he had ignored the crime of getting left at the start. 'Did you see? I got right up her inner!'

He had seen, as had Guy Harwood, who was giving his daughter grief for allowing it to happen.

I saw Grandma walking towards us, putting money into her wallet. She smiled.

'Well done,' she said. 'At least you didn't fall off. That would have been embarrassing.'

'I hope you didn't back me,' I replied. 'I would have hated to lose you money.'

'Don't be stupid,' said Grandma, peering down at me. 'I backed Amanda Harwood. She's a proper jockey.'

\*     \*     \*

The Downe House school prefects are called seniors. They are elected by the whole school and the members of staff, with the person winning most votes being declared the Head Senior. My mother had been Deputy Head Senior in 1966. In 1988, my name was on the voting list. By virtue of being Head of House, I had been heard and seen a lot around school.

When the voting was over, the results were announced in the large dining room. The

254

incumbent Head Senior, Sarah Carter, revealed that I would succeed her. Toe, Heidi, Char, Shorty, KT, Becks and Gerry were all elected seniors as well, and my deputy was a laid-back, kind-hearted girl called Marina Mohammed-Arif. Ours was a band of genuinely close friends, and we were determined to work as a team.

Having been suspended and de-housed in the Lower IV, four years later I was Head of House and Head Girl. Miss Farr pinned the metal badge on my cloak.

'Well, well,' she said. 'I knew you were worth giving a second chance, but even I could not have predicted this. Quite a turn-around, my girl. Quite a turn-around.'

She held my shoulders and smiled.

Now, when I walked into Miss Farr's drawing room to sit in the chair opposite her desk, I could relax. We met once a week, and she would ask me about concerns the girls might have. She always listened to me with patience and consideration. She gave the impression that she valued what I had to say and, in return, I made sure it was worth hearing.

It's hard to know exactly what makes any of us click in our teenage years. It's not an easy time of life, and you need people on your side. I had Miss Farr, and I had a brilliant English teacher called Miss Healy.

I had never met anyone as clever as Miss Healy. She was only a few years older than us, had left Oxford the year before and this was her first job. She taught me that poetry rewards the investigative mind.

'Look beyond the words, Clare. What does it say to you?' She looked at me and silently challenged

255

me to allow my brain to expand.

'The poet is a part of this, but he is not all of it,' she said. 'He writes the words and they mean what they mean to him, but you, the reader, you fulfil the chemical experiment. You complete the poem. Without you, those are just words. With you and your interpretation, it becomes poetry.'

Miss Healy was so detached, so self-contained. She made things happen. She read extensively to arrive at an informed opinion so that she could be governed by what she thought of the world, not what others thought about her.

I wanted to be like that. I wanted to think for myself, not be consumed by what others thought of me. I wanted to be the subject of the sentence of my life, not the object—to control and initiate the things that happened, not to allow life to happen *to* me or be about what other people thought of me. Most of all, I wanted to have an identity that was not linked to my surname or to the achievements of my family. Perhaps that is why I had been so reluctant to embrace horse-racing or even point-to-pointing. It seemed such a cliché. I would be condemned to the title of 'Ian Balding's daughter'.

## 15

# Mailman

'I think I'm having a nervous breakdown,' I said.

'Don't be ridiculous. People like us do not have nervous breakdowns.' My grandmother was standing in our kitchen. 'Only people with too much time on their hands do that.'

Apparently, 'people like us' didn't have depression either.

'Deeply selfish,' said my grandmother.

We weren't obese ('lack of self-control') or anorexic (ditto). We didn't get pregnant out of wedlock and we didn't 'do' divorce. When one of my relatives suddenly left his wife for another woman, Grandma said, 'If he wanted to have sex, I really don't see why he had to make such a fuss about it. Just have an affair and keep quiet. But this—so public and, frankly, so cheap.'

Grandma used to walk every day, her walking stick in hand, striding out across the fields with her greedy Labrador, Chico, or her whippets—first Dawn, and then the ill-fated Dusk. She was a dog person. I always got the impression that she thought cats rather common—which is why it was so out of character that she had two of them: Tommy and Katie.

She always called Tommy by his name, and he followed her around, but Katie she called Titty-Wee.

'It's the ugliest name I can think of,' she said. 'And she is an ugly cat. Useless as well.'

Andrew and I had never had much to do with the cats, apart from carrying out a practical experiment to prove whether or not they always landed on their feet. This involved rolling each one up in a blanket and dropping it over the banister from the top of the stairs. Yes, was the answer, they did land on their feet. We did not get the chance to repeat the experiment—not because Grandma discovered us (she may have approved) but because both cats disappeared whenever we walked into the house.

The tension I was feeling was because my 'A' levels were imminent.

'Pressure?' Grandma scoffed. 'You have no idea what pressure is.'

I expected my grandmother to launch into a list of her most grievous worries: inheritance tax, the problems of finding a good butler these days and the difficulty of cleaning raw silk. Instead, she said, 'I was in the WRNS during the war, you know. I loved it. We drove armoured vehicles, deciphered codes and learned how to fire a gun. I even took an electrician's course. I'm a whizz with a bunch of wires.'

I had never imagined my grandmother doing anything except issuing orders to other people who 'did' things. I knew she was intelligent—she did the crossword every day and she played Scrabble—but I hadn't realized she could be practical as well.

'It was a funny time, the war,' she said. 'The world sort of turned upside down for a while. It was better when the men came back.'

Now here's a thing I have never understood. My grandmother was denied a trainer's licence because of a misogynistic law, she was one of the first female members of the Jockey Club, she was a steward at various top racecourses and a director of Newbury racecourse, she managed a farm and a stud, she was one of the most independent and self-sufficient women I have ever met—and yet she did not believe in equal rights for women. Nor did anyone in my family.

'You can't do that.'

'Why on earth not?'

'Well, you're a girl, for starters.'

My Uncle Toby, whom I adored, used to say 'Women ain't people.' My father and brother would laugh along. My mother treated it as a joke. I never laughed, because I was appalled.

'Are you turning into a *feminist*?' my mother would ask, raising her left eyebrow. She rolled the distasteful word around her tongue and spat it out.

I was reading Mary Wollstonecraft at the time, so I was full of *A Vindication of the Rights of Woman*. She wrote it in 1792, and I was overflowing with righteous indignation that we had achieved so little in the two centuries since.

'I would hope I am a feminist, yes,' I said.

I went on strike, refusing to load the dishwasher or help lay the table unless Dad and Andrew did so as well. Mum never asked them to, so why should I do it?

'Because you're a girl,' said my brother, refusing to budge from the window bench on the inside of the table, where it was nearly impossible to get out anyway. 'It's your job.'

I walked out, in a huff, and heard him saying, 'I just don't know why she gets so wound up about it. It's not as if women can't vote.'

My father has only just stopped putting his coffee mug, still half full, in the kitchen sink and started putting it in the dishwasher, where it belongs. He is seventy-three years old and has never done the supermarket shop. He is not an idiot, but he has found it suits him much better to pretend he can't work the cooker or the dishwasher or the washing machine, and my mother has let him get away with it.

'You will get along a lot better in life if you learn to massage a man's ego,' my mother told me. 'Even if you have a good idea, it's much better to let a man think it's his idea.'

I know what she was trying to do, but I just couldn't see the point of massaging anyone's ego. If they were good at what they did, I'd say so, but if they weren't, why would I lie, just to make a man feel superior?

I vowed that I would not pretend that I was ditzy or uninspired, I would not back down from doing the things I wanted to do and I would not wait for a man to define my position in the world. That did not mean I did not like men, but I could not deal with men who did not recognize a woman's value beyond the size of her breasts.

I tried to say all of that without bursting into tears, which would have rather ruined the whole effect. My mother raised that dangerous left eyebrow again and said, 'Well, I'm sure you feel better now you've got all that off your chest.'

\*       \*       \*

I had been to a meeting with the careers officer at Downe House, a short, round woman called Mrs Trumble. She told me I was being overambitious in trying for law at Cambridge.

'Honestly,' she drawled, in the most acerbically posh accent you can imagine, 'I cannot think what it is that makes you think you are capable of Oxbridge. It is misplaced confidence, I am afraid. The other universities will take it out on you, mark my words.'

In the short term, Mrs Trumble was proved right. The offer from Cambridge was two 'A's and a 'B'. I got an 'A' and two 'C's. Not good enough for my first choice, nor for my second- and third-choice universities. I left the results slip on the kitchen table and ran down to the stud. I tacked up Stuart and disappeared for over two hours. We galloped, we jumped, we stopped to look at the view, and I told him everything as I let the tears flow. By the time I got back, I had dealt with my own disappointment. What was harder to deal with was the disappointment of my parents.

My father could not understand why his old college, Christ's, who had taken him with no 'A' levels at all, on the basis of his ability to catch a book flung at him by the senior tutor, would not take me. Nor would Bristol, nor would Exeter.

'I didn't get the grades,' I explained for the third time. 'It's really simple. They made me an offer and I couldn't match it.'

'But I don't understand,' he kept saying, over and over again.

Many years later, I discovered that part of his anger derived from the knowledge that he had made a rather large donation to the Christ's College fund. He insists that he did not try to buy me into Cambridge but I was not convinced and could happily have drowned him in the horses' swimming pool.

*       *       *

'How much do you weigh?' My father was speaking as he read the *Sporting Life*. I was sitting at the breakfast table, buttering a piece of toast.

'I've no idea.' I hadn't weighed myself since the spring, when I was riding in point-to-points. 'I've been a bit busy taking exams to worry about it.'

'Well, run upstairs and use my scales. I need to know exactly how much you weigh.'

He had bought some new scales with weights along the top which you moved to position for stones and pounds. They were so accurate, they could tell you if you had put on or lost ounces. I moved the weights along to what I hoped I was, and then moved them along a bit more, when I realized I was a bit heavier than I had thought.

'Ten stone five,' I said, as I came back into the kitchen.

'Well, no more of that then.' Dad pointed at the toast and butter. 'You need to be nine stone ten in ten days' time. You're riding in a flat race at Salisbury, so you'd better get sweating.'

He asked me my weight that evening, the next morning and again the next evening. He lent me his sweat suit and showed me how to work the sauna.

'Don't let it get too hot,' he said. 'If you do, you'll just burn. Keep splashing the water on the coals here. That'll make it steam, and it'll help you sweat more. Then lie down on the bed for a while with lots of towels round you, and you'll sweat a bit more. You can lose six or seven pounds in a day if you do it right.'

What he meant was he could lose six or seven pounds in a day. I never could. Two or three, yes, but never more than that. I rode out three horses every morning, went running in the afternoon in the sweat suit or cycled for miles on the exercise bike, wearing the sweat suit and listening to INXS on my Walkman. Then I would sit in the sauna for forty minutes. I tried to read books there, but the glue in the spines melted and the pages fell out, so I turned to magazines and would emerge from the sauna with print all over my hands and face.

I stood on the scales at least six times a day and, if I wasn't moving the weights to the left, I felt worthless. As for eating and drinking: half a cup of tea when I woke up, before I rode out First Lot; a slice of melon at breakfast with half a glass of orange juice and slurp of coffee; a salad for lunch;

and a ready-made Lean Cuisine meal for supper. I was so tired from the running and the sweating that I was good for nothing in the evening, and would collapse into bed by nine o'clock, hoping beyond hope that I would wake up two pounds lighter than I had gone to sleep.

It was hard work, and it was horribly boring, because all I could talk about was how many pounds I had lost or needed to lose and whether chicken and orange or beef stroganoff was my favourite flavour Lean Cuisine. I was obsessed. I trimmed my fingernails, shaved my legs, cut my hair, all to save the odd ounce. I loved being able to fit into slimmer clothes, and I felt more confident about my body, but the dieting was not about looking good, it was all about numbers. How much did I weigh? Dad needed to know exactly.

The answer was that I weighed nine stone thirteen pounds. I nearly fainted if I stood up too fast, and my mouth was dry with dehydration. I was going to have to put up overweight, which would be broadcast humiliatingly on the loudspeaker system, but I could do no more. If I had been born a light-boned waif-like thing, none of this would have been such a heart-breaking effort.

\*         \*         \*

On 9 July 1988, I rode in a mixed amateur race at Salisbury on Mailman, the tall, lean, liver chestnut horse with a white blaze down the front of his face. He was nine years old now, and set in his ways. At home, he was a difficult ride and pulled so hard that only Bill Palmer could ride him. Dad had suggested I ride work on him, just once on the Downs, so

264

that I could get a feel for him. He ran away with me when we were doing our steady first canter and scooted past all the other horses in the string.

I could hear Dad swearing at me, and I swore back because I was grouchy. I was doing the best I could, but my strength had gone. We set off over a mile for a piece of work that was meant to be at three-quarter pace for six furlongs, quickening up to full racing pace for the final two furlongs. I struggled to keep Mailman at three-quarter pace, so we ended up going flat out for six furlongs and steady for the last two, by which time he was exhausted. Dad said I was useless, but he still insisted that I should ride in the race itself.

I was terrified. What if I couldn't hold Mailman and he took off with me? There were fifteen other runners, and I'd look a fool. It would be shown in betting shops around the country. I may not have been getting paid for riding him, but there was plenty at stake.

Salisbury is a right-handed course in the shape of a number 9 with the loop on the left of the tail. The mile-and-a-quarter start is at the top of the tail, and you are fairly quickly into a tight, right-handed bend. I walked the course carefully to see if it was slippery on the inside, or if there were ridges to avoid. The straight was long, more than five furlongs, so I figured there was plenty of time to make up ground if I needed to. That's if I could settle Mailman behind the other runners.

There were twenty-three runners for the Brooke Bond Tea Cup Handicap Stakes for Amateur Riders. I had weighed out at ten stone two, including a saddle and the lightest girths Spider could find. I blocked my ears as the announcement was made on the public-address system that Miss C. Balding would be carrying three pounds overweight. I had had my hair cut even shorter to try to save a few ounces, but it wasn't enough.

It was my first time jumping out of starting stalls and I had watched videos of professional jockeys doing it to try to work out how to avoid bouncing up and down in the saddle as if you're on a space hopper. I decided that the best way was to lean forwards, grip the neck strap tightly and use it to pull myself up into 'race position' as the stalls opened. Professionals do not do this (most of them don't use neck straps), but for a thick-thighed amateur whose bottom had a gravitational force worthy of its own square law, it was a sensible option.

When the stalls open, there is a fractional delay before any of the horses react. In that moment, the world seems to stop and then suddenly bursts into life again. The field set off at a fearsome gallop. There is never any lack of pace in an amateur race, as someone is nearly always getting run away with. In this case, I was grateful it wasn't me. Mailman settled into his stride in the middle of the field, and I waited for things to happen.

What I know now is that, in most flat races, you do not have the luxury of 'waiting for things to happen'. You make them happen. Jane Allison, who was riding a three-year-old trained by Paul Cole, made her move four furlongs from home and shot clear of the field. With apologies to all those who may have had money on Mailman, I have to confess I did not even notice. I was merrily galloping along, saying, 'Good boy,' in Mailman's ear, thrilled that he had settled so well and thinking about how long the straight was.

With three furlongs to go, I could hear shouts and the crack of whips around me and, with two furlongs to go, I figured I'd better try to do something about it. Jane was ten lengths ahead, and the rest of the runners had nothing left to give, so Mailman and I set off in lone pursuit. I could see the orange colours of Storada getting closer and closer. There was a roar from the grandstand that I'd never heard before as punters who had backed Mailman or Storada shouted their chosen horse home. When you're standing in that crowd, it's like listening to an orchestra reaching the end of a crescendo. When you're riding, the wind rushing past your ears means that the music stops and starts.

I tried to move in rhythm with Mailman, urging him to quicken. I didn't use my whip because, despite my father's careful instruction, I did not feel confident at all about taking one hand off the reins for fear of losing my balance. I may have tapped him down the shoulder, but no more than that. We were making ground with every stride, reaching Storada's quarters then drawing level as the winning post came closer.

I looked sideways as we flashed past the post. A stride after it, Mailman was in front. On the line, where it counted, he was a head behind.

'Bloody hell, that was close,' said Jane, as she puffed out her cheeks in relief.

The result of the photo finish was announced as we pulled up.

'First, number 6, Storada. Second, number 22, Mailman.'

I should have been disappointed. I should have

267

been frustrated at my lack of urgency, but I was too busy being elated. It was such a thrill, a total rush of adrenalin to have survived in that big a field, and for a nine-year-old gelding to have run that well against a three-year-old colt. I was beaming as Jo, who looked after Mailman, led him back into the winner's enclosure. Spider had given him a pat and said, 'Well done.' Everyone seemed really pleased.

Except the punter who shouted, 'A few less pies next time, Clare!'

And my father.

'You should have bloody won' were his first words. 'What the hell were you doing? It's a race, not a bloody Pony Club event. There are no rosettes for finishing second.'

I kept smiling, slid down from the saddle, patted Mailman and kissed him on the nose. My mother walked with me back into the weighing room, where I stood on the scales to check that my weight was the same as before the race. Much as I would have loved the experience to have miraculously turned me into a featherweight jockey, the scales read exactly the same.

Dad fumed pretty much the whole way home and made me watch the video again and again while he told me exactly where I should have made my move and what I needed to do to galvanize even more acceleration from my horse. He made me sit on the arm of the sofa, as Andrew and I used to do for the Grand National, and practise using my whip.

'You don't need to use it often,' he explained, 'but the noise will make a horse run faster. You make sure you hit him in the right place, up here.'

He took my arm and showed me how to raise the stick so that I would hit a horse on the top of the quarters, where there is plenty of protection, rather than down the flank, where the skin is thin. I was used to carrying a whip for everyday riding, and for eventing. When you're trying to control half a ton of horse, it helps if you've got something that can get their attention and remind them of your presence, but I had rarely had cause to raise the whip in anger. Dad was trying to show me how to use it effectively, judiciously and tactically—never in anger, and always in rhythm with the movement of the horse.

I had spent so much of my life resenting the hold horse-racing had over the rest of my family that I had deliberately avoided getting too involved. I recognized the good horses and enjoyed the big races but, beyond that, my knowledge and my concern was limited. Overnight, I was interested in racing.

Now I had actually ridden in a race and felt a response from a racehorse, I was intrigued. I rode out each morning with the rest of the yard, rode work on Wednesdays and Saturdays and, steadily, I got the hang of it. I concentrated hard on my diet, ran every day in a sweat suit or went on the exercise bike and weighed myself constantly. The markers on the scales started to go to the left.

Three weeks after that first ride at Salisbury, Mailman and I teamed up again, this time at Ayr. It was the PG Tips Tea Cup Handicap Stakes for Amateur Riders. There were eight runners on a miserable, grey, soggy day on the west coast of Scotland. Mrs McDougald's colours were pale grey and pink. In the rain, they stuck to my skin and became see-through. This was my major concern as I cantered down to the start, having weighed out at ten stone exactly. I had decided to ride in a much smaller saddle so that I could make the weight. Mum was in charge this day, as my father had runners down south, and she raised that damned eyebrow as she collected the saddle from the weighing room.

'Are you sure you'll be all right in this?' She lifted the saddle between her thumb and forefinger. It was barely bigger than her hand.

'I'll be fine,' I snapped. 'Just stop fussing.'

Mailman, on the strength of his good run at Salisbury, was second favourite. I walked into the paddock to join my mother and Andrew, who was on hand as a would-be assistant trainer. In theory, he was meant to give me my instructions, but all he said was: 'Wow, those colours are totally see-through.'

Mum gave me a leg-up in the paddock, and I felt for the stirrups. They were much shorter than I wanted, so I leant down to adjust them. There were no more holes in the leathers—they were at maximum length. I had never ridden in this saddle before and hadn't thought to check the stirrup leathers until now. It was too late.

Of course I said nothing to my mother. I cantered down to the start looking like Lester Piggott, and just hoped that my legs would hold out for the mile and a quarter on the way back. I think my father had told me to ride a similar race to Salisbury—try to settle Mailman in the middle of the field but make my move sooner and be aware of what the other runners were doing.

'Remember, it's a bloody race!' he said.

It's hard sometimes to do exactly what you're told to do, especially if the stalls open and you find yourself in front. So I just let Mailman gallop. He wasn't out of control, he was setting an even tempo, and I didn't have an awful lot of choice about it. I figured he'd run in around fifty races, so he knew what he was doing.

I could feel the rain lashing at my face, and I couldn't hear anything. As we approached the final furlong, still no cracking of whips, no hooves, no shouting. I let my reins out a few inches, Mailman stretched his head forward and we stuck close to the rail as we covered that last 220 yards. With a hundred yards to go, I suddenly heard something.

Dad had told me not, under any circumstances, to look round: just keep looking forward, ride for the line and keep going right past the post. So all I had was this sense of impending doom. A whistling noise, a roaring, a blast of breathing that was intensifying with every stride.

'Grrr. Go-on, go-on!'

It was a man's voice. I could feel a horse's head at Mailman's tail, then at his quarters, then level with his girth. I kept pushing, but I didn't pick up my stick. I was frightened that, if I did, I might fall off. My legs had gone to jelly. I looked up and saw the winning post and, as we passed it, I glanced sideways. We had held on by a neck from Simon Whitaker on the favourite.

I had ridden my first winner on only my second ride. Simon shouted, 'Well done,' as we tried to pull up, and all I was thinking was: Don't fall off, don't fall off.

I clamped my hands down on Mailman's withers and used them for support, as I hoped that he would naturally slow down to a trot. He did, and he turned himself around and started cantering gently

271

back to the entrance to the paddock. That horse could have done it all on his own if he had to. I had merely been a passenger, and I knew it.

Mum was waiting in the number one spot under a large umbrella, her face lit up by a huge grin. I slid off and, as my feet touched the ground, my legs gave way. I tried to cover it up, but my mother is not a fool. I assume that people thought she was hugging me rather than holding me up.

'Those stirrups were much too short,' she whispered. 'Don't make that mistake again.'

I only rode in four more races in 1988, but three of them were sponsored by Brooke Bond, because my father had suddenly realized that I had earned enough points to be in contention for the Brooke Bond Oxo Amateur Riders' Championship, a series of ten races for amateur riders. The winner would get a brand-new Austin Rover Mini. I had not yet taken my driving test.

The final race of the Brooke Bond series was at Haydock on 1 October. No one had ridden more than one qualifying winner, so the points were wide open. I had earned five points for winning at Ayr and three for finishing second at Salisbury, so was the joint leader. The Princess Royal had won one of the qualifying races, as had Jane Allison and the leading female amateur Elaine Bronson. Any one of ten riders could win the Mini outright if they finished in the first four.

If none of them did (and not all were riding in the race), I would be the joint winner with Yvonne Haynes. If she finished in the first four and I did not, she would win the Mini on her own.

There were sixteen women and four men making up the field of twenty and, for the only time in the year, the ladies' changing room at Haydock Park was full. Loudest of the female riders was Sharron Murgatroyd, who three years later would suffer a fall at the final hurdle of a race at Bangor that would deny her the use of her limbs. Since the age of thirty-one, Sharron has been a tetraplegic and has written fabulous prose and poetry about her life then and now.

Murgy, as we called her, was taking the mickey.

'You can't win the car, Balding!' she shouted. 'You can't even drive. How are you going to get it home? In the back of Daddy's horsebox?'

Sharron was never unkind, but she made it clear that I was among the fortunate ones. I did not have to ring unsympathetic trainers begging for rides or travel the length and breadth of the country on no travel expenses riding no-hopers in egg and spoon races. I had my father's support; I had a silver spoon sticking out of my posh little mouth.

Elaine Bronson, another chirpy, chatty, hard-working rider, joined in.

'Give us those 'ands!' she said, grabbing my hands and turning them over in hers. 'Look at 'em. Soft as a baby's bottom. You've never done a hard day's work in yer life, 'ave you?'

'Ah,' I said, 'but look at that line there. That says I'll be lucky and, if you can't be hard-working, you might as well be lucky.'

Elaine and Murgy laughed, and we walked out to the paddock together, past the sparkling red Mini on display just outside the winner's enclosure.

'Lovely, innit?' said Elaine, stroking the bonnet of the car. 'Don't touch it, Clare, you're not allowed. If you haven't got a driver's licence, you can't touch it.'

She cackled with laughter and headed off to meet her trainer, while I looked for my parents in the paddock. For once, my weight was not an issue. Waterlow Park, the horse I was riding, was near the top of the weights in the handicap, so I could have a big saddle with lead weights in it. I had made the most of not having to diet, and my breeches were a little tighter than they should have been.

There are plenty of sports in which you are reliant on the achievements of others to decide your own fate, but the key in each one is to try to control the things within your grasp. The only way I could do that was to do my damnedest to finish in the first four. Dad told me to keep it really simple, to stay out of trouble and, on soft ground, to make sure we had enough left in the tank for Waterlow Park to finish well.

It didn't sound that 'simple' to me, but we did our best. I was in the first four until the last furlong. Murgy came past me to finish second, and then Geraldine Rees, who a few years before had become the first woman to complete the Grand National. I had memorized all the colours of the riders who could overtake me in the standings, and couldn't see any of them ahead of me. If I could just hang on to fourth place, I would win the Mini.

Waterlow Park was starting to get tired, the soft ground sapping his energy. I shouted encouragement at him, slapped him down the neck with my whip and tried my best to move a little bit in rhythm. I could feel another horse coming to our quarters, so I got desperate. I picked up my whip in my right hand and tried to hit him on top of his quarters, just as my father had shown me.

I missed. Honest to God, I did the equivalent of

an air shot, and nearly fell off. That was the first and last time I ever tried to hit a horse behind the saddle. I rode seventeen winners in total over my short, sharp riding career, and I did not hit a single one of them. I couldn't do it. I got overtaken for fourth place and crossed the line in fifth, half a length ahead of Elaine Bronson. Crucially, Yvonne Haynes finished down the field.

My father was busy working out the points situation as I came back into the area of the paddock where the 'also rans' are unsaddled. If he had noticed my failed attempt at a backhand crack with the whip, he didn't say so.

'I don't know how they'll do this,' he said. 'You've both finished on eight points. If they do it on count back, they'll have to go down to fifth places, so today was crucial, but if they do it on overall rides, she's had more than you.'

In the event, Brooke Bond decided to award two cars. Yvonne Haynes was presented with the keys to the Mini that was at Haydock that day, and she drove it home. Ten days later, I passed my driving test and a bright-red Mini (number plate F661 MTF) was presented to me by a man with a moustache on the forecourt of the Austin Rover dealership in Newbury. Unfortunately, in the photo taken for the *Newbury Weekly News*, you can't see any Austin Rover signs—but you can see, clearly in the background, a sign for Magnet kitchens.

I had learned to drive in my mother's Volkswagen Golf and had taken my driving test in it as well. The gear stick for that moved to the left for first and second gears, straight up and down for third and fourth. Driving the Mini home from Newbury, I could not work out why, every time I shifted it up for third, it went back into first gear. I settled for second gear and drove it all the way home in that. I had no idea what 'running in the engine' meant.

Between riding in races and winning the Mini, I retook my history 'A' level and got it up to an A grade. In terms of finding a place at university, I now had decent enough grades with which to go to war.

# 16

# knock knock

The letter was in blue Biro, written in swirly letters on a lined page. It was my first experience of fanmail.

*Dear Clare,*

*You I have chosen to be my wife.*
*First I will tell you about myself and a little about my past. My age, 61. Height 5'4". Going grey and bald. Wear glasses. Unemployed. Only*

277

*income is from Labour Exchange £41 weekly. No savings. Live in 2 bedroom flat rented from council.*

*My Past: been in prison 8 times all for petty frauds. 3 months. 4 months. 6 months. 1 year and 2 years.*

*Clare, I only know that you are not married like myself. I also know your first thoughts will be this man must be some nutcase. A man of 61 years of age and with that prison record asking me to be his wife. That must be your first thought. You may even have a boyfriend. You may even intend to marry him. This I do not know, to me it does not matter.*

*I saw you on TV on Saturday and I liked what I saw. That's why I have chosen you to be my wife. Clare, if you have love, age, looks, wealth, past does not count. I say you will have the love for me even if you have a boyfriend. Even if you do intend to marry him you will not. The love you will have for me will be too strong.*

*Clare, you have read this letter and you will say this man is a real nutcase and it is not even worth the price of a stamp for a reply.*

*Respectfully,*
*George Mathie*

My brother, who for many years had practised his autograph on pieces of paper left lying around the house, thought this was the best letter ever written. He wanted me to frame it. I didn't, but I did keep it, and I reproduce it here, verbatim.

'Could be the only proposal you ever get,' he said, helpfully. 'I think you should think carefully about it.'

278

My mother assumed it was a prank but, if it was, I have never found out who was behind it. Of course, having been taught that good manners are the most important quality in a person, I wrote back. I thanked George very much for his kind words and for his romantic belief that love would conquer all. I told him that I agreed absolutely with his sentiments and that neither his age nor his personal circumstances nor his criminal record would have put me off, but that I just didn't feel I was ready for such a serious relationship. I did not think I could give him the love that he could so clearly offer me. I was only eighteen, I had no idea what love meant; it was me, not him.

I did not hear from George again. I suspect he moved on to another woman in tight jodhpurs that he happened to see on TV.

The reason I had been on television at all was a racehorse called Knock Knock. His sire was Tap On Wood—hence the name Knock Knock. He was owned in partnership by an octogenarian retired headmaster called Mr George Smart and a younger man called Jon Sayer. Knock Knock had arrived at my father's yard with one win to his name and a rapidly decreasing list of achievements. The problem was that he didn't like racing much.

It was a mystery because, at home, you could work Knock Knock with the best three-year-old in the yard and he would outperform it on the gallops. But take him to a racecourse, and he didn't want to know. His handicap mark was on the slide, he was getting a reputation as a bit of a dog, but I thought he was wonderful. He was the most affectionate racehorse I have ever known. He loved to be kissed and cuddled, he loved Polo mints and he detested

279

other horses. Every time one came near he would put his ears flat back and flash his teeth. I liked to think he did it because he was protective of whoever was riding him.

Knock Knock was looked after by Francis Arrowsmith, an apprentice about the same age as me who was known as Scully. Scully would soon become the answer to the quiz question 'Who rode Lochsong to victory in the Ayr Gold Cup?' but, for now, he was competing with Seamus O'Gorman and Andy Whitehall for apprentice rides in our yard. Knock Knock was 'condemned' to apprentice races.

A good trainer makes few mistakes in the placing of horses, and they will win what they are entitled to win. A great trainer finds the key to horses which others cannot work out and wins races that no one else would think them capable of winning. With Knock Knock, no one could work it out. How could he be so talented at home and yet, on a racecourse, when he was smacked and kicked and cajoled to give of his best, so utterly useless?

More in desperation than inspiration, Dad entered him for an amateur race at an evening meeting at Kempton. He told me to walk the course, which I did, with Amanda Harwood, who was also riding a horse trained by her father.

'I've got no chance,' I told her. 'Dad says to ride him like a non-trier, but I'm not really sure what that means.'

'Just the same as you ride all the others,' said Amanda, with a smile.

She really was a proper jockey. She was physically strong, a good judge of pace and she could use her stick in both hands. I could never be in her league, and I knew it, but horses would run for me, perhaps because I more or less let them do what they wanted to do.

Knock Knock was 25–1; the race was restricted to lady riders who were the wives, daughters or secretaries of a trainer. Knock Knock was carrying about a stone more in relation to the other runners than he would have done in a handicap. So I really don't know how to explain what happened next, except to say that the front runners went much, much too fast. As we turned right-handed into the straight at Kempton, I was chatting away to Knock Knock: 'Good boy, that's the way,' I said to him. 'Nice and easy, just like at home.'

*Thwack* went the whip of someone next to me. 'Grrr,' said another jockey. 'Good boy,' I cooed. Everyone else was pushing and shoving and shouting at their horses to close the gap on the leaders, and I realized that Knock Knock was still going easily.

'Go on then,' I said, letting the reins slip through my hands to give him his head. 'Let's go.'

Knock Knock had an engine—I knew that from his work at home—but this was the first time he had ever chosen to use it on a racecourse. He started to pass horses and, as he did so, he pricked his ears. Inside the final furlong, he only had one horse to catch and he did it four strides before the line. There is a photo of him with his ears pricked, me turning to look sideways for dangers and grinning like a daft thing.

There had been no pressure, no expectation, no thought from anyone that we had any chance at all. That had been the key.

Dad was laughing as we came into the winner's

enclosure, really laughing. Scully had run across to greet us, and both of us were patting Knock Knock as we would a pony.

'I said to ride him like a non-trier,' said my father, 'but I never thought it would work that well.'

The key was in the kidding. Knock Knock didn't like pressure, he didn't like the whip and he didn't like to be bullied. He loved to come through narrow gaps, to pass horses and he loved the glory of winning. In his next six races, he didn't finish out of the first four.

The race that inspired the letter from George Mathie was at Sandown later that summer, when we beat Amanda Harwood on a horse owned by Prince Khalid Abdulla and Maxine Cowdrey on a horse owned by Sheikh Mohammed.

'All I could hear,' said Maxine, 'was you saying, "Go on, good boy, go on!" There's no danger of him getting marked from the stick, but he might from you patting him so hard.'

Amanda was getting a bit fed up with it all.

'There I am, riding a proper finish,' she said, 'and you come by with your arse in the air as if you've just joined in.'

The racing papers showered me with plaudits for riding such a patient race. My father said, 'You might have thought she was on Mill Reef!'

Mr Smart, Knock Knock's owner, was thrilled that his seemingly useless gelding was now winning races that were live on television and he told my father that I could ride the horse whenever I wanted. The trouble was that there aren't that many amateur races in the year, and even fewer over Knock Knock's preferred distance of a mile and a quarter, so he was shared around. Scully rode him, Seamus O'Gorman rode him and even the odd professional jockey like Ray Cochrane was allowed, with strict instructions not to hit him.

*     *     *

There were two daily racing papers—the *Racing Post* and the *Sporting Life*—and either they were short of proper stories, or they figured that Amanda Harwood and myself competing for the amateur title made good copy. There was a lot of coverage that summer, including a 'Father and Daughter' feature by Dad and me for the *Racing Post*.

'I'm all for girls riding in amateur races,' he says in the article, 'but I think they will always struggle as professionals. I really don't think they should be getting in the way of the pros.

'I certainly wouldn't want Clare to turn professional . . . Ultimately, I'd rather she evented than race-rode. Obviously, it depends on you having a good horse, but it's easier for girls to get to the top. Anyway, she's not really the right shape to be a jockey!'

That's my father for you. He always struggled to see gender as anything other than an insurmountable hurdle if you were a woman and a huge advantage if you were a man. My education had taught me completely the opposite, and I railed against this myopic view of womankind. I constantly pointed out the successes of women in politics, academia, science, medicine, business and technology.

'Wow, look at this—a woman with a brain,' I would say. 'Do you think she gets in the way of the men around her?'

283

I tried to challenge him and make him question his own preconceptions but, inside, I was crying, because it seemed to make no difference. If I couldn't convince my own father that women were worth an equal place in the world, how could I convince anyone else?

I still have rows, or 'heated discussions', with my father about the respective merits of male and female jockeys. The dedication, strength, skill and success of Hayley Turner has done much to temper his view, but my argument has always been the same—you can't improve if you're not given the chance to ride good horses. There are an awful lot of mediocre male jockeys who will get the call from an owner or a trainer ahead of an equally or more talented female jockey.

It seemed to me that eventing was one area where women could be judged on their merit and were not penalized for being female, so I went to work for the best event rider at the time, Lucinda Green, to discover whether I could be good enough to make it a career.

Lucinda had won Badminton six times on six different horses and was a study in brave but accurate cross-country riding. She was my idol. Suffice to say, I did not last long as her pupil assistant. I let two of her horses loose in the yard, I fed them the wrong amounts, and my brand-new skewbald called Mister Moose had ringworm and was banished back home before the week was out.

'The race riding isn't helping your dressage, and I'm not sure you've got the concentration for it,' Lucinda advised me. 'I can only see you getting frustrated, so, do you know what I'd do? Go to university.'

Lucinda probably saved me a decade of heartache and a fortune in horse-related expenses by being honest. The question of which university was still to be answered, so to keep me busy and prevent me battling my father on a daily basis, Mum sent me to Paris. She enrolled me in a French Civilization course at the Sorbonne, telling me that I needed to improve my language skills. If I were Alan Partridge, I would refer to this as my 'Parisian Period'. Or, more accurately, my baguette phase.

Oh, the joys of a warm baguette with butter and strawberry jam—one mouthful after another of squidgy, comforting dough. So gorgeous, so cheap, so horrifically fattening. My hips expanded, my breasts filled out and my French did not really improve beyond a working knowledge of racing terms. I knew the way to Chantilly from the centre of Paris and drove there each morning at five thirty a.m. to ride out for Criquette Head, whose daughter Patricia was a friend of mine.

I was riding through the woods of Chantilly on the deep, broad 'pistes' accompanied by wizened Rip van Winkles who smoked Gitanes and drank espresso in one gulp. They had low, rasping voices. There were few English speakers and far fewer girls working in the yard than at home. It was a world in which I had only the language of horsemanship.

The French work riders wander around the broad pistes with their stirrups so long their feet almost touch the ground. They have their first canters, just a gentle warm-up, en masse, all of the horses cantering together in a herd. The riders stand bolt upright and shout abuse at each other. Then they gather in a forest clearing while Criquette Head tells them what to do.

285

The stirrup leathers shoot up in preparation for the faster gallop that is about to come. Riding styles differ around the world and, in France, the 'Freddie Head technique' was de rigueur. I have never seen a jockey ride shorter than Freddie. He perched like a tiny sparrow on the back of a hippo, his feet barely coming down below the flaps of his racing saddle. It was a triumph of balance and impossible to replicate for someone of average height and weight. I know, because I tried.

Criquette asked an older lad called Gaston to keep an eye on me, and we made for the main piste. The training area at Chantilly covers 1,900 hectares (4,600 acres) and has around 120 kilometres or 74 miles of gallops. They are all deep sand, so never get firm in the summer or too heavy in the winter. The temperature stays cool for the horses under the trees of the magical forest. As we started to gallop, I was surprised to see horses coming in the opposite direction.

Apart from one horrible fall, when a horse I was riding spooked and I got trampled by the horses behind me, I managed pretty well. I had a quick cup of coffee in the yard or with Criquette and then headed off in my red Mini back to the city. The price I paid for the early mornings was a desperate need for a nap by mid-afternoon, usually in the middle of one of my lessons. That's my excuse for not being fluent in French. On the plus side, I can drive confidently around Paris and know all the short cuts.

All our French Civilization lessons were in French, with none of the multinational class allowed to speak in their own language. I tried to explain that I was one of the leading amateur jockeys in the UK and that I had to fly back to ride in races, but it came out all wrong. Instead, I told them I was *'le premier chevalier dans la monde'*, which, not surprisingly, had them looking perplexed. The first rider in the world? I don't think so.

I also tried to tell my fellow students about the spectacular Grandes Écuries, the Great Stables at the Château de Chantilly. These were built to an unusually high specification because Louis Henri, the Duke of Bourbon and Prince of Condé, believed that, when he died, he would be reincarnated as a horse.

'*Il connait qu'il* would be—damn, what is "would be" in French?'

'Pas d'Anglais!'

'*Qu'il sera un renaissance comme un cheval.*'

I did an impression of a horse, just for good measure. They thought the duke had got a job in pantomime.

When I wasn't revving up the Mini and heading north to Chantilly, I walked everywhere in Paris. I lived in a studio flat in the fourth *arrondissement*, not far from Hôtel de Ville.

I walked past the glorious city hall, re-creating in my romantic teenage brain *The Kiss* by Robert Doisneau. I wanted to be the woman in that photo, so I hung around the Hôtel de Ville hoping someone might kiss me. It didn't work.

My favourite walk to classes was over the bridge to the Île de la Cité and through the flower market. It was an indulgence of olfaction: there was a smell for every mood and every feeling. I never bought any flowers, I just liked to walk through the market as I would through an art gallery, letting the colour and the aroma of the flowers bathe me.

I did have a boyfriend—in the army. We had met at a party that summer, and he had asked for my phone number. He had dark, floppy hair, olive skin and sparkling eyes and was so damned handsome I could not believe he was talking to me. When he kissed me, my knees went trembly and my tummy started flipping. I assumed he would never bother to call, but he did and, for the rest of the summer months, while he was on leave, we were inseparable. He played cricket, rugby and polo, like my grandfather, and knew enough about racing not to be lost in conversation with my family.

Just before I headed off to Paris, I drove the army officer to Brize Norton. He had been deployed to the Falkland Islands for three months. I cried as we parted and told him I loved him. He paused, looked deep into my eyes and said, 'I think, maybe, I love you too.'

We wrote to each other every day. Ours was an old-fashioned long-distance relationship. Occasionally, we spoke on the phone, but it was through the written word that we communicated. I wrote poetic, romantic love letters, while he wrote back about funny encounters of his time surrounded by sheep and men.

It was the perfect relationship because it existed mainly in our heads and neither of us had to change the course of our lives for each other. When he met me, I was fit and thin. It was the middle of the summer, I was riding in races and running in a sweat suit every day. I shall never forget the look on his face when I met him at Charles de Gaulle airport. It had been twelve weeks since we had last seen each other and, during that time, I had gone from the strict starvation diet of a would-be champion amateur rider to the student diet of one baguette a day. Rubens may have appreciated my new-found curves, but the army officer did not. Disappointment registered in his eyes.

'You've been eating well,' he said as we embraced.

The sadness is that I was used to being judged on the size of my waist and hips. I lost weight again the following year for the new season, and my father complimented me on the transformation.

'Do you love me more, now I'm thin?' I asked, breaking the rule my mother had taught me about never asking a question to which you may not want to hear the answer.

My father paused. 'Yes, I think I do,' he said.

Dad hadn't just tossed that answer into the air— he'd thought about it and still said it. Ow, ow, ow. I didn't know that love could be turned on and off like a tap. I thought if you loved someone, you loved them for ever. Good and bad, fat and thin. The army officer did not dump me, but he made it clear that he too loved me more when I was thin.

There is no doubt that I liked myself better when I was fit and light. I walked differently and had more confidence, but I found dieting had no point unless there was a goal at which to aim. Starving and dehydrating my body for the summer had left me craving food, obsessed by it and hopelessly ill disciplined once the shackles of the regime were discarded. I was either on a diet or I was eating everything in sight.

I found it harder to lose the weight I had gained in the off season, and my methods became increasingly unhealthy. I took a particularly disgusting laxative for a while. It came in a pot of granules described as 'chocolate-flavoured'—they could, more accurately, have been described as 'manure-flavoured'. I shovelled down two, three, four teaspoons of this grossness and then waited for the stomach cramps to start. Then I just had to make sure I was near a loo.

Making myself sick, or 'flipping', as some jockeys refer to it, was an option I hated but still felt I had to do if I had overindulged. I was never that good at it, and it really hurt my throat. A few years later, Andrew, having shed his puppy fat, started riding in point-to-points and adopted some of the worst of my habits. I kept going into our bathroom and smelling sick. I remember being appalled that he was flipping.

'You did it.' He sounded accusatory.

'Yes, but that doesn't mean you should. It's really bad for you. Please don't.'

I don't think either of us had an eating disorder, as such, it was just part of what anyone in a weight-related sport will do. I bet any boxer, jockey, lightweight rower or martial-arts fighter has done the same. The scales have to be beaten, just like the opposition, so you do whatever you need to do. With horses like Mailman, Waterlow Park and particularly Knock Knock to ride in races, it was worth it for me.

I rode Knock Knock in fourteen races over three years. We won four of them and were out of the first four only twice. It was a partnership that clicked and gave me more pleasure than anything else in my race-riding career. He won sixteen races on the flat and two over hurdles from a total of eighty-three lifetime starts, amassed over £130,000 in prize money, and gave untold pleasure to his owners, George Smart and Jon Sayer. Knock Knock was adored by everyone in the yard and remained one of the best work horses my father has ever seen.

# 17

# Waterlow Park

Amateur races do not usually elicit much newspaper coverage. A round-up in the *Racing Post* and the *Sporting Life*, perhaps a mention in *Horse & Hound*, yes; amateur races never make the national dailies. Never, that is, unless there is a member of the Royal Family involved.

**THE PRINCESS ROYAL**

# ANNE FURY AT PHOTO DEFEAT

## Princess has rough passage at Beverley

## Tender touch eludes Princess

## Princess is foiled in thrilling finish

## Waterlow has Clare seeking Royal pardon

And, crucially:

## Clare was not guilty

It was all a bit of a hoo-ha, you see. These things happen in races—a bit of bumping here, a bit of boring there: general argy-bargy. You can't legislate for what might occur around the tight turns of, say, Beverley, if a horse happens to jump a path and takes himself to the inside rail and someone else is bumped in the process.

Well, you can legislate, and that is what the Rules of Racing are for but, sometimes, shit happens. That's what I'd have said to the Princess Royal, if she'd still been speaking to me. She wasn't, though. Not after the Contrac Computer Supplies Ladies' Handicap, a race over a mile and a half, worth £2,262 to the winner. Worth nothing to the winning jockey, obviously, apart from a rather nice crystal vase.

It was hardly the Diamond Race at Ascot, which was the highlight of the ladies' season—the winner got a diamond necklace—but if you're a competitive beast, you want to win every race you enter, not just the glamorous ones. Her Royal Highness the Princess Royal rode at the Olympic Games of 1976 in Montreal, won a gold medal at the European Championships of 1971 at Burghley and two silver medals in Luhmühlen in 1975. The Princess Royal is a highly competent horsewoman, of that there is no doubt.

As an amateur rider, her experience was less extensive. She had ridden many times over jumps, had had a few winners, and on the flat had won the Diamond Race in 1987. She had even ridden a winner for my father on a horse called Insular, who was bred by the Queen.

Wherever the Princess Royal rode, the ladies' changing rooms would receive a hasty makeover,

294

which was incredibly useful for the rest of us. She changed alongside us and did not expect any special treatment. I found this rather confusing, given that I had been brought up to curtsey to the Queen and follow official protocol.

When I curtseyed to the Princess Royal in the changing room at Beverley and called her Your Royal Highness, she said, 'Don't be ridiculous.'

She was standing in her underwear at the time, so perhaps a curtsey was inappropriate.

The Princess Royal was riding a horse called Tender Type. He had finished out of the money in his three starts that season and was therefore dropping down the handicap. Waterlow Park, my mount, was having a terrific season. He'd had seven runs by the beginning of August, had won three of them and finished second or third in the others. I had ridden him to victory at Goodwood in June, and he was a lovely ride, even at home. He was a big, strong chestnut with a slightly off-centre blaze of white down the front of his head. He was quiet and gentle, an all-round gent. He was the perfect ride for an apprentice or an amateur.

My mother had driven me to Beverley. As we neared the course, I felt the familiar twinge in my stomach. It wasn't stomach cramps due to laxatives; it was nerves. I rubbed my hands together—they were clammy; and my jaw was tense. I asked Mum if I could put on the lucky songs I needed to listen to before I got to the racecourse and, fairly soon, as we bombed along the A614, Peter Gabriel's 'Big Time' was blasting out of the cassette player.

My mother joined in for the chorus, and we were screaming, 'Big time, so much larger than life!' as a Range Rover sped past us.

'That was Princess Anne,' said my mother. 'Make sure you keep out of her way today.'

'Yeah, yeah, yeah,' I sang back. 'Big time, my house is getting bigger. Big time, my eyes are getting bigger. And my moow-ow-outh.'

I had read the form on all the other runners, I had thought about the race and had memorized the tactics my father wanted me to use. Once the music stopped, I was on an adrenalin wave that lasted for the next couple of hours. I was in a heightened state of nerves, talking ten to the dozen, taking in details and remembering facts that I would never normally digest. If I could have taken exams when my brain was whirring like this, I'd have got straight 'A's.

I loved this stage, and I got more and more nervous before the race, running to the loo more and more often until the point that we were called out to the paddock.

*'Jockeys!'* a voice shouted into the changing room, and we filed out into the weighing room and down the steps into the paddock.

My mouth would go dry and I wouldn't say much, but as soon as I was legged into the saddle, a switch would flick. It was as if it was all happening to someone else. My heart rate slowed, my nerves disappeared and I relaxed. During the race itself, I always felt as if I had all the time in the world. If the pace was too slow, I went on. If the field was going too fast, I waited at the back of it. Gaps seemed to appear when I needed them and, if they didn't, I would yell at someone in front to 'give me some room'.

The same thing happens now when I do live television or radio. I get nervous in the build-up, have to listen to some loud music in my headphones and then, as soon as I see the red light and know we're live, I relax. From the start of the programme, I feel in control, and the more that goes wrong, the more I enjoy it. I am never happier than when the running order has been thrown out of the window, because I reckon that's what I'm there for. Anyone can present a programme that is going well; it's what you do when it's going tits up that makes the difference.

In this particular race, there were ten runners. Elaine Bronson, who had become a firm friend, Amanda Harwood and Tracey Bailey (who was married to the trainer Kim Bailey) were all in the line-up. The Princess Royal was wearing colours similar to mine—hers were chocolate and turquoise, mine turquoise and brown.

'I hope the punters don't get us mixed up,' I said as we circled at the start.

'Unlikely,' she replied.

I swallowed hard, even though there was no saliva to swallow. I was out of my depth.

The mile-and-a-half start at Beverley is right in front of the stands, and the crowd was leaning over the rails, shouting encouragement to us.

'Come on, Cler!' I heard a voice say. 'Don't mess it up. My cash is riding on your backside.'

Waterlow Park had never been that quick to jump out of the stalls. He dawdled, stumbled slightly and broke slower than the horses all around us. We were last of the field as we passed the winning post the first time. At least, I thought we were last. As we turned away from the grandstand, he saw a path made by the pedestrians crossing to the inner section of the racecourse. He jumped it on an angle, took himself to the inside rail and made up about four lengths in the process.

It was at that point that I realized I had not been last out of the stalls. One horse had reared as the gates opened and had been almost ten lengths behind us all. By the time we got to that first bend, he had made up the ground and was just behind me, on my inside as Waterlow Park jumped the path.

'What the hell are you doing? Watch out! Watch out!'

There were other words that were shouted. Naughty words that I need not repeat here.

Oh God, I thought. I've carved someone up. At least it wasn't the Princess Royal. She'd never swear like that.

I heard more chatter behind me, but I was focussed on the horses ahead of me, on where the gaps might appear and what I needed to do to achieve the best possible finish. There was that man who had staked his cash on my backside. I needed to do my best for him.

We swung into the straight, and the field fanned across the course, as they often do in amateur races. It was like the parting of the Red Sea, and I let Waterlow Park accelerate. He didn't find as much as I expected and could not pull clear. I kept pushing and could hear the cracks of whips all around. There were three of us in a line and then I could feel another horse closing fast. As we flashed past the line, I thought I might just have won, but I wasn't sure.

A stride past the line, the turquoise and chocolate colours of Tender Type were ahead. The Princess Royal had made up a huge amount of ground in the straight and had finished faster, but none of us were sure who had been in front on the line.

I took my time pulling up, partly to allow for the result of the photo finish to be called, and partly because I was scared. I'm not sure if I was frightened of having lost or of having won. Either way, it spelt trouble.

My mother was, to quote Procul Harum, a whiter shade of pale as she greeted me in the paddock.

'Do you know what you've done?' she said, in an urgent whisper.

'Yes! I think I've won.' I attempted to win her over with a hesitant smile.

'Not that!' she replied. 'The first bend. The very first bend—what the hell were you doing? You nearly brought down Princess Anne. I have just had the Duke jabbing his finger at my forehead telling me you are effing dangerous and shouldn't be allowed loose on a racecourse in any effing country in the world.'

The Duke was David Nicholson, the Princess Royal's racing guardian. He was a champion jumps trainer, a man who had won Gold Cups at Cheltenham and King George's at Kempton, a man who chewed weak people up and spat them out for breakfast, moving on to idiots for lunch and strong people for supper. He had masterminded the racing career of the Princess Royal, supervising her riding out in the morning and her rides on the racecourse, even if they were for other trainers.

I could imagine him in full flow, accosting my mother (whom he'd known all his life) and taking out his fury on her. Now I could see him giving Princess Anne the full force of his opinion. She had been robbed. Robbed and mugged by a highwayman. Me.

The PA made a noise. The judge had been studying the black-and-white freeze frame of the finish for well over five minutes.

'Here is the result of the photo finish,' the voice intoned. I looked down at my saddle cloth to double-check my number. It was one.

'First'—the PA announcer milked the dramatic pause as if he were presenting a game show—'number one.'

A cheer went up from those punters who had backed Waterlow Park. At least they were on my side. To celebrate too much would have seemed churlish, so I patted him on the neck and practised my 'humble winner' face.

'There is a dead heat for second,' the voice continued, 'between number two and number six. Fourth is number seven.'

The distances were a short-head, dead heat and another short-head back to fourth. You could have thrown a blanket over all four of us but, right on the line, Waterlow Park had stuck his neck out, and his nose, with its sheepskin noseband, had passed the post just in front of Tender Type, who finished best of all to dead-heat for second.

I slid to the ground and took my time taking off the saddle. I really, really did not want to go into that changing room.

I weighed in and went out to the winner's enclosure to receive my trophy. On the way back into the weighing room, I noticed the door to the stewards' room was ajar and they were looking at the film of the race. I poked my head round and made history as the only winning jockey who has ever said the following: 'Could I just check, are

300

you having a stewards' enquiry?' Plenty of beaten jockeys have asked, but if you're declared the winner it's usually a good idea to thank your lucky stars and move on.

'We're not,' said the stewards' secretary, 'but if you'd like to see the film, you're welcome.'

So I saw how far Tender Type had been left at the start—no wonder I hadn't realized he could have been behind me. I saw Waterlow Park jump the path and angle himself towards the inside. Tender Type was knocked sideways, causing the Princess Royal to snatch up.

'We can see clearly from this angle,' said the stewards' secretary, a military man, with an upright back and clipped tones, pointing to the screen with a cane, 'that you did not cause the interference intentionally, Miss Balding. Frankly, we feel that you could have done nothing about it and that it happened too early on to make any difference.'

Armed with my defence, I steeled myself for re-entry into the war zone. I opened the door to the ladies' changing room quietly and heard different voices saying, 'She's always doing it' . . . 'Thinks she can get away with anything.'

Elaine Bronson later told me that she thought the whole thing was hysterical and that she was winding up the Princess Royal for fun. To be fair to the others, I had come on the scene a bit fast and was riding more winners than a second-season amateur should do. I was the new threat.

The Princess Royal was standing with her back to me. As she spun round, my world stopped turning. I swallowed and stood there, not knowing what to say. I looked her in the eye, mainly because she was not dressed and I was embarrassed to look anywhere else.

'So,' she said, 'are they having a stewards' enquiry?'

'No,' I replied. 'I did ask but, no, they're not. They say that it happened too early on to make any difference.'

'Really?' The air had grown chilly. 'Nothing happens too early on to make the difference of a short-head.'

'I'm sorry, Ma'am. I really am,' I said. That's where I should have stopped. I really could have walked on into the room and quietly got changed. But I am me and I don't always know when it's best to stop talking: 'Most genuinely sorry . . . but I was not about to pull up in the straight and let you win.'

In the film version of this moment, I will be Spartacus and my fellow amateur riders will one by one start clapping. In the real version, they sucked in their breath. This was a dangerous move.

The Princess Royal fixed me with a steely glare.

'Well, maybe you should have done,' she said, and turned back to continue dressing. If I had had a weak bladder, I might have wet myself.

The *Sun* reporter wrote: 'The princess had a face like thunder when returning to the weighing room. And she summoned an especially withering glance for an intrepid scribbler who attempted a brief interview.'

There was plenty of talk of me asking for a royal pardon, and the general theme of the articles was 'Upstart amateur, daughter of the royal trainer, carves up the Queen's daughter on the first bend and then beats her in a photo finish.'

On BBC television, Julian Wilson introduced the video footage from Beverley and asked Jimmy

302

Lindley for his opinion.

'Clare Balding has committed the cardinal sin of race riding,' said the former professional jockey. 'She has shown absolutely no regard for the horse behind her. You can't do that, you simply can't. I am surprised she was not disqualified.'

That was my first inside lesson in how the media works. A story will be told from the angle that best suits those telling it.

For the rest of that year, the Princess Royal and I rode in the odd race together and successfully avoided getting too close—either on the course or off it. Two years later, in 1991, we were back at Beverley riding in a one-mile race with only seven runners. The Princess Royal was on a horse called Croft Valley, trained by Richard Whitaker, who had also trained Tender Type. I was on my beloved Knock Knock.

The Duke saw my mother as soon as he arrived at the racecourse and walked towards her. Although tempted to run away, she stood her ground and let him say his piece.

'I've realized that I was a bit harsh,' he said. 'I've watched your daughter a lot since *that race*—and I may have been wrong about her. She's clearly competent. I'm sorry.'

Mum smiled. 'That's all right, but please don't jab your finger at me again. It's rude.'

'I won't, if she stays out of the way this time.'

Croft Valley won by a neck from Knock Knock and, as we were pulling up, I spoke to the Princess Royal for the first time in two years.

'Well done, Ma'am,' I said. 'Happy now?'

I know. I know. I should have just shut up after the 'Well done', but I couldn't help it. The brat in

303

me breaks out sometimes. I thought it was a funny line but, for a joke to work, you need a receptive audience.

*　　　*　　　*

Waterlow Park beating Princess Anne at Beverley had contributed to a fabulous 1989 season during which I rode six winners from nineteen starts at a strike rate of more than 30 per cent. I was leading the amateur championship and the Lanson-sponsored competition to be leading Lady Rider. We came to the last race of the lot at Folkestone in October. I had flown back from Paris to ride, and my fitness as well as my weight had suffered from the baguette diet. Despite riding out in Chantilly, I felt woefully out of practice.

The only rider who could pass my points total was Elaine Bronson. She continued to tease me for being soft, posh and, now, continental.

'Jetting in from Paris, how flash is that? Still not working for a living then?'

The last time we had ridden together, Elaine had offered me CDs and Puffa jackets from the boot of her car, at a 'great discount'.

'Honest, Clare,' she promised me, 'you won't find a better deal.'

She made me laugh but, my God, she was ruthless. She had to win this race. Nothing less would do. If she won, it didn't matter where I finished—she would win the title. If anyone finished in front of her, I would hold on to my points lead and be crowned champion.

Elaine worked for a trainer called David Wilson. He was a renowned form expert and always appeared at the races with a massive book in his hand, in which he noted down all the past runs of various horses, with comments and his ratings. He was a clever trainer, placing his horses well and often pulling off a betting coup. His talent was in targeting a horse at a specific race and making sure it had a handicap mark that gave it a chance of winning. Kovalevskia was the four-year-old filly he had selected for Elaine to ride in this final, championship-deciding race. She had run poorly in her previous three starts, all over further than a mile and a half, so had dropped down the handicap. Now running at her preferred distance again, she had a definite chance but, according to the betting, my chance on Straight Gold was better.

'See you on the other side,' Elaine said as we loaded into the stalls.

Sharron Murgatroyd was riding in the race as well.

'Play nicely, girls,' she shouted. 'And may the best woman win.'

Elaine made all the running. She was five lengths clear and stretching away as we turned into the straight at Folkestone, and as I knew Straight Gold wasn't travelling well enough to catch her, I shouted, 'Someone go after her. Please!'

Straight Gold started to run on, but it was all too late. Kovalevskia won by fifteen lengths. It was a rout.

I cantered up beside Elaine and patted her on the back.

'Well done,' I said. 'Amazing result.'

'She's a flying machine, this filly,' she said. 'I knew I'd beat you, but I never expected it to be so easy.'

She winked at me and grinned. 'Work—it does pay off, you know.'

Part of me was pleased for her. I liked her and, when I saw David Wilson hugging her and lifting her off the ground in the winner's enclosure, I figured that they must have had a major punt as well. Kovalevskia had been backed in from 14–1 to 9–1. There was a lot more riding on the result for them than there had been for me.

It still hurt, though. I may have been the leading amateur, but I went there thinking I could be the champion lady rider as well, and instead I had to stand there watching someone else winning their weight in champagne, someone else being declared the best in the country. The top sportsmen and -women will tell you that it is moments like this they hold on to. They want to remember the pain of losing to spur them on in the dark, cold hours of lonely training. They are masochists, the lot of them. I really don't want to remember it at all.

I knew I would cope, but I couldn't bear the disappointment of others. I didn't want to look at my father as I walked into second place. He had always maintained second was for losers. Now, he surprised me.

'Never mind,' he said. 'You did everything you could and you've had a wonderful year. We gave it our best shot, and we'll make sure we win both titles next year.'

With that, he kissed me on the cheek and patted my shoulder.

'Don't forget to weigh in,' he said, as I tried to pretend that I wasn't crying.

As we were driving home, Dad reminded me that I had at least won something. He gave me a box and a card. In the box was a butterfly brooch and on the card it said:

*To the Champion Amateur*
*(and so nearly the lady's too)*

*With lots of love from*

*A very proud Dad*

# 18

# Song of Sixpence

Many of the lads in my father's yard had worked there their whole lives. Jim Corfield had arrived in his early thirties and was still there, giving the horses their hay every morning, shortly before he died, at the age of eighty-five. My father gave the address at his funeral and said that he was one of the finest horsemen he had ever come across.

There is a black-and-white picture of Jim

cantering up the gallop on a sleek black thoroughbred. His trousers are tucked into his socks, his jodhpur boots pushed firmly into the irons, and he's wearing no hat.

The quotation above the photo is from Sir Winston Churchill: 'There is something about the outside of a horse that is good for the inside of a man.'

Jim had been one of Dad's senior work riders from when he took over the licence in 1964 and was now looking after a six-year-old pot-bellied bay gelding called Song of Sixpence, who had had a decent career but had rather lost his way.

It was evening stables, and Dad was doing the rounds, feeling each horse's legs for any warmth, which could signify an injury. Our assistant trainer, Patrick, was carrying the bucket of carrots, while I stayed a few paces behind, pausing to make a fuss of the horses I knew. I caught the end of a conversation my father was having in the next stall.

'I'm thinking we should try something completely different with him,' said my father.

'Like what?'

'I don't know—maybe an amateur race. Clare could ride him, see if it makes a difference.'

'Oh no, Guv'nor, don't do that. Please give him another chance first!'

I stayed stock still, scared of revealing myself and making the situation worse.

My father was determined. 'Come on, Jim, it's not that bad. There's a race at Newbury in a week or so that is perfect. Let's enter him for that and see how we get on.'

Jim had a sad-looking face at the best of times, but I could see through the bars that it was particularly mournful that evening. I slipped by the front of the stable as he tied up Song of Sixpence, and hoped that he hadn't seen me.

I avoided Jim, and he ignored me on the few occasions that I rode Song of Sixpence at home. He was a sweet, placid horse, but desperately uncomfortable. He had a juddering slow canter that felt like you were on a vibrating tractor but, when he went faster, his stride was much more fluid. Lots of racehorses are poor in their slower paces but, when allowed to stretch their limbs and go on a stride quicker, they move well.

Song of Sixpence could carry weight, which was just as well, because he was going to be at the top of the handicap for any race we had together. He was easily the highest rated and therefore, technically, the best horse I rode.

In the race at Newbury, Maxine Cowdrey was riding a fabulous horse trained by Mary Reveley called Mellottie. They were 9–4 favourite, Amanda Harwood's mount Alreef was second favourite at 15–2 and Song of Sixpence was 14–1.

The race was recorded by BBC television to be shown during that afternoon's coverage. I decided to keep an eye on Maxine and Amanda, to track them and stay as close as I could. Dad had given me simple instructions:

'Just look after him. You know what you're doing and, if you think he can win, go for it. Try to at least look as if you're riding a finish.'

He said that because I had been hauled up in front of the stewards for 'not trying' in a race earlier that month. In my head I had been riding a forceful finish but whenever I watched the video it looked as if I wasn't moving at all.

'Watch any winner I've ever ridden,' I told the stewards. 'I always look like that. I'm doing the best I can. Honestly.'

Jim led me out on to the course and muttered something to the effect that he still didn't agree with running his star horse in an amateur race but, if I was going to have to ride him, to do it properly.

Song of Sixpence juddered his way down to the start and I almost thought of pulling him out because he felt lame. It was lucky I had ridden him at home and knew he was always like this. I thought about Jim and how much I needed to prove to him that I could ride a good horse, and I thought of Mr Mellon, who owned Song of Sixpence. I was wearing the famous black colours with the gold cross, the same ones carried by Mill Reef, and here I was at Newbury, our local course, in a race that was going to be on BBC TV. I couldn't withdraw.

As the field jumped off, I was still in two minds about Song of Sixpence. I decided that, if he didn't feel right at racing pace, I would pull him up straight away. He settled into his stride and felt fine. I was right behind Alreef and alongside Mellottie. Perfect. The straight at Newbury is long, so there is plenty of time to make a move and, as the field had fanned across the course, there was room. I watched Maxine kick Mellottie into the lead and go for home. I watched Alreef follow them, and I sat behind them, waiting for one or both of them to fade. Mellottie ran out of gas first, and I went past, talking to Song of Sixpence as I went: 'That's a good lad. You can do it. Come on now, one more to catch. Let's go.'

He picked up and drew level with Alreef. I tried to push him in rhythm with his stride, feeling his

311

lungs expand and contract as he made his effort. We nudged ahead and, as we passed the line, I raised my hand in an air-punch.

I pulled him up, turned him round and cantered back to the stands. Jim was running towards me, beaming with pride.

'Good lad,' he said, patting Song of Sixpence on the neck. 'I knew this was a good idea. Always said so.'

He was looking up at me and grinning. Dad puffed out his chest as we came into the winner's enclosure.

'See, Jim, I told you she'd look after him. Cheeky bloody thing!' He was looking at me. 'Nearly gave me a heart attack, you did. Barely moving and winning by a head—you want to watch yourself. Now, don't forget to weigh in.'

After the trophy presentation, I was asked to go up to the television studio to be interviewed by Julian Wilson. I was still red in the face from the effort and gave a breathless, gushing interview.

Song of Sixpence was unplaced in his next couple of runs for professional jockeys, then won for Steve Cauthen, but only by a short-head, in a race he should have dominated. He then finished down the field at York, with Seamus O'Gorman on board.

'How is he, Jim?' Dad asked as he went round evening stables.

'I don't think he's quite himself,' Jim replied. 'Can I make a suggestion?'

'Of course you can.'

'Well, the thing is,' Jim said, pausing and then almost whispering, 'I think Clare should ride him again.'

'I'm sorry, Jim, I didn't quite hear you.' Dad was

teasing him.

'I think Clare should ride him again,' Jim said, a little louder this time.

'Really? Well, I'm sure she'll be pleased that you approve. I shall see what there is that might be suitable.'

When Dad told me, he couldn't stop laughing. There was a race at Ayr, the same one that I had won on Mailman a couple of years earlier, which was just the ticket. So Jim and Song of Sixpence made the long journey in the horsebox to just south of Glasgow, and Mum and I met them there. Song of Sixpence justified favouritism and won cosily. He was rated 84 at the time of that race. Steve Cauthen took over again and won on him for the following two Saturdays, including the Chesterfield Cup at Glorious Goodwood. Then he won a Listed Race at Windsor and his rating shot up to 108, way beyond the class of amateur races.

Jim was right: he was far too talented for me— but I caught him at just the right time and benefited with two wins out of two.

\*       \*       \*

I was nineteen and in my second 'gap year', having failed dismally to get an offer from any university I liked. Bristol and Exeter had both turned me down, despite my improved 'A' level grades. In interview I admitted that I had selected universities according to their proximity to racecourses. I now wonder if that was the most intelligent answer. They did not seem impressed.

I wanted to give Cambridge another shot. I had no particular reason to think that I might get in, except for the knowledge that I should never have applied for law and that I was much better suited to reading English. Age was on my side, as I had been young for my year at school and, as long as I promised to do something useful, Mum said it was worth giving it a go.

My father made his one and only contribution to my academic progress by organizing for me to have interview training at Radley College, where my brother was a pupil under the headmastership of one of Dad's old rugby mates, Dennis Silk.

'Everyone says that boys come across more confidently when they're interviewed,' Dad explained. 'I mean, of course they are—they're better at most things—but I think it might do you good to get a little help so that you can sell yourself.

'Now, what is it you're going to read again? Biology?'

'No, Dad.' It always annoyed me that he had no clue which subjects I was any good at. 'English.'

I knew the way to Radley pretty well. I'd driven Andrew back to college a few times in my Mini, with him smoking out of the window, wearing his black 'smoking glove' so that his hand didn't smell. He bought packets of ten, snuck out in the garden at home and sucked so hard he made the filters soggy.

'Oh, don't be such a square.' Andrew was cross because I wouldn't let him smoke in the car.

'It's my car, and I don't like the smell. I'll pull over in the next layby and you can get out.'

I don't think it's much fun to stand on the side of a dual carriageway smoking, but Andrew had no bargaining room. It was my car and, as every teenager knows, your first car is your ticket to an

314

independent life. That little red Mini was more than just a car. So, no, Andrew could not smoke in it—if we were running late, I might let him stick his head right out the window, but he had to keep it out there the whole way through the cigarette. No exhaling once he was back inside.

The speedometer went up to 90 mph, but on the downhill sections of the A34 from Newbury to Oxford, with the wind behind us, we could make it go right past 90 and round to zero. The whole car would shudder, and the steering wheel felt as if it was going to fall off in my hands. Andrew and I screamed in delight and whacked the music up loud. We had grown up with our father weaving in and out of cars on the motorway, undertaking on the hard shoulder and speeding as a matter of honour—of course we thought that was the only way to drive.

*     *     *

Dad used to take us with him for his annual shopping expedition for Mum's Christmas stocking. It was always a last-minute affair. We had to run from shop to shop, Dad dancing from one foot to another like a rugby player running around defenders as he feinted and glanced around bemused shoppers. Andrew and I trotted along behind, attempting to persuade him not to buy lacy underwear or a fluffy bra.

'Dad, I don't think she wants that. Really.'

Andrew stood next to me, mute with embarrassment.

'But what do you think?' Dad turned to the shop assistant, usually a girl in her early twenties, who

315

would blush deep red.

'My wife is about the same size as you—do you think this would fit?' He held the silky negligee up to the shop assistant.

'Yes, sir, I'm sure it would. Now I must just see to a customer over there . . .'

She would scamper away.

I'm sure he meant no harm. I was mortified. We took one basket each, and all three of us selected presents that we thought appropriate. My basket was full of music, books, sensible pants, soap, talcum powder and her brand of shampoo.

Dad selected on a basis of see-buy. If it was in front of him—a handbag, a belt, a pair of gloves, a jar of jam—he would put it in the basket. I reckon department stores are laid out for men who are panic buying. That's why all those leather goods are there on the ground floor as soon as you walk through the door—so that men like my father can scoop up things they think their wife might like.

'Dad, she doesn't like green.' I tossed out a pair of bright-green leather gloves. 'And you know she can't wear wool. Or costume jewellery—it gives her a rash.'

'But it's nice,' my father argued. 'I like it.'

'Yes, but that's not the point.'

I looked in Andrew's basket. There was a football and a packet of jelly sweets. He looked at me hopefully.

When we made it to the cash register, a voice would trill, 'Cash or cheque, sir?'

Dad was allowed to raid the petty cash at Christmas time.

'Cash!' His voice sang out as he produced his wad with a flourish and slapped it down in front of

316

the till.

While Dad counted the notes, Andrew shoved his new football in the bottom of a big carrier bag and covered it up with a dressing gown.

It was my job to wrap the stocking when we got home and weed out some of the less desirable objects. It was also my job to keep all the receipts for the inevitable journey back to Camp Hopson in Newbury.

*     *     *

The interview training from Radley was soon to be put to the test. Mum drove me to Newmarket, where we stayed the night, before she dropped me off at Newnham College for my day of interrogation.

I felt relaxed as soon as I walked past the porter's desk and through the internal doors, admiring the full stretch of Newnham's red-brick buildings, with their high-arched, white-trimmed windows. It has a feeling of space and light and I knew that, if I got in, I would have time to think.

Hidden away from the busy, rather ugly Sidgwick Avenue side of college, there are eighteen acres of gardens. There is a sunken garden, a formal pond, miles of borders and, unlike most Cambridge colleges, you can walk or sit on the lawns almost all year round. Hardly any tourists know about Newnham, so you can do so relatively undisturbed.

I liked the place. I didn't want to admit to anyone how much, but I really, really liked it. I was ready to study again, and I wanted it to be here.

Such was my desire to impress the director of studies, Mrs Gooder, that I almost fell over myself in my enthusiasm to get into her drawing room and

317

start my interview. Mrs Gooder had one of those warm faces turned at the pottery wheel of love and laughter and it made me want to hug her straight away. I restrained myself and shook her hand instead.

The study was on the ground floor of Clough Hall and had a huge desk facing out into the garden. It was large enough to have an array of sofas and chairs, which later that year would be filled with up to twenty girls exchanging views with Mrs Gooder about Shakespeare and Dickens, Henry James and Emily Dickinson.

I have no idea what I did in that interview, other than be wildly enthusiastic about the books I liked and the challenge of prose and poetry I had yet to discover, but it seemed to work. Mrs Gooder did not so much ask me questions; it seemed to me that we had a conversation in which we both took part.

I didn't want the interview to end. Mrs Gooder finally looked at her watch and politely ushered me towards the door. As I walked backwards I said, 'This place has the most wonderful aura. I could learn so much here. I really hope you will give me that chance.'

I meant it. I may even have come out in an immediate rash, such was my feverish desire to study at Newnham.

'We'll see,' said Mrs Gooder, looking at me kindly—or perhaps noticing the rash.

Less than a month later, I received a letter from Newnham College, Cambridge, saying they had accepted my application and looked forward to seeing me for the start of the new academic year in September 1990. I would be following in the footsteps of A. S. Byatt, Margaret Drabble, Iris

318

Murdoch, Joan Bakewell, Eleanor Bron and Emma Thompson, who had all studied there.

So many people had told me that I wasn't clever enough to get into Cambridge; that I was mad taking another year to apply again. My mother was quietly and completely thrilled for me.

'Must have been the interview practice Dennis Silk gave you,' said my father. 'Mind you, I knew they'd see sense in the end. Just ridiculous they turned you down in the first place. Ridiculous.'

'Dad,' I said, for the hundred and fiftieth time, 'they didn't turn me down. I didn't get the grades. Remember? Bristol and Exeter—they turned me down.'

Lovely as it was that he cared, I wasn't sure Dad really understood that this is what happened in the real world—some people liked you and some people didn't. They would select you or not select you for universities and jobs accordingly. The real world was almost entirely subjective. His world was based on hard facts; mine would rest on whether people liked me or not. It wasn't a case of how many winners you trained or where you stood in a table.

\*       \*       \*

There was a lot of reading to be done that summer in preparation for my first term, but there was a lot more riding. In my third season as an amateur jockey, I was throwing everything at what might be the only chance I would ever have of being champion and winning the Lady's Championship I had narrowly missed the season before.

Every week, the racing calendar would arrive.

This is the equivalent of the *Radio Times*—it is the forward planner that contains all the races in the country and the conditions required for entry. Some trainers now use a computer program to suggest every horse that is qualified for each race, but Dad didn't have that luxury—nor would he have used it. He preferred to plan individually for every horse in the yard and write, with his all-colour Biro, the name of the horses he wanted to be entered next to the relevant races. No wonder he didn't have a lot of time for us as children.

Throughout the summer of 1990, it was not the Group races that would catch his attention first—it was the amateur ones. He looked at all of them in the calendar and tried to find a horse that was qualified and suitable. He and I both knew that my amateur career was not going to last for ever, so it was now or never. I rode at Catterick, Ayr, Pontefract, Redcar, Beverley, Brighton, Goodwood, Yarmouth—it didn't matter how far away or how little the race was worth, if it was a points-scoring opportunity, I had to be there.

I rode horses for other trainers, and I rode a few that were probably unsuitable for amateur races. I had a horror fall at Kempton, when my stirrup leather snapped and I landed like a sack of cement then was kicked in the head by a horse who trampled over me. I couldn't remember much about it but when I came round from the concussion I kept saying, 'I would have won, I would have won.'

The hospital staff patiently replied, 'Of course you would have done, dear. Now drink this glass of water, tell me your name, your date of birth and the name of the prime minister.'

I missed a few races but, two weeks later, I was riding again.

One morning on the Downs, in a thick pea-souper of a fog, I was on a filly called Skazka. She had never been much of a work horse, only ever doing as much as she had to, but, on this morning, when we couldn't see further than fifty yards in front of us, she emerged from the fog fifteen lengths clear of her work companion. I had hardly been able to hold one side of her, but she'd kept going all the way to the top of the gallop and I struggled to pull her up.

'Interesting,' said my father. 'I've seen that happen before in the fog. It can act like a pair of blinkers. She couldn't see behind her so was trying to get away from the sound of being chased.'

For a while during her two- and three-year-old career, Skazka had looked as if she might be a decent filly. She was out of a mare called Winter Words, and Paul Mellon had chosen a name that is Russian for 'fairy-tale' in the hope that this filly might be a bit special. Unfortunately, that early promise faded, and this piece of work in the fog was the first time she had shown enthusiasm in ages.

Dad entered her in the same race at Beverley—the Contrac Computer Supplies Handicap—that I had won the previous year on Waterlow Park, at the expense of the Princess Royal. He was worried that Skazka didn't really get a mile and a half, so told me to conserve her energy. Mum and I made the familiar journey up the M1 to Doncaster, east on the M18 past Goole, and headed north of Hull to what had become my favourite racecourse.

After I had walked the course, I bumped into Elaine Bronson, who was riding an old favourite of hers called Cathos.

'What do you reckon?' she asked.

'The ground's all right,' I said. 'A bit rough just off the rail, but smooth right on it or out wide.'

'I don't care about the effin' ground,' she said. 'What do you reckon to your chances? Bookies have got you as favourite.'

'Oh,' I said dismissively, 'I'm not sure she'll stay, to be honest. She's never won over more than a mile.'

I wasn't lying—I wasn't sharp enough for that—but I hadn't predicted that we would go no pace at all for the first two furlongs. Nothing seemed to want to make the running so, as we crossed the path that Waterlow Park had jumped a year earlier, I found myself near the front of the field. Skazka heard something that scared her and she started to motor.

I did my best to hold her, but I didn't want to upset her rhythm by fighting too hard. Within a furlong, we were ten lengths clear of the rest and, as we turned into the straight, nothing was closing. I kept her right on the inside rail, trying to find that strip less than four feet wide that was smooth, fresh grass. My boot was scraping the rail and, as we passed the furlong marker, Skazka bumped the rail and momentarily lost her balance. I could hear someone wailing like a banshee and the thundering of hooves, but I dared not look round.

Skazka was tiring, and I just sat there, holding her together and barely moving, willing the line to come before we both fell in a heap. The dreadful noise, which I knew could only be Elaine, was getting closer but, luckily, the winning post came just in time. Two strides after it, she passed us.

'I thought you said your horse wouldn't stay?' Elaine was shouting at me.

'I didn't think she would,' I puffed.

I didn't know at the time why Elaine was so annoyed but, when I saw her boss David Wilson's face, I realized that, once again, they had had a big bet and, this time, it hadn't worked out.

'That's why she's going to Cambridge,' he shouted at her. 'And you never will! She had you fooled, you idiot.'

When my father rang to give me a bollocking for not following his instructions, I told him that I had deliberately exploited the rest of the field's assumption that Skazka wouldn't stay.

One thing I had learned in my study of the world away from school was that men seemed to take credit for success, even when it happened by accident. They did not immediately point out their own mistakes. My mother knew the truth, of course, and I suspect my father did too, but Elaine Bronson and David Wilson were convinced I was shrewder than I appeared.

My first job when I got to Newnham would be to persuade Mrs Gooder to let me keep a car there and to give me time off to ride in the final race of the season at Chepstow.

# 19

## Respectable Jones

'You would like to go where?' asked Mrs Gooder.

I had explained that I needed a favour. I knew that it was not necessarily a good start to turn up at the university of your dreams and immediately ask for a day off.

'The thing is . . .' I started.

'Please, my dear,' said Mrs Gooder, 'let's try not to start any sentence with "the thing is". I don't think you'll find that any of the great writers lean on that phrase as a literary frame. You can do better.'

'It's the last race of the season,' I said, a hint of desperation in my voice. 'And I need to win it, otherwise Lydia Pearce is going to beat me, and I got beaten last year in the very last race, and I don't want it to happen again, and Uncle Toby says I can ride a horse for him called Respectable Jones at Chepstow, and I might win my weight in champagne, and I promise I'll mention Newnham if I do and . . .'

Mrs Gooder raised her hand.

'Take a breath, please. You and I shall make a deal. There is one page in the newspaper that I do not understand and, if you promise that you will explain this to me, you may ride at Chepstow.'

She opened a copy of the *Guardian* to the racing page and gestured.

'Might as well be gobbledegook. I do not like to feel ignorant.'

I nodded solemnly.

'I promise. Thank you so much. Thank you, thank you, thank you.'

'One thank-you is enough,' said Mrs Gooder. 'Any more and you rather start to lose the impact. Now go, before I change my mind.'

She waved me towards the door and then added, as an afterthought, 'While you are there, you might like to read Wordsworth's lines on Tintern Abbey. I think you'll find it's not far from Chepstow.'

As I shut the door, I could hear Mrs Gooder reciting to herself, 'Five years have past; five summers, with the length/ Of five long winters.'

I had to pace myself that first week of term, because I didn't want to put on too much weight. It

325

wasn't easy, as there was a 'squash' every night. The first week of any university year is like the January sales, with each society playing the part of the big department stores and the first-year students, known as freshers, being the gullible shoppers.

Posing in alphabetical order for our matriculation photo, I had made friends with the girl standing next to me, Louise Arter, who was reading modern languages. We decided we would explore Cambridge together by way of whatever squash we could get into. Each one offered a free glass of something and hoped to get you tipsy enough to sign up straight away and pay a year's subs.

We went to the Newnham College Boat Club squash and both signed up for the novice boat; we went to the Union Society and both joined the debating society; we went to the Wine Society, the Cheese Society, the Film Society and the Cricket Society. We walked into the Tiddlywinks Society squash at Queen's College but decided that they looked a little too intense for us. The Beagling Society were a fun bunch, but we didn't join. I felt a little guilty that we raided the free wine at the Christian Society and left without even having a conversation, let alone a conversion.

How anyone gets any academic work done in the first term of university is beyond me. It was a whirl. Any friend network that we had from school was busted. The two other girls from my school year who had got to Cambridge were one or two years ahead of me and, although I knew of other people, the links were as fragile as candyfloss. Louise and I embarked upon our adventure with open minds. We would be friends with anyone who seemed fun, chatty and didn't take themselves too seriously.

My self-preservation streak always kicked in just before midnight, when I would drag Louise away and we would head back to Newnham before the porter locked the main door. You could get in after midnight, but it involved ringing the doorbell and looking ashamed as the porter made a big show of getting out his keys and granting you entrance, while staring suspiciously.

*　　*　　*

I was still firmly attached to the army officer, who had been sent to fight in the First Gulf War. Before he left, he had asked me to marry him. The romantic in me was desperate to say yes. I thought I could never love anyone as much as I loved him. The realist in me told me that this was the situation talking. He was going to war, I was going to university, it was all a bit weird. So I said, 'Ask me again when you come back.'

We were saying goodbye at Brize Norton airport. It's a desperate place for farewells. I held him tight and whispered, 'And make sure you do come back.'

I walked away, turning one last time to see him standing there in his Desert Rat uniform. His fringe was falling over his left eye and, as he moved his hand up to adjust it, he turned his palm towards me and held it there until I had disappeared out of view. I had to stop the car three times on the way home because I couldn't see through the tears.

We wrote to each other every day (we were good at that) and I threw myself into university life, ensuring that I was always busy so that I did not have time to be terrified of where he was or what he might be doing. It was a triumph of action over thought.

I watched the lunchtime and six o'clock news, hoping that there were no reports of Allied casualties. I waited for the letters, which arrived in batches of five or six at a time, and I rang his mother occasionally to see what she had heard. I was living parallel lives. One was the faithful girlfriend waiting and worrying, the other was the fresher student exploring an invigorating new world.

Then, of course, there was the pull of home and the challenge of the championship. I had successfully persuaded the college of my need to have a car and, those first couple of weeks, I headed off to Newmarket at 5 a.m. to ride out for a trainer called David Morley. The effect this had on my ability to concentrate in lectures was fatal. By ten o'clock in the morning, my eyes felt as heavy as sheets of metal.

Germaine Greer was in full flow—something to do with Shakespeare and his obsession with phallic symbols. I thought that if I just put my head on my arms on the desk, I would be able to take it in better. If I just . . .

'You there!' The Australian voice was in my dream, shouting at me.

I felt Colette, who was sitting next to me, dig me in the ribs. I sat up.

'Yes, you,' said Dr Greer. 'Am I boring you?'

'No,' I flustered, 'no, not at all. It's fascinating.'

'And what, precisely,' she asked, 'do you find most fascinating?'

Dr Greer was staring at me. The whole lecture theatre had turned to look at me. Oh God. What the hell had she been going on about?

'Shakespeare's portrayal of strong, independent, witty women on equal terms with men . . . I had not thought of him as a feminist icon but, yes, I see it now.'

I was stabbing in the half-light, because the title of the lecture was 'Shakespeare: A Proto-feminist Icon'.

'Yes,' said Dr Greer. 'And?'

I had no more to offer. I glanced at Colette's notes. She had written in capital letters: 'TAMING OF THE SHREW. MISOGYNISM OR EXPLORATION OF FEMALE INDIVIDUALITY?'

'And . . . Kate,' I said. 'In *The Taming of the Shrew*. An intriguing exploration of female individuality and the challenge of protecting the spirit of a woman within the confines and restrictions of traditional patriarchal marriage.'

Germaine nodded. I was off the hook.

'If you could make the effort to stay awake in my lectures, you might find that you take even more in,' she said, before moving on to discuss the use of the skull in *Hamlet* as an ironic reference to erectile dysfunction.

\*     \*     \*

My mother had lent me her mobile phone, a heavy brick of a thing with a battery that lasted about an hour before it needed recharging. I was the only student in college with one. My father rang me every couple of days to check on my weight. He didn't have anything suitable to run in the final race of the season, a six-furlong handicap, but he had

329

been in touch with Uncle Toby.

'He says he's got just the horse,' Dad said. 'So you make sure you're fit and ready because, if Uncle Toby says a horse will win, it will win.'

I sleepwalked through lectures on Monday morning and then drove to Kingsclere. Dad sent me upstairs to weigh myself as soon as I walked in the door. I was heavy, but it didn't matter too much as Respectable Jones, the horse selected by Uncle Toby, was carrying eleven stone seven pounds. What I did not discover until I was in the changing room at Chepstow at one o'clock the next day was that my legs had expanded so much that my breeches and boots were too tight. The thin leather boots strained as I battled to zip them up.

For the millionth time, I asked myself why I couldn't be tiny and featherweight like Lydia Pearce. She barely weighed eight stone, without even trying. Her horse, A Little Precious, was also carrying eleven stone seven, and Lydia could barely lift the saddle and weight cloth to get on the scales. She was carrying three stone of lead.

'Live weight's better than dead weight,' Uncle Toby said as he met me in the weighing room. He took me to the side of the room and put an arm conspiratorially around my shoulder.

'Now listen,' he said. 'Respectable Jones is a lovely ride. Just be careful cantering down to the start. Don't let him out of a hack canter. He's a sprinter, and that's all he knows how to run—flat out.

'He'll jump out pretty smartish, so be ready. Let him stride along, and you'll be fine. I know he's not favourite but, believe me, he'll win.'

Unlike my father, who never had a bet, Uncle

Toby was not averse to the odd gamble and, as we walked out to the paddock, I heard the PA announcer say that Respectable Jones had come in from 14–1 to 12–1 to 10–1. Someone was confident in his ability, if not in mine.

I had driven my Mini to Chepstow, with Andrew as my co-pilot. He had left school that summer, was riding out for Uncle Toby and thinking of applying to read Equine Business Studies at Cirencester Agricultural College. This meant that a day at the races was, technically, 'work'.

'I don't want to miss history in the making,' he said as he climbed into the car, which made me nervous.

We walked the course together, me with a serious look on my face, him looking like a protégé trainer with, naturally, a hint of Lionel Blair. Chepstow has a long straight that rolls up and down like a big dipper. The last climb to the winning post is draining.

'Make sure you save a bit for this,' said Andrew, as he started to run towards the winning post. I ran with him, knowing that, for good luck, I had to cross the line before he did. We were sprinting as hard as we could and, in the last few strides, I caught him and put my hands in the air, feeling like Harold Abrahams as played by Ben Cross in *Chariots of Fire*. He smiled at me. I think he might have let me win.

My father was driving down later to support me, but my mother said she couldn't come. I tried not to show it, but I was really hurt. If I was going to win the championship, I wanted her to be there— she had driven me halfway round the country chasing after rides—and if I *wasn't* going to win it, I needed her there even more. I knew I was getting a little old to believe that the world revolved around me but, on this Tuesday in October, I thought that, just for an hour or so, it could.

Racing is not a sport in which you can control the movements of others—not unless you box them in or deliberately rev up another horse to make it pull too hard or upset its stride pattern. Most of the time, you can only influence your own horse, and the rest will be whatever it is going to be. The changing room was buzzing. Sharron Murgatroyd had brought a bottle of champagne and promised to spray whichever one of us won the prize. Elaine Bronson was winding us all up, promising that she would crush me again, as she had done last year. She needed to win on Profit à Prendre with Lydia and me out of the first four.

Lydia was quiet. Her two small children had come to watch her, and she was desperate not to disappoint them. She had a narrow lead in the championship and just needed to finish in front of me to seal her first title. I needed to win. Nothing less would do.

It really bothered me that Mum wasn't there. She said that I never noticed when she was supporting me, that it was always Dad I wanted to impress, but now she wasn't there, and I noticed. It didn't feel right. Dad's attention was like a spotlight—almost blinding for the length of time it was on you but soon off to another part of the stage. Mum's was not so bright, but it was a constant, warming light—like sunshine.

I went to the loo for the fourth time in ten minutes, and heard the call.

'*Jockeys!*'

Murgy shouted at me, 'Come on, Balding, you can't have any pee left. We're going. Hurry up!'

I struggled to do up my breeches and ran to catch up with the other women. I couldn't move freely, as everything was so tight. Uncle Toby, Dad and Andrew were standing together.

'Minder says you've got two horses to watch out for,' said Uncle Toby. He always called Andrew 'Minder' because, when he was young, he looked as if he was going to be too big to be a jockey and Uncle Toby joked that he would have to be his minder instead.

'So, it's simple: don't let them get anywhere near you.'

The three of them wished me good luck, and Uncle Toby walked me to the edge of the paddock, where Respectable Jones was being led round. We ran alongside him, me with my left leg sticking out as I hopped up and down on the right leg. As he gave me a leg-up, I heard the sound of ripping. My breeches had split down the back seam.

I said nothing and thanked God that I had not had to take off my pants to save an ounce or two. As I was walking around the paddock, I heard a whistle. It was the familiar two-note whistle that my mother always used when she was trying to find us in a crowd. I started to scan the faces and heard the whistle again.

'Mum?' I shouted.

'Ah, she wants her mum,' I heard a punter say.

There was the whistle again and, just as we turned to walk out of the paddock, I saw my mother in the crowd. She smiled and gave me the thumbs-up, mouthing 'Good luck.' I swallowed hard and patted Respectable Jones on the neck. It was the first time I had ever sat on him.

'He takes a fair old grip,' said the lad leading him up. 'So don't let him get going with you on the way to the start. Trot if you have to.'

He let me go, and I anchored the horse's chestnut head to the left, turning it towards the rail so that he couldn't get into any sort of a stride. It looked awful, but it worked. It also meant that I could point my bottom towards the middle of the course, away from the crowd. That way they wouldn't see that I had split my breeches. I'm not sure which was worrying me more—the risk of being run away with before the race had even started, or the risk of exposing my backside to the world.

We arrived at the start safely, and I felt round the back of my breeches to see if the split had spread. I would have to ride without restraint if I was going to have any effect, so to hell with modesty. In the pursuit of success, you have to risk your dignity.

I patted Respectable Jones as we waited for the other horses to be loaded into the stalls and looked at the straight six furlongs ahead of me. In little over one minute and ten seconds, my fate would be decided. I was completely calm, despite the tear in my breeches. This would either happen or it wouldn't, and I knew I could cope if I was beaten. I had before.

The stalls opened, and Respectable Jones jumped straight into his stride. We were in the front line of four, with Lydia Pearce directly to my right. I am only aware of this because I have since seen the photos. In the race, all I know is that I had clear green turf ahead of me and a horse that was galloping underneath me. I held his head steady, a firm but constant contact on the reins, tried not to go too fast and counted down the furlong markers. In America and Australia, the clock is king and every work rider learns to cover furlongs in exact times—twelve seconds per furlong is the rate of a really good middle-distance horse. Sprinters can go faster and can cover a furlong in ten seconds, but they can't keep that rate up for long. I had to conserve Respectable Jones's energy, allow him to cover the furlongs at an even pace, keeping up his momentum for that last uphill surge to the line.

My mind went blank. I didn't worry about the championship, the punters, my father or anything else. I was, as they say, 'in the zone'. More importantly, so was Respectable Jones. His pace did not weaken, his stride kept covering the ground with the same length and power, and it sounded like music, like the beat of a drum. We passed the one-furlong marker, and I could hear the crowd shouting. I did not dare look round and kept my eyes firmly on the strip of grass we were taking, keeping Respectable Jones straight, pushing him out as best I could up that hill. As we crossed the line, my body acknowledged the feat, even if my brain couldn't take it in. I took my right hand off the reins and gave a low punch.

I looked round to see Lydia Pearce half a length behind me in second place. She shouted, 'Well done!'

Elaine Bronson cantered up and whacked me on the back. Murgy smiled and said, 'About time, too!'

I did not feel immediate elation. I suspect few people do in the seconds after a big win. I think I was in shock. I tried to think how I should behave.

My mother would be appalled if I appeared too triumphant, and I also knew that, if I stood up in the irons as I walked into the winner's enclosure, everyone would see that my breeches were split.

I patted Respectable Jones, who was hardly even blowing. For him, it had been an afternoon canter. I had managed to lose my fitness so fast that I was breathing hard, even though all I'd had to do was sit there and steer.

The walk back to the winner's enclosure was fabulous. All the punters who had backed us had got a decent return for their money and were cheering. The PA announcer knew the score, and announced me into the winner's enclosure as 'the *new* Champion Lady Rider!'

As I slid off Respectable Jones, I tried to turn my bottom towards his body so that no one would be able to take a photo. It was not an elegant dismount.

'Walk behind me to the weighing room,' I hissed to Andrew.

'What?' he asked loudly.

'Walk as close as you can behind me, like a minder.'

This he understood, and he shadowed me back to the scales. I weighed in but, before I could run back into the weighing room to change into another pair of breeches, I was ushered straight back out for the trophy presentation. It was neither the biggest nor the best trophy of my life but, of all the winners I rode, it was the most significant, because it sealed the deal.

I had won the Ladies' Championship. This was going to look a lot more impressive on my list of certificates than Piano Grade 2.

As I walked back into the changing room, Murgy unleashed the champagne bottle she had been shaking for the last five minutes. It exploded over me, and the room roared with laughter. I saw Lydia Pearce packing her stuff up and went over for a quiet word. I knew only too well how she was feeling.

'At least you've got years to keep at it,' I said, trying to sound encouraging. 'Look at me—you don't get many years of race riding out of a body this big.'

She laughed, and we both knew it was true. The one advantage was that the return in champagne on my weight would be considerably more than any other champion lady jockey before or after me.

I dropped in at home on my way back to Cambridge, and Grandma came over for supper. It was my favourite—roast chicken with as much bread sauce as I wanted.

'I hear you split your jodhpurs,' she said. I stared at Andrew, who looked guilty. He must have grassed on me. 'I'm not surprised. You're clearly eating well at Cambridge.'

'I'm rowing,' I said. 'It builds up your muscles.'

'Huh,' said my grandmother. 'A boatie, eh? Whatever next!'

She glanced at my father and tapped the side of her nose.

'Toby rang me, and I got 14–1. Thank God she didn't mess it up.'

# EPILOGUE

1990 was the last year that I rode with any great intent in amateur races. I had a few more winners, but never again challenged for the championship. Lydia Pearce won the Ladies' Championship the following year and took home considerably fewer cases of champagne. Her son, Simon, now rides as an apprentice jockey for my brother.

The pink Lanson champagne was saved for my twenty-first birthday party, where my school and university friends helped drink to the exploits of Knock Knock, Waterlow Park, Song of Sixpence and Respectable Jones.

I became president of the Cambridge Union at the end of my second year and graduated from Newnham College with a 2.1 in English.

Mrs Gooder and her husband, who was director of studies at Clare College, came to stay at Park House for a weekend. She loved seeing the horses in their home environment and watching them on the gallops. We went racing at Newbury, and she could read the form perfectly.

My relationship with the army officer did not survive our living in the same country. We had been better in long-distance letters and, when he returned from the Gulf War, mercifully unhurt, he did not propose again. I went out with a few more boys, because that's what I thought I was meant to do, taking them out like books from the library and returning them when I didn't get into the story. I did not treat them well, and didn't much like the way I was around them. It was another few years before I realized I'd been looking in the wrong section of the library.

My brother moved into Park House with his wife and children a few years ago. My parents built a new house at the end of the garden. Andrew took over the trainer's licence in January 2003 and that year trained his first Classic winner when Casual Look won the Oaks. I attempted to conduct a live TV interview with my father and my brother, but none of us could speak because we were all crying. Andrew now trains over 150 horses and employs 60 staff. He may one day be a champion trainer.

I had no intention of working in racing and left Cambridge wanting to be a writer. A chance meeting with the BBC radio racing correspondent Cornelius Lysaght led to a voice test for Radio 5. The following week, I started as a freelance reporter on racing. I became a trainee sports reporter for a new station called 5 Live, which started in 1994. I had a screen test for television a couple of years later and, when Julian Wilson left, I took over as the BBC's racing presenter in January 1998. I have been doing the job ever since.

My grandmother died in 2010, at the age of ninety. Her last words were to her doctor, who had withstood her decline with admirable patience, as he urged her to sip from a glass of water.

'What the hell do you think you're doing? Trying to drown me?'

I keep a postcard from her in my desk drawer. It says, 'I'm sorry I said you were talking nonsense.' It was the only time, to my knowledge, that she ever apologized for telling someone they were an idiot.

I ride rarely now, and I am often asked if I miss it. It was a huge part of the first twenty years of my life and may yet be a huge part of my later life, but these last twenty years have been dedicated to a career that is stimulating, exciting and rewarding. Deep in my heart, I know my working life would not be what it is had I stayed at home.

I have learned not to take too much notice of those who disapprove of my lifestyle choices, because I know that I was not designed to be part of the crowd. If I am different, I make no apology, and I hope that others will have the courage to be themselves and stand up for what they believe in, fight for those who need protection, love who they want to love, and be proud of it.

Alice and I have been together for ten years and counting. We had our civil partnership in 2006. My parents adore her, and my father even accepts that she is better than he is at golf. My nephew Toby asked me the other day, 'You and Auntie Alice are married, aren't you?'

'Yes, effectively, we are,' I replied, deciding that, at three years old, he was a little young to understand the finer points of how civil partnership and marriage differ.

'Can women marry men as well?' he asked.

'They can if they want to, and most women do. But not all.'

He stared at me with big blue eyes and smiled. 'I love Auntie Alice,' he said.

'I know. I do too.'

As I write this, Archie the Tibetan Terrier is asking for his evening walk. We live our days according to his needs, but I would admit that his needs suit us very well—a long walk in the morning, a shorter one in the evening. Breakfast in the morning, and tea at four o'clock on the dot.

He sleeps on the bed at night and the sofa during the day. He is thoroughly spoilt and he is far from perfect, but he is part of the life that Alice and I have carved for ourselves. We wouldn't have it any other way.

# ACKNOWLEDGEMENTS

The idea for *My Animals* has been working around my brain for many years, and I'd like to thank Lee Durrell, who gave me permission to flip the title of Gerald Durrell's great work and the confidence to go for it.

I have never written a book before, partly because I was scared and partly because I kept telling myself I didn't have time.

It turns out I did have time and I loved doing it. The breakthrough moment was finding 'the key', and thanks to the gorgeous Dawn French for that— reading her memoir, *Dear Fatty*, made me realize that I could tell stories, sad or funny, without being tied down by chronology or the need to share every detail. She used letters; I have used animals as the way into each chapter.

When it comes to the practicality of actually writing, I have been very lucky to have the kick up the backside I needed from Nicola Ibison at James Grant Group, who banged on and on about it so much that it was easier to write than to tell her I wasn't. She hooked me up with the dashing and charming Ivan Mulcahy, who went through every comma of the early chapters and was there whenever I needed him. I like to think that I've helped him acknowledge and open up to the love of his life—a bichon frise called Charlie.

At Penguin, Joel Rickett has been an absolute joy. He is kind, consistent and patient; I take his advice because he makes things better. Sarah Day did a brilliant job with the copy-editing, and many thanks to Gill Heeley, who has drawn the wonderful illustrations for each chapter.

Most of all, I would like to thank my family. Mum: for reading an early draft and, despite me giving her three vetoes, not using any of them. Dad: for saying I would never get it finished on time, which made me so angry I made sure I did. Andrew: for being quietly excited about it. My sister-in-law Anna Lisa: for being loudly excited about it. Alice: for encouraging me, motivating me, listening to me and reading every page at every stage.

JJ, Toby and Flora: I hope you enjoy reading about your daddy and Auntie Clare and that you have a childhood as fun as ours, but maybe without the stealing!

Thank you to all the animals who have filled my life with happiness and love—especially Frank, for understanding me. Archie and Itty the cat have both watched me write, and I like to think they'd enjoy reading this, if they could. Walking Archie was essential, because it gave me space and time to think.

Finally, thank you to *you* for reading this.